Welcome to Express Track German

Maybe you have never learned German, and feel that now is the time; or you learned German years ago, and want to take it up again. Perhaps you are interested in learning more about Germany and its people, their customs, culture and language. Or maybe you are going to work with Germans, and need a basic business vocabulary. Whoever you are, the authors of Express Track German wish you a warm welcome - in German: Herzlich willkommen! - and offer you this carefully designed, step-by-step guide to the German language.

What you will find in Express Track German

• This full-colour textbook contains dialogues, vocabulary lists, exercises, games, articles about Germany and the German people, a short story, a tourist guide and an alphabetic glossary;
• Four cassettes, total playing time nearly 6 hours, with dialogues, games and numerous exercises;
• A separate booklet with translations of the dialogues, further grammar, and a complete transcript of the cassettes.

How to use Express Track German

Each lesson begins with a dialogue in simple but natural everyday German. Read it through once in the textbook, and check the translation in the booklet. Then listen as often as necessary, until you can distinguish all the words. Key phrases are highlighted at the end of each dialogue. Listen for the signal, and repeat each phrase and sentence aloud until you achieve an easy rhythm and intonation.

Important words and phrases from the dialogues are translated and explained in the sections VOCABULARY and HOW TO SAY IT, together with further useful vocabulary on the same topic. The meanings given are only those relevant to the context. To explore deeper, you should also have a good bilingual dictionary.

ORAL PRACTICE gives you a series of structured exercises on tape (with sound signals and pauses for you to respond). Grammar buffs will find explanations of all the structures in the grammar sections of the accompanying booklet.

After every five units you will find WRITTEN PRACTICE - a series of exercises covering everything you have learned in those five units. This is followed by a section of MORE VOCABULARY.

Finally, for lighter moments, in each unit you will find short, humorous accounts of some of the good and not so good things about Germany and the Germans; a selection of famous German songs with translations; listening games, word puzzles, quizzes and crosswords to fill in on the page; and a selection of the sort of German colloquial sayings and expressions that you may hear any day in the streets.

So plan your route, and let's get on the Express Track to German. Viel Glück!

TABLE OF CONTENTS

EXPRESS TRACK

A self-study course for business and pleasure

by
HILKE OPITZ ● *BARBARA PAUL*

English text by
Henry Strutz, MA and Kath Boothman, MA

Illustrations by
Anne-Gildas Langevin, Juliette Planque and Zaü

EUROPEAN
SCHOOLBOOKS
PUBLISHING

All enquiries should be
addressed to:
European Schoolbooks
Publishing Limited
The Runnings,
Cheltenham, GL51 9PQ
England

ISBN 0 85048 155 4
© copyright 1991
Editions Nathan, Paris
English edition first
published in the
United States 1992 by
Barron's Educational
Series, Inc.

This revised edition
published in the United
Kingdom and Eire by
European Schoolbooks
Publishing Ltd in May
1994 by arrangement
with Barron's
Educational Series Inc.,
Hauppauge, N.Y.

TABLE OF CONTENTS

Frankfurt: old and new.

UNIT 1

1.1 *DIALOGUE*

LISTEN **RHEIN-MAIN FLUGHAFEN, FRANKFURT**

Journalist Silke Peters and Hans-Jürgen Krumbach, managing director of Krumbach Books, welcome the French writer Marcel Bosquet to the Frankfurt Book Fair.

Silke Peters: *Da kommt Herr Bosquet.*

Marcel Bosquet: *Guten Tag, Frau Peters.*

Silke: *Guten Tag, Herr Bosquet.* (turning to Mr Krumbach) *Das ist der Schriftsteller Marcel Bosquet.*

Hans-Jürgen Krumbach: *Angenehm. Krumbach. Willkommen in Frankfurt.*

Marcel: *Verzeihung, wie heißen Sie?*

Hans-Jürgen: *Krumbach. Mein Name ist*

Krumbach: *K-R-U-M-B-A-C-H. Ich bin Verleger hier in Frankfurt.*

Marcel: *Ach, das ist interessant.*

Silke: *Ich rufe jetzt ein Taxi.*

Hans-Jürgen: *Woher kennen Sie Silke Peters, Herr Bosquet?*

Marcel: *Ich kenne sie aus Paris.*

Hans-Jürgen: *Schön, gehen wir. Das Taxi wartet.*

LISTEN AND REPEAT
See translation on page 1 of the booklet.

Frankfurt: the Autobahn and the airport

1.1 VOCABULARY

NOUNS

der Flughafen — airport
der Tag — day
(der) Herr — gentleman, Mr
(die) Frau — lady, Mrs
der Mann — man
der Mensch** — person, human being
das Kind, pl. die Kinder — child
der Schriftsteller — writer
der Name* — name
der Verleger — publisher
das Taxi — the taxi
ein Taxi — a taxi

_____

das Flugzeug }
die Maschine } — aeroplane
der Abflug — flight departure
die Ankunft — arrival
der Vorname* — first name
der Nachname* — surname
der Journalist** — journalist
die Journalistin (1) — journalist (female)
die Schriftstellerin — writer (female)
die Verlegerin — publisher (female)
das Buch — book
die Messe — fair
die Buchmesse — book fair
die Ausstellung — exhibition

ADJECTIVES

angenehm (2) — pleasant (here) nice to meet you
interessant — interesting

schön — beautiful (here) fine
unangenehm — unpleasant
uninteressant — uninteresting

VERBS

kommen — to come
sein — to be
heißen — to be called or named
rufen — to call
kennen — to know (a person)
gehen — to go
warten — to wait

MISCELLANEOUS

da — there
hier — here
dort — there, over there
in — in, to
wie — how
jetzt — now
woher — where from
aus — out of (here) from
Verzeihung — I beg your pardon
ach — oh!

_____

Entschuldigung — I'm sorry, excuse me

* mixed masculine noun
** weak masculine noun

HOW TO SAY IT

Guten Tag — how do you do; hallo (formal)
Willkommen! — welcome!
Guten Morgen — good morning
Guten Abend — good evening

Gute Nacht — good night
Hallo! — hallo! (informal)
Auf Wiedersehen — good-bye
Tschüß (3) — 'bye; cheerio

Wie heißen Sie? (4) — What's your name?
Ich heiße Krumbach (5) — I'm (called) Krumbach
Mein (6) Name ist Krumbach — My name's Krumbach
Angenehm — Pleased, delighted (to meet you)
Darf ich Ihnen Herrn (7) Krumbach vorstellen?
Darf ich Sie mit Herrn Krumbach bekanntmachen? } — May I introduce you to Mr Krumbach?

Woher kommen Sie? — Where do you come from?
Ich komme aus Paris — I come from Paris
Ich bin Verleger in Frankfurt — I'm a publisher in Frankfurt

Was machen Sie? — What do you do (for a living)?
Was sind Sie von Beruf?
Welchen Beruf haben Sie? } — What kind of work do you do?
Ich bin Schriftsteller (8) — I'm a writer

See grammar on page 40 of the booklet.

REMARKS   REMARKS   REMARKS   REMARKS

(1) The suffix -IN forms the feminine of nouns expressing a profession, function etc. e.g. der Verleger (the publisher), die Verlegerin (the female publisher). — (2) Predicate adjectives take no ending. e.g. die Buchmesse ist interessant (the book fair is interesting). (See grammar on page 38 of the booklet.) — (3) GUTEN TAG and AUF WIEDERSEHEN are more formal than HALLO and TSCHÜß. — (4) The pronoun SIE takes a capital letter when it means "you" (polite). — (5) When introducing yourself you give your surname. — (6) MEIN (my) is a possessive pronoun. (See grammar on page 41 of the booklet.) — (7) For the declension of DER HERR see grammar on page 38 of the booklet. — (8) The indefinite article is omitted when stating a person's profession.

1.1   *ORAL PRACTICE*

1. THE VERB „SEIN"

(● ●) LISTEN AND REPEAT

ich bin,
du bist,
er/sie/es ist,
wir sind,
ihr seid,
sie/Sie sind

See grammar on page 44 of the booklet

2. REGULAR VERB: PRESENT TENSE

(● ●) LISTEN

ich komme,
du kommst,
er/sie/es kommt,
wir kommen,
ihr kommt,
sie/Sie kommen

Now give the present tense of the following verbs:
heißen, rufen, kennen, gehen, warten.

See grammar on page 43 of the booklet

3. HOW TO ASK QUESTIONS

(● ●) LISTEN

du heißt Silke
● *heißt du Silke?*
er ruft das Taxi
● *ruft er das Taxi?*

Now ask some questions, following the examples:
Sie sind Herr Krumbach — er heißt Marcel Bosquet — wir kennen Silke Peters — sie warten hier — ihr seid in Frankfurt — er kommt aus Paris — die Buchmesse ist interessant — sie ruft ein Taxi — sie heißt Silke Peters — er kennt Herrn Krumbach.

See grammar on page 47 of the booklet.

4. QUESTIONS

(● ●) LISTEN

Wie (du - heißen)
● *Wie heißt du?*
Woher (er - kommen)
● *Woher kommt er?*
Woher (Sie - kennen - Frau Peters)
● *Woher kennen Sie Frau Peters?*

Now ask some questions:
Wie (du - heißen) — Woher (er - kommen) — Woher (du - kennen - Silke) — Wie (Sie - heißen) — Woher (ihr - kommen)

See grammar on page 47 of the booklet.

5. PRONUNCIATION

(● ●) LISTEN AND REPEAT

Frau - aus
Herr - er
er - woher
ich - ach
mein - heißen

See grammar on page 36 of the booklet.

6. INTONATION

(● ●) LISTEN AND REPEAT

Frankfurt — Flughafen — Guten Tag — Krumbach — Mein Name ist Krumbach — Verzeihung, wie heißen Sie?

See grammar on page 36 of the booklet.

WHO ARE THE GERMANS, ANYWAY?

"What does it mean to be German?" If you're ever in a café frequented by intellectual Germans you may hear them discussing this question, when they've had a few beers. Do they perhaps worry about being one race with two identities? Or is it that they've found a new sense of nationhood, now the country is reunified? It used to be said that Germany's population was ageing because of the declining birthrate; now the influx of immigrants from Eastern Europe is expected to send the birthrate up. Even among the original population you'll come across various groups. For example, there's the Schickeria (smart set) who enjoy a cosmopolitan lifestyle. They're all more or less involved in the "alternative scene" which consists of the Greens and the numerous pacifist groups, with their art galleries, cinemas and publishers of books on "alternative" art. Theirs is an "alternative" culture - things like the Tempodrom in Berlin, a privately-funded old-fashioned circus which recreates fond childhood memories, and also, by contrast, the UFA, Berlin's old Cinecittà (cinema city), now occupied by young people and turned into a workers' community. They have unorthodox political ideas too: rejecting "the system", which they say is corrupt, they start up their own "alternative" taxi services, shops and even banks.

The Green movement grew out of the pressure groups known as B.I.s (Bürgerinitiativen or Citizens' Initiatives): an anti-noise B.I., for instance, a B.I. opposing the expansion of Frankfurt airport, B.I.s campaigning for children's playgrounds and youth centres, B.I.s for the protection of forests and against dioxin dumping and nuclear installations. The B.I.s bring together citizens of every age, class and political persuasion. The generation gap is bridged and everyone enjoys being kontaktfreudig (sociable), now that the idea of self-help has caught on. There are self-help organisations for the unemployed, for tenants, for retired people (not to mention "The Grey Panthers", another senior citizens' association) and any number of support groups. Twenty-year-olds say: "Germany doesn't exist. For me, there's just Europe and the world."

On the other hand, there are also the German flag wavers and singers of the Deutchlandlied who are to be seen at football matches, apparently seeking a

The Grey Panthers - pensioner power!

German identity in the victories won by "their" team. Is this a sign of reviving nationalism? Since there was not just one Germany but two until recently, it used to be necessary to specify which Germany you were talking about!

Then again, there are the worthy middle classes. They invite one another to cocktail parties where wine and canapés are served, the guests bring flowers (remember, when in Germany, to take the paper off before handing them over!) and conversation is likely to turn - perhaps rather complacently - to environmental issues. These people hold liberal views, even if they vote for right-wing parties. They consider themselves anti-racist, though you may well hear grumbles about "too many foreigners". They feel (and East Germans seem to feel this even more strongly than West Germans) that the law granting political asylum should be amended to prevent so

many foreigners from flooding in and trying to share Germany's high standard of living. They are staunch supporters of law and order; should they see a neighbour fuelling his Golf Diesel with heating oil, they are quite capable of reporting him to the authorities.

They take their environmental concerns seriously, and set high standards in their own homes too: the toilet paper is white to protect underground aquifers, tea is green because it's healthier, and coffee comes from Nicaragua as a token of support for the Third World. No bottles are thrown into bottle banks after eight o'clock in the evening to avoid disturbing the neighbours, and those who have rediscovered the church (especially its links with pacifism) may be found joining hands before a meal to say a little prayer, just as their grandparents did. One way and another, there's no lack of variety in today's Germany!

TAKE-A-BREAK

1.2 DIALOGUE

◉◉ LISTEN

IM HOTEL

Silke Peters drops Marcel Bosquet at an hotel. Now he is at the reception desk.

Empfangsdame: *Guten Abend.*

Marcel: *Guten Abend. Ich habe ein Zimmer für eine Nacht reserviert.*

Empfangsdame: *Wie ist Ihr Name bitte?*

Marcel: *Bosquet.*

Empfangsdame: *Ja, Moment bitte. Bosquet, Bosquet... Es tut mir leid, „Bosquet" finde ich nicht.*

Marcel: *Wie bitte? Das ist unmöglich.*

Empfangsdame: *Bosquet. Bitte, wie schreibt man das?*

Marcel: *Bosquet. B-O-S-Q-U-E-T. Das ist französisch.*

Empfangsdame: *Ach so, ich verstehe. Sie sind Franzose.*

Marcel: *Ja, richtig.*

Empfangsdame: *Natürlich. Sie haben ein Einzelzimmer ohne Bad für eine Nacht reserviert.*

Marcel: *Nein, ein Einzelzimmer mit Dusche.*

Empfangsdame: *Hier ist der Schlüssel für Zimmer 16.*

Marcel: *Danke.*

Empfangsdame: *Der Lift ist rechts.*

Marcel: *Wann kann ich frühstücken?*

Empfangsdame: *Wann Sie möchten.*

Marcel: *Wo kann ich telephonieren?*

Empfangsdame: *Hier links ist die Telephonzelle. Gute Nacht, Herr Bosquet.*

◉◉ LISTEN AND REPEAT
See translation on page 2 of the booklet.

The Park Hotel, Regensburg.
The Golden Lamb Hotel, Rothenburg.

1.2   VOCABULARY

NOUNS

die Empfangsdame — receptionist
das Zimmer — room
die Nacht — night
der Franzose(1) (weak masculine noun) — Frenchman
das Einzelzimmer(2) — single room
das Bad — bath
die Dusche — shower
der Schlüssel — key
der Lift — lift
die Telefonzelle(2) — telephone booth/box

das Telefon — telephone
das Hotel — hotel
die Rezeption/der Empfang — reception
der Zimmerschlüssel(2) — room key
das Doppelzimmer(2) — double room
das Bett — bed
der Personalausweis(2) — identity card
der Ausweis — identity card, proof of identity
der Paß — passport
der Führerschein — driving licence
das Frühstück — breakfast
das Abendessen — dinner, supper

ADJECTIVES

möglich — possible
unmöglich — impossible
französisch — French
richtig — right, true
falsch — wrong, untrue
wichtig — important
sicher — certain, sure

deutsch — German
englisch — English
spanisch — Spanish
italienisch — Italian
amerikanisch — American

VERBS

haben — to have
reservieren — to reserve
finden — to find
schreiben — to write
verstehen — to understand
können(3) — to be able
frühstücken — to have breakfast
mögen(4) — to like
ich möchte — I should like
telefonieren — to telephone

MISCELLANEOUS

für(5) — for
bitte — please
nicht(6) — not
man — one, "you", "they" (speaking generally)
das — (here) that
natürlich — naturally, of course
ohne(5) — without / *mit(5)* — with
ja — yes / *nein* — no
danke — thank you
wann? — when?
wo — where (location)
rechts — on the right
links — on the left

aber — but

HOW TO SAY IT

Danke! — Thank you
Vielen Dank! — Many thanks
Danke schön! — Thank you very much
Ich danke Ihnen! — Thank you (formal)

Bitte!
Bitte schön } — That's all right!
(responding to thanks)
Gern geschehen! — Glad to help!
Nichts zu danken! — Don't mention it!

(einen) Moment, bitte!
(einen) Augenblick, bitte! } — Just a moment, please!
Warten Sie, bitte! — Please wait

Wie bitte? — I beg your pardon?
Wie schreibt man das? — How do you spell that?
Können Sie wiederholen? — Could you repeat that please?
Ich verstehe (das) nicht — I don't understand

Es tut mir leid — I'm sorry (about that)

REMARKS   REMARKS   REMARKS   REMARKS

(1) The noun, not the adjective, is used to express a person's nationality, eg Er ist Engländer/Sie ist Engländerin (He/she is English). — (2) Compound nouns are normally written as one word, with the last component determining both number and gender of the whole word, eg das Telefon + die Zelle = die Telefonzelle. — (3) Können (to be able) is a modal verb; see U1-L2 or the grammar on page 45 of the booklet. — (4) In this lesson we're studying only the conditional form of MÖGEN (to like): ich möchte, du möchtest etc (I should like, you would like, etc). The conditional form of MÖGEN is a polite way of expressing a wish. — (5) FÜR (for), OHNE (without) and MIT (with) are prepositions. — (6) NICHT (not) usually follows the verb, eg er versteht (he understands); er versteht nicht (he doesn't understand). For more information about the negative see U1-L5 or the grammar on page 48 of the booklet.

1.2   ORAL PRACTICE

1. ALPHABET

(● ●) LISTEN AND REPEAT

Wie schreibt man ,,Bosquet"?
● *B O S Q U E T*

Now repeat the following:
Wie schreibt man ,,Krumbach"? — Wie schreibt man ,,Frankfurt"? — Wie schreibt man ,,Jürgen"?
See grammar on page 36 of the booklet.

2. CONJUGATION OF VERBS

(● ●) LISTEN

ich reserviere, du reservierst, er/sie/es reserviert, wir reservieren, ihr reserviert, sie/Sie reservieren.

Now conjugate the following verbs:
finden — schreiben — verstehen — frühstücken.
See grammar on page 43 of the booklet.

3. MODAL VERBS

Mögen (conditional: möchten) and können.

(● ●) LISTEN AND REPEAT

Mögen:
  ich möchte, du möchtest, er/sie/ es möchte, wir möchten, ihr möchtet, sie/Sie möchten.
Können:
  ich kann, du kannst, er/sie/es kann, wir können, ihr könnt, sie/Sie können.
See grammar on page 45 of the booklet.

4. MODAL VERBS + INFINITIVE

(● ●) LISTEN

er (schreiben / mögen)
● *er möchte schreiben*
Sie (hier / warten können)
● *Sie können hier warten*

Now try making similar changes in the following sentences:
er (jetzt / frühstücken / mögen) — sie (ein Zimmer / mögen) — wir (verstehen / können) — er (ein Hotel / finden / können) — Sie (jetzt / gehen / können).
See grammar on page 45 of the booklet.

5. ,,HABEN"

(● ●) LISTEN AND REPEAT

ich habe, du hast, er/sie/es hat, wir haben, ihr habt, sie/Sie haben.
See grammar on page 44 of the booklet.

6. NEGATION

(● ●) LISTEN

er telefoniert
● *er telefoniert nicht*

Now make the same change, following the example:
das Taxi wartet — du schreibst — ich verstehe — ihr kommt — er schreibt — wir frühstücken.
See grammar on page 48 of the booklet.

7. ASKING QUESTIONS

(● ●) LISTEN

er telefoniert nicht
● *telefoniert er nicht?*

Now turn the sentences in exercise 6 into questions.

8. ADJECTIVE PRACTICE

(● ●) LISTEN

möglich
● *Dies (this) ist möglich, aber das ist unmöglich.*

Now try making similar sentences using the following words:
sicher — interessant — wichtig.
See grammar on page 38 of the booklet.

9. PRONUNCIATION

(● ●) LISTEN AND REPEAT

Guten Abend — ich habe das Zimmer reserviert — das ist unmöglich — natürlich — der Schlüssel — der Lift — der Lift ist rechts — die Telefonzelle ist links.

THE PRESS

Germany's federal politics naturally give rise to pluralism in other areas of life too. There is, for example, a multiplicity of newspapers: Germans have a trifling 1,250 to choose from. They generally prefer to place a regular order for their favourite papers and have them delivered.

First of all, there are the big daily newspapers, the Tageszeitungen, such as the Frankfurter Allgemeine Zeitung (Frankfurt) or the Süddeutsche Zeitung (Munich), which, though basically regional, are read all over Germany. They syndicate some of their features to local newspapers. Only Die Welt (Bonn) and Die Tageszeitung or TAZ (Berlin) claim to be national dailies. Whereas Die Welt is aimed at right-wing readers, the TAZ is an independent daily associated with the alternative left. It was founded in 1979 by intellectuals who felt unrepresented by the conventional press. Innovative and highly provocative, it attracts a large readership as a result of its enquiries into taboo or off-beat subjects neglected by other newspapers. Most of the major newspapers published in West Germany are increasingly widely read in the East as well, though some tend to be rather expensive for East German pockets. Neues Deutschland, formerly the dreary organ of the East German communist régime, has become an interesting newspaper dealing with post-reunification social and political problems. The eastern Länder also have numerous local and regional papers of their own.

Press baron Axel Springer and the publishing house of the same name are particularly well known for the tabloid Bildzeitung. This paper for the "man in

Titles galore

the street", der kleine Mann, not only has the biggest circulation of any European daily (5.4 million copies), but also, alas, takes first prize for vulgarity. Die Bild, as it's popularly called, feeds on scandal. It presents a reactionary view of the world, promotes nationalist propaganda and reduces its news coverage to sensational headlines. Bild's recipe for success can be summarized in two words: sex and crime. Its editors are often accused of lying and defamation.

Alongside the dailies and innumerable magazines there are the weekly papers, die Wochenzeitungen, which offer their readers both news and in-depth analysis. Of these Die Zeit (circulation 500,000) is the undisputed leader. It is published in Hamburg, the great stronghold of the press. Founded by members of the resis-

tance in 1946, this liberal weekly has become an institution in German intellectual life. Its articles are written in literate, if somewhat laboured German and are aimed primarily at thinking people - academics, writers, politicians, captains of industry and so forth. For some years it has been oriented towards European integration and has collaborated closely with other newspapers, notably Paris's Le Monde. The two papers publish joint supplements ("Liber") and organise conferences in which prominent literary figures and journalists take part.

The other big weekly published in Hamburg, the news magazine Der Spiegel, differs from Die Zeit both in style and in its penchant for investigative reporting. It is written in typical journalese, usually takes right-wing politics as its target and

has exposed numerous political scandals. Like the rest of the West German press, Der Spiegel was launched after the war under Allied supervision. Its format and cover layout were modelled on those of the American Time magazine.

The development of the German press is closely bound up with the history of West Germany. Anxious to promote democracy after twelve years of Nazi censorship and propaganda, the Allies introduced an Anglo-American style of journalism which is still recognisable. Many dailies, for example, publish voluminous Sunday supplements (Sonntagsausgaben) packed with information on sports and cultural events, as well as literary, artistic and economic reviews - plenty to keep the reader occupied in those long winter evenings!

No. 1

Fill in the form for Mr Bosquet

Hotel „Zur Post"

Veranstaltung/event/manifestation

Zimmerbestellung/reservation/réservation   für/for/pour   ☐ Pers.

Preisgruppe/category/catégorie   A ☐   B ☐   C ☐   D ☐

Anzahl number nombre	Zimmer/room/chambre	Ankunftstag arrival arrivée	Abreisetag departure départ
	Einzelzimmer/single/à 1 lit		
	2-Bettzimmer/with 2 beds/à 2 lits		
	3-Bettzimmer/with 3 beds/à 3 lits		

Besondere Wünsche/special requests/désirs particuliers . . . .
. . . .

Anreise mit Flugzeug ☐ | Bahn ☐ | Pkw ☐ | Bus ☐ | um . . . . . Uhr
arrival   by   air | train | car | coach | at . . . o'clock
arrivée   par avion | train | auto | bus | à . . . . heures

Name und Anschrift/ . . . .
name and address/ . . . .
nom et adresse/ . . . .
           Unterschrift/signature . . . .

Datum/date . . . .

Listen closely to the tape, then in the box below each picture put the number corresponding to the scene of the action.

A ☐

B ☐

C ☐

D ☐

(See answers on page 3 of the booklet)

DIALOGUE

●●● LISTEN

AUF DER BANK

Marcel Bosquet goes to the bank to change some money.

Marcel: *Guten Tag, ich möchte Geld wechseln.*

Der Bankangestellte: *Hier vorne bitte, Schalter drei.*

Marcel (am Schalter): *Ich habe französische Francs und möchte in D-Mark umtauschen. Wie steht der Kurs?*

Der Bankangestellte: *Sie bekommen 28 Mark und sechzig Pfennig für hundert Francs.*

Marcel: *Da steht aber dreißig Mark und*

vierzig Pfennig für hundert Francs.

Der Bankangestellte: *Das ist Verkauf. Wir verkaufen dreißig Mark und vierzig Pfennig für hundert Francs. Ankauf ist achtundzwanzig Mark und sechzig.*

Marcel: *Wieviel bekomme ich für tausend Francs?*

Der Bankangestellte: *Sie bekommen... äh... Moment bitte,... Sie bekommen zweihundertdreiundachtzig Mark.*

Marcel: *Wieviel? Das stimmt nicht. Tausend Francs... das macht zweihundertsechsundachtzig Mark.*

Der Bankangestellte: *Sie müssen drei Mark Gebühren zahlen. Das macht zweihundertdreiundachtzig.*

Marcel: *Ach so... Ich möchte bitte fünf Zwanzigmarkscheine haben. Und ich brauche Kleingeld für das Telefon. Wo kann ich ein Taxi finden?*

Der Bankangestellte: *Dort hinten ist ein Taxistand.*

Mr Bosquet leaves the bank.

Marcel: *Hallo, Taxi!*

Eine Passantin: *Hier können Sie lange warten!*

Marcel: *Warum?*

Die Passantin: *Hier hält kein Taxi an. Hier ist Halteverbot. Gehen Sie hundert Meter weiter. Da ist ein Taxistand.*

●●● LISTEN AND REPEAT
See translation on page 3 of the booklet.

*Frankfurt:
Opening of a new "alternative" Bank.
The Römerberg and the banking district.*

VOCABULARY

NOUNS

das Geld — money
der Bankangestellte — bank clerk
der Schalter — window (in a bank, etc)
die DM/die deutsche Mark — 100 Pfennig
der Pfennig — pfennig
das Geldstück — coin
der Kurs — exchange rate
der Verkauf — sale
der Ankauf — purchase
die Gebühren — charges
der Schein — banknote
das Kleingeld — small change
der Taxistand — taxi rank
kein Taxi — no taxi *(1)*
die Passantin — passer-by *(f)*
das Halteverbot — no stopping allowed
der Meter — metre

___

die Wechselstube — bureau de change
der Scheck — cheque
die Kreditkarte — credit card
das Konto — bank account
französische Francs — French francs
österreichische Schilling — Austrian Schillings

englische Pfund (das Pfund) — pounds sterling

VERBS

wechseln — to change money
umtauschen — to change money (into another currency)
bezahlen — to pay
verkaufen — to sell
einkaufen — to buy, purchase; to shop
bekommen — to get, receive
brauchen — to need
anhalten — to stop *(2)(3)*
weitergehen — to continue walking *(2)(4)*
müssen — to have to, be obliged to... *(5)*
stehen — to stand; here: to be written

MISCELLANEOUS

vorne — in front / hinten — behind
wieviel? — how much?
ach so! — oh, I see!
lange — for a long time
warum? — why?
und — and

NUMBERS

1: eins (ein Schalter, eine Mark, ein Taxi) — 2: zwei — 3: drei — 4: vier — 5: fünf — 6: sechs — 7: sieben — 8: acht — 9: neun — 10: zehn — 11: elf — 12: zwölf — 13: dreizehn — 14: vierzehn — 15: fünfzehn — 16: sechzehn — 17: siebzehn — 18: achtzehn — 19: neunzehn — 20: zwanzig — 21: einundzwanzig — 22: zweiundzwanzig — 23: dreiundzwanzig — ... — 30: dreißig — 40: vierzig — 50: fünfzig — 60: sechzig — 70: siebzig — 80: achtzig — 90: neunzig — 100: hundert/einhundert — 200: zweihundert — 278: zweihundertachtundsiebzig — 350: dreihundertfünfzig — 1 000: tausend — 1 000 000: eine Million

HOW TO SAY IT

Ich möchte Francs in DM umtauschen — I'd like to change some francs into German marks
Wie steht der Kurs? — What is the exchange rate?
Da steht 3,40 DM — It says there [ie on the board] 3 marks 40 pfennig

Hundertfünfzig minus drei macht hundertsiebenundvierzig — 150 - 3 = 147
Fünf plus drei macht (ist) acht — 5 + 3 = 8
Fünf mal drei macht (ist) fünfzehn — 5 x 3 = 15

Ich möchte telefonieren — I'd like to use a telephone
Ich möchte Geld wechseln — I'd like to change some money

Sie müssen 3,- DM bezahlen — You have to pay 3 marks
Ich brauche Kleingeld — I need some small change

Das stimmt — That's right
Wo kann ich telefonieren? — Where can I use a telephone?
Wo kann ich ein Taxi finden? — Where can I find a taxi?
Hier können Sie lange warten! — You will have a long wait here / you will have to wait a long time here

---

REMARKS   REMARKS   REMARKS   REMARKS

(1) The negative KEIN is used before a noun in place of the indefinite article: -- ein Taxi - kein Taxi (no taxi) -- ein Scheck - kein Scheck (no cheque) -- eine Telefonzelle - keine Telefonzelle (no telephone booth). It can also be used with nouns not usually preceded by an indefinite article: Ich habe Geld (I have money) -- Ich habe kein Geld (I have no money) (see grammar on page 48 of the booklet).— (2) Many German verbs take prefixes that alter their meaning. Separable prefixes usually go to the end of the clause or sentence. Eg: umtauschen - ich tausche DM um (I (ex)change some German marks) -- weitergehen - Herr Bosquet geht weiter (Mr Bosquet goes on walking). Some prefixes are inseparable. Eg: bezahlen - er bezahlt das Zimmer (he pays for the room) (See grammar on page 43 of the booklet). -— (3) Some strong verbs (see grammar on page 43 of the booklet) change their stem vowel in the second and third persons singular of the present tense. Eg: anhalten - das Taxi hält an (the taxi stops)— (4) The separable prefix weiter (further) can be used with many verbs. Eg: weiterschreiben - Silke schreibt weiter (Silke writes on, continues writing) — (5) Müssen (to have to, be obliged to): see grammar on page 45 of the booklet. When used with a negative, müssen means to have no need or obligation to do something. Eg: Ich muß Geld wechseln (I must change some money); ich muß KEIN Geld wechseln (I don't need to change any money).

1.3 ORAL PRACTICE

1. NUMBER PRACTICE

(• •) LISTEN

100,-DM
* *Ich möchte 100,-DM wechseln.*

Following the example, say how much you want to change:
250 Francs — 230 belgische Francs — 50 Dollar — 80 Pfund — 600 Schweizer Franken — 750 Pesetas — 900 Schilling.
See grammar on page 48 of the booklet.

2. CALCULATIONS

(• •) LISTEN AND REPEAT

Wieviel ist 2 x 7?
* *14 (Zwei mal sieben ist vierzehn)*
Wieviel ist 2 + 7?
* *9 (Zwei plus sieben ist neun)*
Wieviel ist 7 - 2?
* *5 (Sieben minus zwei ist fünf)*

Your turn to calculate:
3 x 3? — 4 + 15? — 10 - 6? — 8 + 16? — 12 x 12? — 5 x 20? — 8 + 7? — 12 - 4? — 320 + 15? — 150 - 45?

3. MODAL VERBS

Müssen
(• •) LISTEN AND REPEAT

ich muß, du mußt, er/sie/es muß, wir müssen, ihr müßt, sie/Sie müssen.

Müssen + Infinitive
(• •) LISTEN

Herr Bosquet (lange warten)
* *Herr Bosquet muß lange warten.*

Change the following into sentences in the same way:
Wir (ein Zimmer reservieren) — Herr Bosquet (ein Taxi anhalten) — Ich (französisch sprechen) — Silke Peters (50,-DM Gebühren bezahlen) — Sie (Geld wechseln).
See grammar on page 45 of the booklet

4. INTERROGATIVE SENTENCES

(• •) LISTEN

Herr Bosquet muß lange warten.
* *Muß Herr Bosquet lange warten?*

Change the sentences in exercise 3 into questions in the same way:
See grammar on page 47 of the booklet

5. NEGATIVE SENTENCES

(Be careful of the difference between nicht and kein!)
(• •) LISTEN

Muß Herr Bosquet lange warten?
* *Nein, Herr Bosquet muß <u>nicht</u> lange warten.*
Müssen wir ein Zimmer reservieren?
* *Nein, wir müssen <u>kein</u> Zimmer reservieren.*

Change the sentences in exercise 3 into negative sentences in the same way:
See grammar on page 48 of the booklet.

6. SEPARABLE PREFIXES

(• •) LISTEN

Herr Bosquet (Geld <u>um</u>tauschen)
* *Herr Bosquet tauscht Geld um.*

Change the following into sentences in the same way:
Silke Peters (Kaffee <u>ein</u>kaufen) — Wir (ein Taxi <u>an</u>halten) — Wir (jetzt <u>weiter</u>gehen).
See grammar on page 45 of the booklet.

7. PRONUNCIATION

(• •) LISTEN AND REPEAT

Ich möchte Geld wechseln — Ich möchte französische Francs umtauschen — Sie bezahlen drei Francs — Das ist Verkauf — Hier ist Halteverbot — Gehen Sie hundert Meter weiter.
See grammar on page 36 of the booklet.

FRANKFURT AM MAIN

Goethe, who was born in Frankfurt, called it Germany's secret capital. He was proud of the city's distinguished past: for three hundred years, the emperors of the Holy Roman Empire had been crowned there. Less than twenty years after his death, moreover, Frankfurt's Paulskirche (St Paul's church) became the seat of the first German parliament. Although this assembly met for barely two years (1848-1850) it had a lasting influence, for it drafted Germany's first democratic constitution, on which the modern Grundgesetz *(Basic Law)* of the German Federal Republic is largely based.

Today, commerce and banking make Frankfurt one of Germany's most important cities. It has been a financial centre since the 16th century; in the 17th, the mighty Rothschilds founded their financial empire there. Nowadays German Hochfinanz *(high finance)* is concentrated in Frankfurt. It is the headquarters of several major German banks, such as the Deutsche Bank, the Dresdner Bank and the Commerzbank. The stock exchange, of course, is there too. So is another important institution, the Deutsche Bundesbank, the German national central bank, which is responsible for the country's monetary policy. Like the American Federal Reserve Bank, but unlike its French and English counterparts, it is completely independent. Neither the Chancellor nor the government can impose their policies on the all-powerful Zentralbankrat *(Central Bank Council).* This independence ensures the stability of the German economy. But Frankfurt isn't only finance. It is, after all, Goethe's birthplace, and as host to the world's largest book fair, die Frankfurter Buchmesse, it attracts literary people from far and wide. Frankfurt University is also held in high regard.

In politics Frankfurt has traditionally been a trend-setter: even the radical Daniel Cohn-Bendit calls it home! He is assistant to the city's mayor, responsible for intercultural relations (- foreigners make up more than 20% of Frankfurt's population). Cosmopolitan and dynamic, Frankfurt is a young city despite its venerable past.

The old town is now reduced to a small nucleus around the Römerberg. Its medieval façades are, however, only meticulous reproductions of the originals which, like most of the city, were heavily bombed in the Second World War. Since 1945 Frankfurt has taken on a new look.

The Frankfurt Stock Exchange

It now bristles with huge tower blocks, the tallest of which, the Messeturm, is some 70 storeys high.

And what of the people? First and foremost, they enjoy the good life. It's no accident that they're famous for their Frankfurter sausages. They're accomplished cooks, and their real specialities are sauerkraut and gateaux. Cider, known locally as Appelwöi, is the staple beverage. The best cider bars are to be found in the Sachsenhausen district, Frankfurt's "left bank"; here people sit cheek by jowl at long tables convivially sharing the latest news and gossip. The people of Frankfurt are not without a sense of humour. "Bankfurt" is their nickname for the city. As more and more skyscrapers spring up around them, they also joke about living in "Mainhattan".

1.3   **TAKE-A-BREAK**

No. 1   🎧 LISTEN

Listen and write out in full the numbers you have just heard:

1. ....

2. ....

3. ....

4. ....

5. ....

No. 2

Tick R. (richtig) when the sentence is correct and F. (falsch) when it is wrong.

1. *Herr Bosquet möchte DM umtauschen* .... $\boxed{R}$ $\boxed{F}$

2. *Der Kurs steht 4,46 Francs* .... $\boxed{R}$ $\boxed{F}$

3. *Er will 1.000 Francs wechsein* .... $\boxed{R}$ $\boxed{F}$

4. *Er bekommt 278 Mark und 90 Pfennig* .... $\boxed{R}$ $\boxed{F}$

No. 3

Make out the cheque.

ABC   271,20 DM

ABC-BANK

271,20 DM

Form compound nouns!

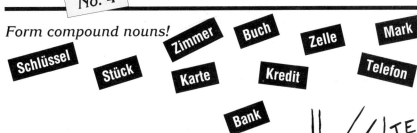

Schlüssel · Stück · Zimmer · Karte · Buch · Kredit · Zelle · Telefon · Mark · Angestellte · Bank

1. Das ist ein ....

4. Das ist der ....

2. Das ist eine ....

5. Das ist eine ....

3. Das ist ein ....

6. Das ist ein ....

(See answers on page 4 of the booklet)

LISTEN

Back at the hotel, Marcel Bosquet wants to telephone the publisher Hans-Jürgen Krumbach to arrange a meeting. But he hasn't got his number. So he calls directory enquiries:

Auskunft: *Hier Auskunft, bitte warten Sie! ... Hallo? Ja bitte?*

Marcel: *Guten Tag. Ich möchte die Telefonnummer von Hans-Jürgen Krumbach. Er ist Verleger hier in Frankfurt.*

Auskunft: *Es gibt viele Verleger hier in Frankfurt. Wie heißt der Verlag genau?*

Marcel: *Krumbach Verlag.*

Auskunft: *Augenblick bitte -- hallo? Die Nummer ist 502 43 20.*

Marcel: *502 43 20. Vielen Dank, auf Wiederhören.*

Marcel Bosquet lifts the receiver again and dials the number. But...

Stimme am Telefon: *Wolff & Söhne AG, guten Tag.*

TELEFONIEREN

Marcel: *Guten Tag. Ist Herr Krumbach da?*

Stimme am Telefon: *Wer? Krumbach? Kenne ich nicht.*

Marcel: *Wie bitte?*

Stimme am Telefon: *Das ist ein Irrtum. Sie sind falsch verbunden.*

Marcel: *Oh, Entschuldigung!*

Marcel Bosquet redials the number.

Stimme am Telefon: *Krumbach Verlag.*

Marcel: *Ja, guten Tag, hier ist Marcel Bosquet. Herr Krumbach, sind Sie es?*

Stimme am Telefon: *Nein, ich bin Udo Bartels. Herr Krumbach ist nicht da. Er besucht die Messe. Kann ich etwas für Sie tun?*

Marcel: *Ich möchte Herrn Krumbach treffen. Ich bin Schriftsteller und brauche Informationen über die Publikationsmöglichkeiten in Deutschland.*

Udo Bartels: *Ich verstehe. Am besten, Sie gehen direkt auf die Messe. Herr Krumbach ist dort jeden Tag morgens von neun Uhr bis zwölf Uhr und nachmittags von sechzehn bis achtzehn Uhr. Halle drei, Stand vierzehn.*

Marcel: *Gut, richten Sie bitte aus : ich komme heute nachmittag.*

Udo Bartels: *In Ordnung, mach' ich. Wiederhören.*

Marcel: *Auf Wiederhören.*

LISTEN AND REPEAT
See translation on page 4 of the booklet.

Bonn:
the statue of Beethoven in front of the main post office.
Telephone booths.

1.4   ***VOCABULARY***

NOUNS

die Auskunft — information
die Telefonnummer — telephone number
der Verlag — publishing house
der Sohn/pl. die Söhne — son *(1)*
der Irrtum — mistake
die Information — information
die Publikationsmöglichkeit —
possibility of getting something published
die Halle — hall
der Stand — stand
die Uhr — hour, time; clock, watch
die Ordnung — (good) order; routine
die Stimme — voice

_____

der Morgen — morning
der Vormittag — morning
der Mittag — midday, noon
der Nachmittag — afternoon
das Viertel — quarter
die Zeit — time
die Stunde — hour
die Zahl — number
eine halbe Stunde — half an hour
eine Viertelstunde — a quarter of an hour

ADJECTIVES

genau — exact
viele — many *(2)*
direkt — direct
am besten — best, the best thing *(3)*

VERBS

geben — to give, *es gibt* — there is, there
are *(4)*
verbunden sein — to be connected
besuchen — to visit
tun — to do, make; put
treffen — to meet
ausrichten — to deliver (a message); arrange

_____

wählen — to select; (here) dial
abheben/abnehmen — to lift, take off
auflegen/aufhängen — to hang up
beginnen — to begin
beenden/aufhören — to finish, stop
anrufen — to ring up, call (on the telephone)

ADVERBS

heute — today

_____

gestern — yesterday
morgen früh — tomorrow morning
morgens }— in the morning, every
vormittags }— morning

MISCELLANEOUS

von — from, of *(5)*
etwas — something
über — over, on; concerning
auf — (here) to *(5)*
alle — all
wer — who

HOW TO SAY IT

Krumbach (6), guten Tag — Hallo, Krumbach here
Krumbach am Apparat — Krumbach speaking
Hier ist Herr Krumbach — (This is) Mr Krumbach here

Geben Sie mir bitte... — Please could I speak to...
Bleiben Sie am Apparat — hold on, hold the line
Ich verbinde — I'm putting you through

Was? — What? Können Sie das bitte wiederholen? — Could you repeat that please?
Was sagen Sie? — What did you say?
Sprechen Sie (bitte) lauter — (please) speak up
Ich verstehe Sie schlecht — I'm having difficulty understanding you

In Ordnung — OK, no problem
na gut — all right, fine
alles klar — I see, that's quite clear

Wie spät ist es? — What time is it?
Wieviel Uhr haben wir? — What's the time?
Haben Sie/hast du die Uhrzeit? — Have you got the time?

08.00	*es ist (genau) acht Uhr (7)*	**08.30**	*es ist halb neun*
08.45	*es ist viertel vor neun*	**09.15**	*es ist viertel nach neun*
09.50	*es ist zehn vor zehn*	**10.10**	*es ist zehn nach zehn*
10.35	*es ist fünf nach halb elf*	**07.20**	*es ist zwanzig nach sieben*

REMARKS	*REMARKS*	*REMARKS*	*REMARKS*

(1) The plural of the definite article for all three genders is DIE; DER SCHEIN — DIE SCHEINE; DIE UHR — DIE UHREN; DAS BUCH — DIE BÜCHER. — (2) VIELE has adjectival endings when it precedes a plural noun (eg Silke hat viele Bücher = Silke has many books). It takes the form VIEL, which is invariable, when it precedes a singular noun (eg Herr Krumbach hat viel Geld = Mr Krumbach has lots of money) and when it is an adverb (eg Herr Bosquet schreibt viel = Mr Bosquet writes a lot). — (3) AM BESTEN is the superlative of GUT. See grammar on page 39 of the booklet. — (4) ES GIBT means both "there is" and "there are". For the conjugation of GEBEN see grammar on page 43 of the booklet. — (5) For prepositions see page 43 of the booklet. — (6) Germans normally give their name when answering the telephone. — (7) UHR, like the English "o'clock", is used with the full hour but not with fractions of the hour, eg Es ist drei Uhr = it is three o'clock, but es ist viertel vor drei = it is a quarter to three. Note, however, es ist zwei Uhr zwanzig = it is 2.20 / twenty past two. See exercise 5 on page 36.

1.4   ORAL PRACTICE

1. NUMBER PRACTICE

(●●) LISTEN TO THE TELEPHONE NUMBERS GIVEN BY DIRECTORY ENQUIRIES, AND REPEAT THEM:

040 47 4623   2136   32593   7805
506 32 98   78 64 10   7004

2. VERB PRACTICE

(●●) LISTEN

das Taxi anhalten (sie)
● *sie hält das Taxi an.*
Now make some sentences yourself!
das Buch geben (du) — das Taxi anhalten (es) — Silke treffen (er) — die Information geben (ich) — da anhalten (du) — Frau Peters treffen (ihr).

See grammar on page 41 of the booklet.

3. PRACTISING THE PLURAL

(●●) LISTEN

Das Bad
● *Es gibt viele Bäder.*
Now form the plural of:
der Irrtum — das Buch

(●●) LISTEN

Die Information
● *Es gibt viele Informationen.*
Your turn:
Die Uhr — der Herr — die Frau — der Journalist — die Ausstellung — das Bett

(●●) LISTEN

der Tag
● *Es gibt viele Tage.*
Your turn:
Der Schein — das Telefon — der Abend — der Ausweis.

(●●) LISTEN

der Schalter
● *Es gibt viele Schalter.*
Your turn:
das Zimmer — der Koffer — der Verleger — der Schlüssel.

4. TELLING THE TIME

(●●) LISTEN

Wann endet das Konzert?
● *Um halb elf.*
Wann beginnt die Messe?
● *Um viertel nach neun.*
Now answer these questions by giving the time:

16.45 *Wann beginnt die Ausstellung?*
17.40 *Wann kommt Udo Bartels?*
08.55 *Wann geht Silke Peters?*
06.50 *Wann ist der Abflug?*
08.15 *Wann telefoniert Herr Bosquet?*

See grammar on page 40 of the booklet.

5. TWO WAYS OF TELLING THE TIME

(●●) LISTEN

20:10
● *Es ist zwanzig Uhr zehn (Minuten)*
● *Es ist zwanzig (Minuten) nach acht*
Now tell the time in a different way:
15:25 — 13:15 — 7:45 — 3:30 — 11:45 — 14:30 — 16:00 — 23:15 — 0:10 — 6:30 — 12:20 — 18:50 — 20:30 — 10:00.

6. PRONUNCIATION

(●●) LISTEN

Hecke - Ecke
In German "h" at the beginning of a word is always pronounced.

Repeat:
Haus — aus / hier — ihr / Herde — Erde / heilig / eilig / hoffen — offen / Hund — und.

See grammar on page 36 of the booklet.

RADIO AND TELEVISION

As with the press, the history of German radio and television is closely linked to that of the country itself. In West Germany it was influenced primarily by the British, who after the war remodelled German broadcasting along the lines of the BBC. To guarantee freedom of expression, public service radio and TV (der öffentlich-rechtliche Rundfunk) is not state-controlled. There are nine publicly-owned companies, each broadcasting radio and TV programmes within its own specific area, which may be one Land (federal state) or a group of Länder. The legislative bodies of the Länder regulate these companies, which are each governed by a council made up of representatives of different sections of society (political parties, churches, etc). The seats are allocated in proportion to the importance of the various interest groups. The composition of these media "parliaments" varies from one region to another: in the Protestant north, liberal ideas predominate, while the south inclines toward a more conservative, Catholic set of values. Although the Rundfunk is required by its operating code to take account of the different elements within society, key positions are often held by people belonging to the ruling political party...

The öffentlich-rechtliche Rundfunk consists of three networks: the ARD, the ZDF and a third network of local stations. They jointly finance films and TV productions and co-ordinate their output so that there are never two similar programmes on at the same time. The two big evening news reports, the ARD's Tagesschau and the ZDF's Heute are spaced an hour apart. Since the mid-eighties the public broadcasting service has faced increasing competition from independent networks. Having first tried to fight back by offering more fiction and light entertainment, the ARD and the ZDF finally decided to concentrate on increasing their news coverage. Now almost half their output consists of news programmes and documentaries.

Not that the German public doesn't revel in American series such as Dallas! German television zealously produces and broadcasts its own soap-operas too. Die Schwarzwaldklinik, for example, was a success because it was all about health, which is a favourite topic of conversation in Germany. Programmes about the police also get impressively high ratings.

Inspector Derrick, TV hero

It's the investigative process itself that fascinates the audience, whether the officer in charge is Inspector Derrick or one of the detectives on Tatort (Scene of the Crime). All such series depict a police force of high integrity and the everyday moral and ethical problems a police officer has to face.

However, even on television, fiction isn't as interesting as real life. This explains why, ever since 1967, people have been staying home in droves to watch a programme called Aktenzeichen XY ungelöst (Case XY unsolved), which is not unlike the BBC's Crimewatch. Its purpose is to help the police track down criminals by mobilising the television audience. To this end the programme-makers reconstruct the crime, which is usually a hold-up, murder or rape. The presenter then gives the viewers all the clues so far gathered by the police as to the identity of the criminals. According to the producers, 40% of the cases shown have been solved, thanks to the viewers and their one-night stand as detectives.

As public radio and TV are financed by the State, commercial advertising plays almost no part in it. It's strictly limited to twenty minutes a day, between the hours of 6.00 pm and 8.00 pm, and is shown only on the two main channels ARD and ZDF. On Sundays and public holidays German viewers are spared commercials. Audiences in other countries may well envy them!

Because it doesn't allow itself to be influenced too much by the superficiality of some of the programmes on independent radio and television, the public broadcasting service is very highly regarded in Germany. Over the years many notable Hörspiele (radio plays) have been produced; German radio runs contests for aspiring writers and gives commissions to established playwrights.

1.4 TAKE-A-BREAK

Who is talking to whom? Finish the sentences!

1. .... spricht mit ....

2. ....ruft............an.....

3. .... telefoniert mit ....

4. ....ist mit ....verbunden.

KARIN: Hallo, hier ist Karin. Ich möchte Rolf sprechen.

MANNI: Petra, bist du es? Oh, Verzeihung.

THEODOR KRAMER: Wie bitte? Ich kann Sie nicht verstehen. Wer? Sprechen Sie lauter!

KARSTEN: Ich will die Ausstellung besuchen. Und du?

HERR MÜLLER: Müller

Ja, einen Moment bitte.

Ich glaube, Sie sind falsch verbunden.

HERR STREICHHOLZSCHÄCHTELCHEN: Guten Tag. Hier ist Herr Streichholzschächtelchen. Ich bin Herr Streich·holz·schäch·tel·chen!!!

HERR XY

KARL MARTIN: Was machst du heute nachmittag?

Ich arbeite.

What time is it? Write it down!

1. Es ist ....

5. Es ist ....

2. Es ist ....

6. Es ist ....

3. Es ist ....

7. Es ist ....

4. Es ist ....

8. Es ist ....

(See answers on page 5 of the booklet)

1.5   *DIALOGUE*

    DIE BUCHMESSE IN FRANKFURT

Marcel Bosquet, Hans-Jürgen Krumbach and Silke Peters meet at the Krumbach Books stand. Udo Bartels, a colleague of Hans-Jürgen Krumbach, joins them.

Udo: *Tag, Hans-Jürgen!*

Hans-Jürgen: *Na endlich! Da bist du!*

Udo: *Entschuldigung, mein Bus hatte Verspätung.*

Hans-Jürgen: *Wir haben Gäste: Silke Peters kennst du ja. Und das ist Herr Bosquet aus Paris.*

Udo: *Hallo, Silke. Guten Tag, Herr Bosquet, mein Name ist Udo Bartels. Sind Sie auch Verleger?*

Marcel: *Nein, ich bin kein Verleger. Ich bin Schriftsteller. Und Sie?*

Udo: *Ich arbeite mit Herrn Krumbach zusammen.*

Marcel: *Ach so, dann waren Sie das heute morgen am Telefon.*

Udo: *Ja, das war ich. Ich hatte Telefondienst...*

Hans-Jürgen: *Udo ist mein Mitarbeiter. Er ist verantwortlich für...*

Marcel: *Das trifft sich gut. Sind Sie Lektor? Ich möchte mein Buch in Deutschland veröffentlichen.*

Udo: *Da kann ich nicht helfen. Das ist nicht meine Aufgabe. Das macht Herr Krumbach persönlich.*

Silke: *Ja, Herr Krumbach, das Buch ist wirklich spannend. Es geht um die Finanzaffäre bei Molten & Co.*

Hans-Jürgen: *Normalerweise verlege ich keine Kriminalliteratur.*

Silke: *Aber das ist ein Tatsachenbericht!*

Marcel: *Ich habe hier ein Exemplar für Sie, Herr Krumbach.*

Hans-Jürgen: *Ja, dann zeigen Sie mal. Ich lese das Manuskript vielleicht morgen oder übermorgen.*

Silke: *Darauf müssen wir anstoßen!*

Udo: *Ja, das finde ich auch. Haben wir Sekt?*

Hans-Jürgen: *Ja, ich glaube. Kannst du die Flasche und die Gläser holen?*

Udo Bartels brings the bottle and pours drinks all round.

Hans-Jürgen: *Na denn, zum Wohl!*

Silke: *Zum Wohl und auf eine gute Zusammenarbeit!*

Marcel: *C'est un grand jour pour moi! Levons nos verres!*

Udo: *Prost!*

● ● LISTEN AND REPEAT
See translation on page 6 of the booklet.

A German bookshop.

1.5 VOCABULARY

NOUNS

der Bus — bus
die Verspätung — delay
Die Gäste / sing.: *der Gast* — guest(s)
Telefondienst haben — to mind the telephone
der Mitarbeiter — colleague
der Lektor — publisher's reader
die Aufgabe — job, task
die Finanzaffäre — financial scandal
die Kriminalliteratur — crime novels/stories
der Tatsachenbericht — factual report
die Tatsache — fact
der Bericht — report
das Exemplar — copy
das Manuskript — manuscript
der Sekt — sparkling wine (German equivalent of champagne)
die Flasche — bottle
die Gläser / sing.: *das Glas* — glass(es)
das Wohl — well-being, health
die Zusammenarbeit — collaboration

---

das Wasser/das Mineralwasser — water/ mineral water
das Bier — beer
der Wein — wine
die Arbeit — work

ADJECTIVES/ADVERBS

persönlich — personally, personal
wirklich — really, true
spannend — exciting
gut — good, well

---

zuständig — responsible

ungefähr — approximately
pünktlich — punctual, punctually
schlecht — bad, badly

VERBS

zusammenarbeiten — to collaborate, work together
verantwortlich sein (für) — to be responsible (for)
helfen (1) — to help
verlegen — to publish
zeigen — to show
lesen (1) — to read
anstoßen — to drink a toast
glauben — to believe
publizieren — to publish
herausgeben — to publish, edit
arbeiten — to work
fahren — to go (by transport), drive

MISCELLANEOUS

endlich — finally, at last
bei (2) — at, with, at the house of
normalerweise — normally
dann — then
vielleicht — perhaps
auch — also
na denn — now then, well then

---

manchmal — sometimes
oft — often
selten — seldom
nie — never
immer — always

HOW TO SAY IT

Es geht um...
Es handelt sich von } — it's to do with...
Es ist die Rede von — it's a question of

Zum Wohl — all the best!
Auf Ihre Gesundheit — (Your) good health!
Auf eine gute Zusammenarbeit — here's to a successful collaboration
Auf bald — here's to the next time
Prost — cheers!

Wie geht es Ihnen? — how do you do? (polite)
Wie geht es dir? — how are you? (informal)
Wie geht's (3) — how are things with you? / how goes it? (informal)
Danke, gut. Und Ihnen / Dir? — Fine, thanks. How about you?
Hervorragend — excellent, great
Blendend! — terrific
Nicht (4) so gut — not very well
Es geht
So lala } — so-so, could be better
Schlecht! — badly
Alles klar? — everything all right? (can be question or statement)

Wie schaut's aus? — how does it look? What's the picture?

REMARKS   REMARKS   REMARKS   REMARKS

(1) For the conjugation of HELFEN and LESEN see grammar on page 45 of the booklet. — (2) BEI is a preposition. — (3) The apostrophe indicates that an 'e' is omitted: wie geht's = wie geht es. — (4) Negation with NICHT (see note 6, page 19): where the verb has an object, the word order is subject + verb + object + NICHT. Eg: Er versteht das Buch nicht = he doesn't understand the book.

1.5 *ORAL PRACTICE*

1. MAKING SENTENCES

(••) LISTEN

Herr Bosquet trifft Silke Peters (da)
● *Da trifft Herr Bosquet Silke Peters.*

Make some sentences, following the example and using the adverb given.
Herr Krumbach besucht die Messe (dann) —
Die Ausstellung beginnt (endlich) — Udo war
in Frankfurt (gestern) — Wir trinken Kaffee
(jetzt) — Er hat Verspätung (morgens) — Udo
kommt pünktlich (normalerweise) — Das
Hotel ist angenehm (natürlich).
See grammar on page 47 of the booklet.

2. PRACTISING THE NEGATIVE

(••) LISTEN

sie ruft Peter an
● *sie ruft Peter nicht an.*

Put the following sentences into the negative:
Wir brauchen die Uhr — ihr kennt Frankfurt
— ich reserviere das Zimmer — du schreibst
das Manuskript — er besucht die Ausstellung
— ich glaube das.
See grammar on page 48 of the booklet.

3. VERB PRACTICE

fahren, lesen, helfen *belong to the same group of verbs as* **anhalten, geben.**

(••) LISTEN AND REPEAT

ich fahre — ich lese — ich helfe — du fährst
— du liest — du hilfst — er,sie,es fährt —
er,sie,es liest — er,sie,es hilft — wir fahren —
wir lesen — wir helfen — ihr fahrt — ihr lest
— ihr helft — sie fahren — sie lesen — sie
helfen. See grammar on page 43 of the booklet.

4. IMPERFECT TENSE OF „SEIN"

(••) LISTEN

*sein: ich war, du warst, er /sie / es
war, wir waren, ihr wart, sie waren.
Er ist da*

● *Er war da.*

Put the following sentences into the imperfect tense:
Ich bin in Frankfurt — sie ist interessant — ihr
seid hier — sie sind in Paris — es ist wichtig
— wir sind sechs. See grammar on page 44 of the booklet.

5. IMPERFECT TENSE OF „HABEN"

(••) LISTEN

haben:
● *ich hatte, du hattest, er / sie / es
hatte, wir hatten, ihr hattet, sie hatten.
Er hat es*
● *Er hatte es.*

Put the following sentences into the imperfect tense:
Du hast Geld — Udo und Silke haben Sekt —
er hat Telefondienst — wir haben Verspätung
— ihr habt Zeit — sie hat das Buch.
See grammar on page 44 of the booklet.

6. THE INDEFINITE ARTICLE

(••) LISTEN

Herr Krumbach verlegt ein Buch
● *Herr Krumbach verlegt Bücher.*

Remember that the indefinite article has no plural. Now put the following sentences into the plural:
Udo holt ein Glas — Silke ruft ein Taxi — Herr
Bosquet reserviert ein Zimmer — Sie braucht
eine Information — Er tauscht eine Münze um
— Sie trinken eine Flasche Sekt.
See grammar on page 37 of the booklet.

7. PRONUNCIATION

Listen to the difference between the long vowel in schie̲f *and the short vowel in* schi̲ff

(••) REPEAT

schief / Schiff — Beet / Bett — Weg / weg —
Miete / Mitte — ihn / in — Ruhm / Rum —
Wahl / Wall — Rose / Rosse — Heer / Herr —
Ofen / offen.
See grammar on page 36 of the booklet.

The library in the Wim Wenders film "Wings of Desire"

BOOKS

"The German nation is by nature literary and philosophical", remarked the French writer Madame de Staël on returning from Germany almost 200 years ago. She saw her neighbours across the Rhine as a Volk der Dichter und Denker (a people of poets and thinkers). There is still much to be said for this view.

Germans are avid readers. In Gutenberg's native land books are loved both for their content and as things of beauty in themselves: there is a tradition of fine binding, and many hardback books are very handsomely bound.

The Buchhandel (book trade) is thriving. About 70,000 titles a year are produced in what used to be West Germany alone, roughly the same as in Britain. Nevertheless there is no literary "establishment", and German reading tastes remain largely a personal and private matter. Politically and culturally, and thus in publishing too, the absence of centralisation has always been a significant factor in Germany. Munich, where 10,000 titles are published each year, has some claim to be called the

literary centre of Germany; but so have other big cities, most notably Frankfurt, home of the Börsenverein, the all-powerful German Book Trade Association. Publishers, broadcasters, booksellers and most other professionals from the world of books belong to this organisation. Frankfurt is also the site of the world's largest book fair which, every autumn, welcomes German and foreign publishers alike. But it would be wrong to overlook Stuttgart, Hamburg (headquarters of the German press) and especially Berlin with its countless small publishing houses — artistic, esoteric, committed, "alternative" — the best known of which are Wagenbach and Rotbuch. Since reunification it seems likely that Berlin, and Leipzig too, will eventually become once again the major publishing centres they used to be.

Book lovers read literary reviews in the Feuilletons, the cultural sections of the major newspapers such as Die Zeit, Frankfurter Allgemeine Zeitung or Süddeutsche Zeitung. Or they simply ask their bookseller's advice. Booksellers are often very knowledgeable and can supply almost any title within 24 hours with the aid of the Barsortimente,

wholesale distributors offering instant stock of almost all books in print. It is largely thanks to this system that the book trade is so prosperous, because it enables booksellers to satisfy customer demand quickly without having to carry large stocks. The small "fringe" publishers, however, tend to be left out of the catalogues, and consequently accuse the Barsortimente of influencing the market by offering only selected titles and discriminating against the less well-known publishers.

The undisputed giant of German publishing is the Bertelsmann group, a world leader in communications. Bertelsmann controls about 15 publishing houses in Germany and has subsidiaries involved in paper manufacture, printing, distribution and all the media. The sheer size of the organisation worries people in German publishing circles who fear for the survival of the many smaller companies within the industry.

Faced with this trend, the small publishers will have to make it their business to preserve, if they can, the tradition of cultural diversity for which Germany is envied the world over.

1.5　TAKE-A-BREAK

No. 1 🔊 LISTEN

Find the right answer:

1. Wie heißen Sie?
a. Danke, gut.
b. Mein Name ist Udo Bartels.
c. Nein, ich heiße nicht Silke Peters.
d. Ich heiße Bankangestellte.

2. Was machen Sie?
a. Ich bin Schriftsteller.
b. Ich bin Udo Bartels.
c. Ich heiße Schriftsteller.
d. Ich mache Schriftsteller.

3. Wie spät ist es?
a. Er ist Viertel nach fünf.
b. Es hat Viertel nach fünf.
c. Wir haben Viertel nach fünf Stunden.
d. Es ist genau Viertel nach fünf.

4. Wie geht es Ihnen?
a. Gut, und Ihnen?
b. Danke ich bin gut.
c. Nein, ich gehe nicht.
d. Mir geht.

No. 2

Find the hidden words (horizontally, vertically, diagonally):

```
K O F F E R Q E A S D V I Y O Ü N W I L E F G
A S E C V F T Z N E Z U J A W Ö I R R V L E Ä
Z K M A Y X G H K I O Y Ö U K O C T E E P M X
D T A X I K Ö F U J A A T S I J H M C W Q P M
R E R S A D W B N N I Ä C W G V T I H S W F F
Q E K F F T I L F L U G Z E U G S Q T W U A Ö
L I E G R I U R T B I Ü O I F H V X S G K N G
R E S Q A E N G M H S A U S S T E L L U N G W
M S Y E U I Ä D O T Z B I U Z B V Y X S A Q W
B I T T E J V G E L D E L Ö N E U N Z I G M C
Ä Ö Ü B N K M H K N U N L P I Z T R E X Q M L
K H Z T N B Ä O Ä P I D O P P E L Z I M M E R
E H U N D E R T O Z I J Ö V S E I N U F E S A
Ä L K J G F B E T T O I U Z T O F L Ö O E S Z
E N T S C H U L D I G U N G L Ö T Ä I Z W E R
E S S E N O U T N B J E T Z T R B X Y W Q I J
```

(See answers on page 7 of the booklet)

Figures of Speech

EINEN FROSCH IM HALS HABEN

To have a frog in one's throat

EINEN KATER HABEN

To have a tomcat
To have a hangover

EINEN VOGEL HABEN

To have a bird
**To have a bee in one's bonnet
(or "bats in the belfry")**

SCHWEIN HABEN

To have a pig
To be lucky

1.   WRITTEN PRACTICE

1.1

Supply the missing verbs: *Da ...... Herr Bosquet. Das ...... Der Schriftsteller Günter Grass. Wie ...... Sie? Mein Name ...... Krumbach. Ich ...... ein Taxi. Ich ...... Frau Peters aus Paris. Das Taxi .... *
Translate: *Wie heißen Sie? Woher kennen Sie Silke Peters? Ach, das ist interessant.*
Mr Bosquet is a writer. Mr Krumbach is a publisher. Silke Peters is a journalist.

1.2

Fill in the gaps: *Sie haben ...... ohne ...... reserviert. Nein, ich habe ...... mit ...... für ...... reserviert. Hier ist ...... für .... 16. ...... ist rechts, und ...... ist links. ...... ist angenehm.*
Translate: *Er möchte ein Zimmer reservieren. Sie möchten frühstücken. Du möchtest telefonieren. Wir können kein Taxi finden. Könnt ihr verstehen?*
I can come. He can have his breakfast. We can find a taxi. I'd like to telephone.

1.3

Put the verbs in the right form. (Be careful with the prefixes!): *Er ...... Geld ...... (umtauschen). Das Taxi ...... (anhalten). Er ...... das Zimmer ...... (bezahlen). Die Bank ...... 3,34 Francs für eine Mark ...... (verkaufen). Herr Bosquet ...... jetzt ...... (weitergehen).*
Translate: *Schalter drei ist hier vorne. Der Taxistand ist dort hinten. Hier ist Halteverbot.*
I'd like to change some money. How much is 1,000 francs worth? I need change for the telephone.

1.4

Put the nouns in brackets into the plural: *Silke Peters hat viele ..... (das Buch). Herr Krumbach braucht viele ...... (die Information). Herr Bosquet hat sechs ...... (der Koffer). Das Hotel hat hundertzwei ...... (das Zimmer). Es gibt in Frankfurt viele ...... (die Ausstellung).*
Translate: *Es ist fünf Uhr. Es ist Viertel nach sechs. Es ist halb sieben. Es ist zwanzig vor acht. Es ist fünf vor neun.*
It is noon. It is half past three. It is quarter past seven. It is ten past five.

1.5

Make four sentences out of the following words: *Udo Bartels -- Herrn Krumbach -- das Buch -- der Bus -- Verspätung -- ich -- das Manuskript -- arbeitet -- hatte -- ist -- lese -- vielleicht -- wirklich -- spannend -- mit -- morgen -- zusammen.*
Translate: *Herr Bosquet war in Frankfurt. Das Taxi hatte Verspätung. Das Buch war interessant. Silke hatte kein Geld.*
Udo was my collaborator. It wasn't my job. We had guests. I had a copy for you.

(See answers on page 31 of the booklet)

MORE VOCABULARY

CONTINENTS

Africa — Africa
Amerika — America
Antarktis — Antarctica
Asien — Asia
Australien — Australia
Europa — Europe

EC COUNTRIES **

Belgien — Belgium
Dänemark — Denmark
Deutschland — Germany
Frankreich — France
Griechenland — Greece
Großbritannien — Great Britain
Irland — Ireland
Italien — Italy
Luxemburg — Luxembourg
die Niederlände — the
Netherlands
Portugal — Portugal
Spanien — Spain

NATIONALITIES

der Italiener — Italian
die Italienerin — Italian (f)
*der Franzose** — Frenchman
die Französin — Frenchwoman
der Engländer — Englishman
die Engländerin —
Englishwoman
der Spanier — Spaniard
die Spanierin — Spaniard (f)
der Deutsche — German
die Deutsche — German (f)
der Portugiese — Portuguese
die Portugiesin — Portuguese (f)
der Belgier — Belgian
die Belgierin — Belgian (f)
der Luxemburger —
Luxemburger
die Luxemburgerin —
Luxemburger (f)
der Holländer — Dutchman
die Holländerin — Dutchwoman

*der Grieche** — Greek
die Griechin — Greek (f)
*der Däne** — Dane
die Dänin — Dane (f)
der Ire — Irishman
die Irin — Irishwoman

OTHER COUNTRIES **

Ägypten — Egypt
Algerien — Algeria
Angola — Angola
Argentinien — Argentina
Bosnien — Bosnia
Croatien — Croatia
Brasilien — Brazil
Bulgarien — Bulgaria
Burkina Faso — Burkina Faso
Chile — Chile
China — China
die Elfenbeinküste — Ivory
Coast
Finnland — Finland
Indien — India
Indonesien — Indonesia
Israel — Israel
Japan — Japan
Jordanien — Jordan
Kanada — Canada
der Libanon — Lebanon
Libyen — Libya
Marokko — Morocco
Mexiko — Mexico
Neuseeland — New Zealand
Nigeria — Nigeria
Norwegen — Norway
Österreich — Austria
Polen — Poland
Rumänien — Romania
Rußland — Russia
Saudiarabien — Saudi Arabia
Schweden — Sweden
die Schweiz — Switzerland
der Senegal — Senegal
Serbien — Serbia
die Slowakei — Slovakia
Slowenien — Slovenia

Südafrika — South Africa
die Tschechische Republik —
The Czech Republic
Tunesien — Tunisia
die Türkei — Turkey
Ungarn — Hungary
die Vereinigten Staaten —
United States
Vietnam — Vietnam
Zaire — Zaire

TRAVEL

die Reise — journey
*die Bus-, die Flug-, die Zug-,
die Auto-, die Gruppenreise* —
journey by bus, air, train, car, with a
group
das Gepäck — luggage
die Buchung — booking,
reservation
das Reisebüro — travel agency
der Reisende — traveller
die Fahrt — journey, trip
das Abteil — compartment
*das Raucher-/Nicht-
raucherabteil* — smoking / nonsmoking compartment
der Fahrschein / Flugschein
— train/plane ticket
der Bahnhof — railway station
die Eisenbahn — railway
das Gleis — (railway) track
die Wartehalle — waiting room
der Zoll — customs
die Autobahn — motorway
die Strasse/die Landstrasse —
street, road/trunk road
der Koffer — suitcase
die Fahrkarte — ticket
das Auto — car

* weak masculine noun
** Countries are always neuter (das)
except where shown.

1. TEST YOURSELF

1. TRUE OR FALSE? (RICHTIG ODER FALSCH)

1. Silke Peters ist Schriftstellerin. ....

2. Herr Krumbach kommt aus Paris. ....

3. Herr Bosquet hat ein Zimmer reserviert. ....

4. Udo Bartels und Herr Krumbach arbeiten zusammen. ....

5. Die Buchmesse ist in Frankfurt. ....

6. Herr Bosquet möchte Dollars umtauschen. ....

7. Der Krumbach Verlag hat die Telefonnummer: 5024302. ....

8. Alle trinken Sekt. ....

2. COMPLETE WITH: „WIE, WOHER, WANN, WO, WIEVIEL, WARUM, WAS, WER"

1. ....heißen Sie?   *2.* ....kommt Herr Bosquet?

3. .... kennen Sie Silke Peters?   *4.* ..... hat Udo Bartels Verspätung?

5. ....Geld wechselt Herr Bosquet?   *6.* .... kann ich ein Taxi finden?

7. .... macht Herr Krumbach?   *8.* .... ist am Telefon?

3. WHAT WOULD YOU SAY IF YOU HAD TO ....

1. Introduce yourself? ....

2. Ask someone's name? ....

3. Thank someone? ....

4. Reserve a hotel room? ....

5. Change money? ....

6. Ask how someone was getting on? ....

7. Indicate your agreement? ....

8. Ask what time it is? ....

4. FIND THE RIGHT VERB

kenne / kennst / frühstücke / kann
1. Ich .... Frau Peters aus Paris.
schreibt / liest / versteht / möchte
2. Bosquet .... man: BOSQUET.
verkauft / finde / heißt / braucht
3. Herr Bosquet .... Kleingeld für das Telefon.
wechselt / macht / geht / beginnt
4. Silke Peters .... direkt auf die Messe.

5. FIND THE QUESTION THAT FITS THE ANSWER

1. Wie heißen Sie?
2. Woher kommt Herr Bosquet?   *A. Aus Paris.*
3. Was liest Herr Krumbach?   *B. Silke Peters.*
4. Wann beginnt die Messe?   *C. Um fünf Uhr.*

6. ONLY ONE OF EACH GROUP IS CORRECT. WHICH ONE?

Tick the right box

A. Ich ist Verleger hier in Frankfurt. .... ☐
B. Ich war Verleger hier in Frankfurt. .... ☐
C. Ich war Verleger links in Frankfurt. .... ☐

A. Woher kennen Sie Silke Peters? .... ☐
B. Wer kennen Sie Silke Peters? .... ☐
C. Wo kennen Sie Silke Peters? .... ☐

A. Ich möchte meine Buch in Deutschland veröffentlichen. .... ☐
B. Ich möchte mein Buch in Deutschland veröffentlicht. .... ☐
C. Ich möchte meine Bücher in Deutschland veröffentlichen .... ☐

A. Kennst du die Flasche und die Gläser holen? .... ☐
B. Kannst du die Flasche und die Gläser holen? .... ☐
C. Kannst du die Fläsche und die Glaser holen? .... ☐

(See answers on page 33 of the booklet)

LONDON - BERLIN, ONE WAY

*S*imon Lambert did not usually read the classified adverts in the newspapers. Since coming to London two years ago he had always turned first to the financial section, as a young executive should. Now, sitting in a fashionable pub with a tall glass of lager in front of him, he reflected that his diligence was being rewarded: he was doing well at his job and the future looked rosy...

It was a fine spring evening, and the pale blue sky visible through the window made the soft lights over the bar seem warm and welcoming. Simon relaxed.

Yes, life was pretty good. He could see himself running the London office of his firm within a few years... if only he could keep up his present rate of progress. Frowning slightly, he ordered another lager and leafed through his newspaper in search of distraction from unwelcome thoughts. He came across the personal column. "Handsome romantic male seeks fun-loving female" it said. Hmmm... An attractive blonde sitting nearby diverted his attention for a moment - until he realised she wasn't alone. Regretfully, he returned to the paper.

The fact was that he didn't feel like going home to his desirable bachelor flat just yet. He would have to get on with the project his boss had given him, which was a market research study to do with an after-shave lotion his firm wanted to promote in Germany, and he couldn't work up any enthusiasm for it. Not only did he dislike the heavy scent of this particular product, but his knowledge of German and Germany wasn't really up to the job, and he knew he was going to have to do something about that. Germany was, after all, his firm's most important export market...

With a sigh he glanced again down the personal column, and to his surprise some German words caught his eye. „Deutsche sucht Engländerin" (German girl seeks English girl), the advert began, then continued in English: " I'm from Berlin, and I want to improve my English and learn about England by corresponding with a Londoner. I suggest you write mostly in English and I write mostly in German, then we should both learn something." It was signed Lore Brinkmann.

Simon sat back and thought. Perhaps this was the sort of thing he needed. He knew he wasn't going to immerse himself in grammar books to improve his German; at most, he might try picking up one of the bronzed and beautiful German girls to be found at any European holiday resort... but he had already made holiday plans for August with his girlfriend Laura, so that wouldn't work. Anyway, the summer holidays were still a long way off, and the real problem was that his boss was asking him to translate more and more letters from German companies now; sooner or later the firm would be sending him to Germany to find things out on the spot.

Why this mantle had fallen on his shoulders he wasn't sure. No doubt it was partly because he had claimed, at his job interview, that he had learned German at school (as indeed he had, after a fashion). Perhaps his appearance had something to do with it too: people seemed to think he looked like a German. The junior typist said he was just like the tall blond Nazi officer in some war film she had seen. „Jawohl, Herr Major!" she chirped, whenever he asked her to do something. Even though she was a very pretty girl, Simon was not amused.

What a pity the German girl wanted a female penfriend... but on the other hand, why should it matter? And what was to stop him from pretending to be a girl for this purpose? She need never know... He decided to answer the advert, just for the hell of it. Finishing off his second lager, he began drafting a letter on the back of an envelope.

Albrecht Dürer: The martyrdom of ten thousand Christians.

,,Sehr geehrtes Fräulein Brinkmann..." *he began, in formal business-letter style; then realised that she could equally well be a Frau, a married woman. He remembered his German teacher commenting wrily that no such distinction was drawn between single and married men.* "In German" *she had said* "Fräulein is die kleine Frau, *the little woman. So why is a young unmarried man not* Männlein, *the little man? But no, a man is addressed as* Herr, *which means lord". However, Simon knew that in Germany nowadays any adult woman can be addressed as* Frau. *So he settled for* ,,Sehr geehrte Frau Brinkmann"...

CONTINUED ....

The port of Hamburg at night.

UNIT 2

AM ARBEITSPLATZ

Back in Hamburg, Silke Peters returns to her job in the editorial offices of Der Spiegel.

Frauke von Hohen, Redakteurin: *Hallo, Silke, wie war's in Frankfurt?*

Silke: *Schön, aber anstrengend. Wo ist denn meine Post?*

Frauke: *Hier ist deine Post. Ist dein Artikel über die Buchmesse fertig?*

Silke: *Nein, er ist noch nicht ganz fertig,*

ich brauche noch die Besucherzahlen, Fotos und den Pressebericht aus Frankfurt.

Frauke: *Dieter Hartmann hat den Pressebericht. Du kannst ihn sicher fragen.*

Silke: *Danke für den Tip. Na, dann will ich mal...*

She heads for the office of her boss, Dieter Hartmann...

Silke: *Tag, wie geht's? Hast du den Pressebericht aus Frankfurt?*

Dieter Hartmann: *Ja, hier hast du ihn. -- Was macht der Artikel?*

Silke: *Ich gebe ihn heute nachmittag ab.*

Dieter: *O.K. Übrigens, du darfst den Termin mit Werner Gebert nicht vergessen.*

Silke: *Wer? Was sagst du? Wann denn?*

Dieter: *Ja, du sollst die Reportage über die Yuppies übernehmen. Und Gebert ist Unternehmensberater, weltweit aktiv, er kennt Gott und die Welt.*

Silke: *Und wann soll ich ihn treffen?*

Dieter: *Ab Dienstag ist er in Hamburg. Sein Hotel ist das „Plaza".*

Silke: *Gut, dann rufe ich ihn an.*

Dieter: *Auf jeden Fall muß ich die Reportage am Freitag haben.*

Silke: *Am Freitag? Das ist zu knapp!*

Dieter: *Gut, dann eben nächste Woche.*

The Volkswagen factories at Wolfsburg.

A range of products marked "Made in Germany"

NOUNS

der Arbeitsplatz — place of work
die Post — post; Post Office
der Artikel — article
der Besucher — visitor
die Besucherzahl — number of visitors
die Pressebericht — press report
das Foto — photograph
der Tip — tip, advice
der Termin — appointment; deadline
der Unternehmensberater — management consultant
der Berater — consultant, adviser
die Reportage — report, ongoing coverage
Gott — God
die Welt — world
der Fall — case
der Brief — letter
der Besuch — visit
das Datum — date
das Unternehmen — enterprise, company
die Antwort — answer

Montag — Monday
Dienstag — Tuesday
Mittwoch — Wednesday
Donnerstag — Thursday
Freitag — Friday
Samstag or *Sonnabend* * — Saturday
Sonntag — Sunday

die Woche — week
der Tag — day
der Wochentag — weekday
der Monat — month
Januar — January
Februar — February
März — March
April — April
Mai — May
Juni — June
Juli — July
August — August
September — September
Oktober — October
November — November
Dezember — December

ADJECTIVES

anstrengend — strenuous, tiring
fertig — ready
aktiv — active, dynamic
knapp — short, meagre; (here) tight

VERBS

fragen — to ask
dürfen — to be allowed to *(1)*
vergessen — to forget
sagen — to say
sollen — to be supposed or expected to *(2)*
abgeben — to hand in
wollen — to want to (see grammar on page 43 of the booklet)
antworten, übernehmen — to take over, take charge of

MISCELLANEOUS

denn — (here) because
dann will ich mal — then I'll just...
ab — from, starting from
auf jeden Fall — in any case
nach — to (towns, countries etc)
weltweit — worldwide
zu — too *(3)*
dann eben — well then
Gott und die Welt kennen — to know everybody, know one's way around
zu — (here) at the house of *(4)*
übrigens — by the way; moreover
noch — still
noch nicht ganz — not yet quite

* *Sonnabend* is more usual in Northern Germany, *Samstag* in South Germany, Austria and Switzerland.

HOW TO SAY IT

Ich brauche die Besucherzahlen — I need the number of visitors
Ich danke für den Tip — Thanks for the tip
Du darfst den Termin nicht vergessen — You mustn't forget the appointment
Du sollst die Reportage übernehmen — You're to take over the report

Der Artikel ist interessant.   → *Silke schreibt den Artikel.*
The article is interesting.   → Silke writes the article.
Die Reportage ist interessant.   → *Silke schreibt die Reportage.*
The report is interesting.   → Silke writes the report.
Das Buch ist interessant.   → *Silke schreibt das Buch.*
The book is interesting.   → Silke writes the book.
Die Artikel/Die Reportagen/die Bücher sind interessant. → *Silke schreibt die Artikel/die Reportagen/die Bücher.*

(Der Artikel) Er ist interessant. → *Silke schreibt ihn.*
(Die Reportage) Sie ist interessant. → *Silke schreibt sie.*
(Das Buch) Es ist interessant. → *Silke schreibt es.*
(Die Artikel/Die Reportagen/die Bücher) Sie sind interessant. → *Silke schreibt sie.*

Du sollst die Reportage schreiben — You're to write the report
Ich muß die Reportage am Freitag haben — I must have the report by Friday
Du darfst den Pressebericht lesen — You can/may read the press report
Dürfen wir hier rauchen? — May we smoke here?

Wie war's? — How was it? What was it like?
Was macht die Arbeit? — How is the/your work going?

Ich bin von Dienstag bis Freitag hier — I'm here from Tuesday.to Friday
Er ist ab Mittwoch hier — He's here from Wednesday onwards
Nächste Woche — next week
Letzte Woche — last week
Heute ist Montag, der zweite November — Today is Monday, the second of November *(5)*

REMARKS   REMARKS   REMARKS   REMARKS

(1) DÜRFEN = to be permitted or allowed (to do something). Not to be confused with KÖNNEN = to be able (to do something); see grammar on page 45 of the booklet. — (2) There is a difference between MÜSSEN (absolute obligation) and SOLLEN (more of an expectation or moral obligation; can often be translated by "should"). See grammar on page 45 of the booklet. — (3) ZU means TOO when followed by an adjective: zu schön = too beautiful / zu viel = too much. — (4) For prepositions see grammar on page 42 of the booklet. — (5) der erste Mai = the first of May / der zweite Mai = the second of May (see grammar on page 48 of the booklet).

2.1 ORAL PRACTICE

1. DIRECT OBJECTS

(••) LISTEN

schreiben / der Artikel
- *Ich schreibe den Artikel*
anrufen / die Redakteurin
- *Ich rufe die Redakteurin an.*

Try making your own sentences in the same way:
lesen / das Buch — haben / der Pressebericht — treffen / der Unternehmensberater — abnehmen / das Telefon. See grammar on page 37 of the booklet

2. PERSONAL PRONOUNS

in the nominative

(••) LISTEN

Der Mann / arbeiten
- *Er arbeitet*
Das Café / schön sein
- *Es ist schön.*

Use pronouns to replace nouns as in the examples:
Der Verleger / veröffentlichen — Die Uhr / richtig gehen — Das Kind / schreiben.
See grammar on page 40 of the booklet.

3. PERSONAL PRONOUNS

in the accusative

(••) LISTEN

Sie schreibt den Roman.
- *Sie schreibt ihn.*
Er gibt die Romane heraus.
- *Er gibt sie heraus.*

Use pronouns to replace nouns in the accusative as in the examples:
Er besucht die Messe. — Er ruft Frau Peters an. — Sie liest den Bericht. — Wir treffen die Franzosen. See grammar on page 40 of the booklet.

4. ,,DÜRFEN''

(••) LISTEN AND REPEAT

ich darf, du darfst, er/sie/es darf, wir dürfen, ihr dürft, sie/Sie dürfen.

5. ,,SOLLEN''

(••) LISTEN AND REPEAT

ich soll, du sollst, er/sie/es soll, wir sollen, ihr sollt, sie/Sie sollen.
Ich arbeite samstags.
- *Ich soll samstags arbeiten.*
Er ruft morgen an.
- *Er soll morgen anrufen.*

Change the following sentences in the same way:
Er veröffentlicht sein Buch in Deutschland. — Sie macht Telefondienst bei Krumbach. — Ich stelle Herrn Bosquet vor. — Am Donnerstag trifft er Silke. See grammar on page 45 of the booklet.

6. ,,WOLLEN''

(••) LISTEN AND REPEAT

ich will, du willst, er/sie/es willt, wir wollen, ihr wollt, sie/Sie wollen.
Ich arbeite samstags.
- *Ich will samstags arbeiten.*
Er ruft morgen an.
- *Er will morgen anrufen.*

Change the sentences given in exercise 5 in the same way. See grammar on page 45 of the booklet.

7. INVERSION

(••) LISTEN AND REPEAT

Wann gehst du arbeiten? / Dienstag.
- *Am Dienstag gehe ich arbeiten.*

Answer:
Wann ruft Silke Herrn Gebert an? / Freitag. — Wann gibt Silke den Bericht ab? / Mittwoch. See grammar on page 47 of the booklet.

8. PRONUNCIATION

(••) LISTEN AND REPEAT

Silke — wie war's? — hier ist — der Pressebericht — sicher — was sagt sie? — du sollst — Dienstag — nächste Woche — diese Woche — übrigens.

Natural break

THE WORLD OF WORK

Incredible, but true: on average the Germans spend less time at work than the British, French or Americans. German workers have achieved the 35-hour week (to take effect in 1994) without any drop in earnings. Nevertheless, Germans have a strong work ethic, as their booming economy testifies.

So what exactly is the secret of their success? It is efficient organisation at the "time and motion" level (,,eins nach dem anderen", one thing after another). Punctuality is the norm, of course, and many people munch sandwiches at their desks rather than take the official twelve-to-two lunch break. (,,Zeit ist Geld", time is money). On the other hand, don't expect to find anyone in the office after 5.00 pm!

Shop opening hours are regulated by a law, the Ladenschlußgesetz. All shops are supposed to close at 6.00 or 6.30 pm on weekdays and for the whole afternoon on three Saturdays out of four. There is controversy about these strict hours, because workers and professional people alike resent having their Einkaufsbummel (leisurely shopping trips) curtailed.

Recently some towns have authorised their shopkeepers to stay open late on Thursday evenings: token resistance to the Ordnung (order) so dear to the German heart! Nothing is done ohne Anweisung (without instructions); everything is regulated. Germans value stability and are not given to compromise and petty manoeuvring. A German convinced he is right will stick to his guns until stronger arguments prevail.

Now that the discrimination suffered by women at work has been generally recognised, a debate has arisen over the Chancengleichheit (equality of opportunity) which is guaranteed to women under the Grundgesetz (Basic Law).

The left, the Greens and various liberals have proposed the introduction of a Quotenregelung (compulsory quota) obliging companies to recruit as many women as men at every level. The idea is that the present excess of male employees should be gradually eroded by the increased intake of women. The quota system isn't mandatory yet, but some companies and the civil service in a few Länder already apply it.

Meanwhile, for working women in Germany the battle is far from won. Trying to work and raise a family at the same time is a nerve-racking business; the chances of getting a place at a day nursery are slim, and things don't get easier when the children are older because they're at school only in the mornings. Women often find themselves compelled to work part-time or entrust their children to Tagesmütter (child-minders). The father who turns Hausmann (househusband) to look after his offspring isn't exactly a common species!

It's a disastrous situation. What has become of the much-vaunted German efficiency? Germans are still strongly attached to the notion of the devoted stay-at-home mother. This Hausmütterchen is the antithesis of the Karrierefrau, the single independent career woman.

It's not surprising that the birth rate is so low. German women no longer accept rigid old-fashioned conventions about the social order. They reject this Schubladendenken (pigeon-hole thinking) and want something better than the grim choice between work and children. Eventually, they hope, people will realise that the German economy cannot do without a whole generation of qualified and capable women.

2.1 TAKE-A-BREAK

Look at Mr. Hartmann's diary, listen to the questions, and reply:

1. **MONTAG, 10 UHR** : *TREFFEN BEI KRUMBACH*
2. **DIENSTAG, 14 UHR** : *EINKAUFEN MIT SILKE*
3. **MITTWOCH, 16 UHR** : *TELEFONDIENST*
4. **DONNERSTAG, 12 UHR** : *REISE RESERVIEREN*
5. **FREITAG, 17 UHR** : *TREFFEN MIT GEBERT*
6. **SAMSTAG, 20 UHR** : *APERITIF MIT HEINO*
7. **SONNTAG** : *REISE NACH FRANKFURT*

Write the answers in complete sentences:

Was macht Herr Hartmann diese Woche?

1. ....
2. ....
3. ....
4. ....
5. ....
6. ....
7. ....

No. 2 (●●) LISTEN

Enter R (richtig) or F (falsch) in the boxes:

1. *Silke* : .... ☐   5. *Silke* : .... ☐

2. *Frauke* : .... ☐   6. *Gebert* : .... ☐

3. *Silke* : .... ☐   7. *Gebert* : .... ☐

4. *Silke* : .... ☐   8. *Silke* : .... ☐

No. 3

Fill in the blanks:

Die Messe dauert ...... Montag ..... Sonntag. Herr Krumbach ist mittwochs und samstags hier, und ...... Montag und ...... Dienstag ist er in Hamburg. Silke schreibt den Artikel ...... Freitag. Herr Gebert ist ...... Dienstag in Frankfurt.

Describe what the people are doing:

1. ....

4. ....

2. ....

5. ....

3. ....

6. ....

(See answers on page 8 of the booklet)

IM RESTAURANT

After their day's work Silke Peters and Werner Gebert are dining at the "Fischerhaus".

Silke: *Herr Ober, die Speisekarte bitte!*

Der Ober: *Ja, sofort... bitte schön.*

Silke: *Danke! Ich hoffe, Sie mögen Fisch?*

Werner Gebert: *Oh ja, sehr gerne sogar. Leider essen wir in Süddeutschland nur wenig Fisch.*

Silke: *Das Restaurant ist typisch für Hamburg. Man kann hier sehr gut essen, und es ist auch nicht zu teuer.*

Was nehmen wir?

Werner: *Was können Sie empfehlen?*

Silke: *Möchten Sie eine Vorspeise?*

Werner: *Nein, lieber nicht. Ich habe keinen großen Hunger.*

Silke: *Hier, vielleicht Labskaus... ?*

Werner: *Was ist das?*

Silke: *Das ist ein Brei aus Kartoffeln, Fleisch -- corned beef -- Essiggurken, ein Spiegelei und Salat.*

Werner: *Hm, ich mag keine Eier und keinen Salat.*

Silke: *Dann vielleicht Scholle nach Finkenwerder-Art? Das ist Scholle mit Speck und Salzkartoffeln als Beilage.*

Werner: *Ja, das klingt gut. Und als Nachtisch?*

Silke: *Da nehmen wir rote Grütze. Das ist Himbeergelee mit Vanillesoße.*

Werner: *Gerne, das möchte ich probieren.*

Silke: *Herr Ober, können wir bestellen?*

Der Ober: *Was wünschen Sie?*

Silke: *Also -- einmal Scholle mit Salzkartoffeln für den Herrn, Aalsuppe und Labskaus für mich; als Nachtisch rote Grütze für uns beide.*

Der Ober: *Und was trinken Sie?*

Werner: *Ich trinke nur ein Mineralwasser.*

Silke: *Ein Bier für mich bitte... Ich habe einen Bärenhunger!*

◖●●◗ LISTEN AND REPEAT
See translation on page 9 of the booklet.

*Cologne's "Altstadt" (Old Town).
The Black Forest, heaven for hikers...
and for hearty eaters.*

2.2 VOCABULARY

NOUNS

das Restaurant — restaurant
der Ober — waiter
die Speise — food
die Karte — menu
Süddeutschland — South Germany
der Süden — south
der Westen — west
der Osten — east
der Norden — north
der Fisch — fish
die Vorspeise — hors d'oeuvres, starter
der Hunger — hunger
das Labskaus — lobscouse (Hamburg speciality)
der Brei — purée, mash
die Kartoffel — potato
das Fleisch — meat
die Gurke — cucumber
der Essig — vinegar
die Essiggurke — gherkin
das Spiegelei — fried egg
der Salat — salad
die Scholle — sole
die Art — style, manner
der Speck — bacon
das Salz — salt
die Salzkartoffel — boiled potato
die Beilage — (here) garnish, side dish
der Tisch — table
der Nachtisch — dessert
rote Grütze — a typical Hamburg dessert
das Gelee — jelly
die Himbeere — raspberry
die Soße — sauce
die Vanille — vanilla
der Aal — eel
die Suppe — soup
das Mineralwasser — mineral water *(1)*
ein Bärenhunger — (literally:) a bear's hunger

das Getränk — drink
die Rechnung — bill
der Durst — thirst

ADJECTIVES

typisch — typical(ly)
teuer — expensive   billig — cheap
rot — red

VERBS

hoffen — to hope
mögen — to like *(2)*
essen — to eat *(3)*
nehmen — to take
empfehlen — to recommend
probieren — to try or sample something
bestellen — to order
wünschen — to wish, want
schmecken — to taste (intransitive)

MISCELLANEOUS

sofort — at once, immediately
sogar — even   gern(e) — gladly, willingly *(4)*
leider — unfortunately
wenig — little   sehr — very
lieber — comparative of gern: *(5)* rather,
preferably
als — (here) as   nur — only
also — so, then   einmal — once
zweimal — twice
beide — both

HOW TO SAY IT

Herr Ober, die Speisekarte bitte! — Waiter, the menu please!
Können Sie uns bitte die Speisekarte bringen? — Can you bring us the menu please?

Was können Sie empfehlen? — What can you recommend?
Was nehmen Sie als Vorspeise? Beilage? Nachspeise? Getränk? — What will you have as a starter? side order? dessert? drink?

Das klingt gut! — That sounds good!
Das schmeckt gut! — That tastes good!
Das schmeckt hervorragend! — That tastes wonderful!
Ich mag das gern(e)! — I like that very much!
Ich mag das nicht! — I don't like that!

Ich habe Hunger } — I'm hungry
Ich bin hungrig }
Ich habe einen Bärenhunger! — I could eat a horse!
Ich habe Durst } — I'm thirsty
Ich bin durstig }

Herr Ober, die Rechnung, bitte! — Waiter, the bill please!
Fräulein, wir möchten bezahlen! — (addressed to the waitress:) We'd like to pay.

| REMARKS | REMARKS | REMARKS | REMARKS |

(1) Generally, if you ask for mineral water, it will be carbonated. Non-sparkling water is called: stilles Wasser. — (2) We have already met the conditional of this verb: ICH MÖCHTE (I should like). See U1 — L2. Here we're learning the present tense of MÖGEN. Eg: Ich mag Salat (I like salad); ich mag Salat essen (I like eating salad). — (3) ESSEN (to eat). Caution! Do not confuse er ist (he is) with er ißt (he eats). — (4) GERN or GERNE (willingly, with pleasure) is used (a) as a polite response to an offer or invitation, eg: Möchten Sie ein Bier? (Would you like a beer?) — Ja, gerne! (Yes, I'd love one!); (b) when one likes doing something, eg: Ich trinke gern Kaffee (I like (drinking) coffee). — (5) LIEBER (preferably, more willingly) is the comparative form of GERN. It can sometimes be translated as "rather", eg: Möchten Sie ein Bier? (Would you like a beer?) — Nein, lieber Wein! (No, I'd rather have wine).

2.2   ORAL PRACTICE

1. „NEHMEN"

(●●) LISTEN AND REPEAT

ich nehme, du nimmst, er/sie/es nimmt,
wir nehmen, ihr nehmt, sie/Sie nehmen.

Listen to NEHMEN *followed by a direct object*
in the accusative case:
ich (nehmen / ein Fisch)
● *ich nehme einen Fisch*
er (nehmen / ein Bier)
● *er nimmt ein Bier.*

Now it's your turn:
du (nehmen / eine Aalsuppe) — sie (nehmen / ein
Spiegelei) — wir (nehmen / Spiegeleier) — ich
(nehmen / eine Scholle) — Sie (nehmen / ein Salat)
— er (nehmen / Salzkartoffeln) — wir (nehmen /
ein Nachtisch) — ihr (nehmen / Himbeergelee ohne
Vanillesoße) — wir (nehmen / Wein).
See grammar on page 43 of the booklet.

2. NEGATION

(●●) LISTEN

ich nehme einen Fisch.
● *ich nehme keinen Fisch.*
er nimmt ein Bier.
● *er nimmt kein Bier.*

Put the sentences in exercise 1 into the
negative:
See grammar on page 48 of the booklet.

3. „ESSEN" AND „TRINKEN"

(●●) LISTEN AND REPEAT

ich esse, du ißt, er/sie/es ißt, wir essen,
ihr eßt, sie/Sie essen.
ich trinke, du trinkst, er/sie/es trinkt, wir
trinken, ihr trinkt, sie trinken.

Listen, then replace the verb nehmen *in*
exercise 1 with essen *and* trinken:
ich nehme einen Fisch.
● *ich esse einen Fisch.*
er nimmt ein Bier.
● *er trinkt ein Bier.*
See grammar on page 43 of the booklet.

4. THE PREPOSITION „FÜR"

(Give the accusative case of the personal pronoun)

(●●) LISTEN

die Aalsuppe ist für... (Silke Peters).
● *die Aalsuppe ist für sie.*

die Vorspeise ist für... (ich).
● *die Vorspeise ist für mich.*

Change the following sentences in the same
way:
das Spiegelei ist für...(Herr Gebert) — der Fisch
ist für...(du) — der Salat ist für...(Frauke) — die
Salzkartoffeln sind für...(ihr) — das
Mineralwasser ist für...(Herr Krumbach) — die
Bücher sind für...(wir) — die Reportage ist
für...(ihr). See grammar on page 42 of the booklet.

5. „MÖGEN"

(●●) LISTEN AND REPEAT

ich mag, du magst, er/sie/es mag, wir
mögen, ihr mögt, sie/Sie mögen.

Listen to MÖGEN *followed by gern and lieber*
ich(Bier/Wein)
● *ich mag gern Bier, aber ich mag lieber*
Wein.

Change the following sentences in the same way:
er(Tee/Kaffee) — sie (Wein/Sekt) — ich
(Aalsuppe/Labskaus) — wir (Frankfurt/Paris)
— Sie (Deutschland/Frankreich).
See grammar on page 45 of the booklet.

6. „ZU"

(●●) LISTEN

Das Restaurant ist teuer.
● *Das Restaurant ist zu teuer.*

Change the following sentences in the same way:
die Zeit ist knapp — die Arbeit ist anstrengend
— der Artikel ist schlecht — es ist spät.

7. PRONUNCIATION

(●●) LISTEN TO THE DOUBLE CONSONANTS AND REPEAT:
Bitte — ich hoffe — wir essen Kartoffeln
— Scholle mit Speck — Aalsuppe.

German "daily bread" and its usual accompaniments

FOOD AND DRINK

To some people, the very idea of German "cuisine" is mildly amusing: all those dumplings and sauerkraut! And black bread, Westphalian pumpernickel for example - ugh! There's a story about how this bread got its name. During the French occupation of Westphalia in the 18th century a French officer asked for something to eat and was given a piece of pumpernickel. He tried it and declared: "C'est bon pour Nickel" (this will do for Nickel) - that being the name of his horse. "Pumpernickel" supposedly derives from bon-pour-Nickel.

Bread plays an important part in the German diet. Ask for Brötchen (diminutive of Brot) and you'll get rolls anywhere. They're always to be found on the breakfast table. But different regions have different names for them. In Berlin they're Schrippen, in Hamburg Rundstücke and in Munich Semmeln or Wecken. Many new varieties of bread have appeared in recent years, and the Germans have a vast array of cold meats and cheeses to eat with them.

Although German eating habits have changed tremendously since the advent of the Common Market, some typically German tastes remain. Beer, of course, is the great thing. Statistics reveal that the average German drinks 150 litres of it per year. Then there's Schnaps too... or preferably both: a tot of Schnaps followed by a beer chaser. In Berlin this is called 'ne Molle und 'n Korn, in Cologne 'n Kurzer und 'n Bier, in Hamburg 'ne lüttje Lage. Popular brands of beer are "Jever", "Dortmunder", "Kölsch" and many more, varying from region to region. Germans also drink a lot of coffee and mineral water, perhaps sometimes to help them get sober: in 1988 there were 1.8 million alcoholics in West Germany alone.

The potato (Kartoffel), long considered the mainstay of German cooking, has lost ground to a multitude of other vegetables, though even now, as in the English-speaking world, it is considered a normal part of a main meal.

Much more meat and fruit is eaten now than 30 years ago, but the quality of nutrition still leaves much to be desired. Some 30% of West Germans are over-weight, and many consequently suffer from cardio-vascular disorders. Just as the French worry about their livers and the British about their digestion, so the typical German has "circulation problems".

An old German proverb advises eating "in the morning like an emperor, at midday like a king and in the evening like a beggar", which means that breakfast should be a really hearty meal. German breakfasts can be very substantial, con-sisting of copious quantities of coffee or tea, jam, cold meats, a slice or two of Emmenthal cheese, a boiled egg and plenty of rolls and bread.

How about regional cooking? Specialities vary, but north, south, east and west, the sausage is king. Standard favourites such as Bockwurst, Bratwurst and Currywurst are found everywhere alongside innumerable local varieties like Thüringer and Bavaria's Weißwurscht. Berliners also enjoy their Buletten (meat balls) and Frikadellen (rissoles) - notice the Huguenot influence in these names!

On any street you can buy chips (Fritten or Pommes). They are sold mit oder ohne Majo (with or without mayon-naise), and in some places the vendor will ask "Weiß oder rot?", ie with mayonnaise or ketchup? Turkish immigrants have brought the kebab, and Nordic influence shows in Rollmops. Bismarck-Hering and Schillerlocke (marinated and smoked herring, respectively) are much eaten in the north along with a wide variety of other fish. One notable feature of some northern dishes (lobscouse, eel stew) is the marriage of meat or meat broth with fish. Schweinshaxe mit Sauerkraut (pig's trotter with sauerkraut) and Weißwurst und Klöße (white sausage with dumplings) are Bavarian specialities, while Spätzle (noodles) are popular in Baden-Württemberg. There is a tradi-tional Rhineland dish called Himmel und Erde mit Blutwurst (heaven and earth with black pudding), in which "heaven" is mashed potato and "earth" hot apple sauce. As a rule, hors d'oeuvres are served only in restaurants.

Last, but perhaps not least, there are the cakes and pastries on offer in the Konditoreien (cafés) where middle-aged ladies meet to enjoy their Kaffeeklatsch, that is, to gossip over a cup of coffee while savouring such delights as Windbeutel (cream puffs) and Schwarzwälder Kirschtorte (Black Forest gateau).

No. 1

RECIPE FOR EEL SOUP

HAMBURGER AALSUPPE

für 4 Personen (Zubereitung : 30 Minuten)

200 g Räucheraal
1 Bund junges Gemüse wie Sellerie,
Petersiliewurzel, Möhren,
Frühlingszwiebeln
1 1/4 Liter Brühe
100 g Backpflaumen
200 g kleine Birnen
frische Kräuter wie Majoran,
Basilikum, Salbei,
Rosmarin, Thymian, Petersilie
Prise Salz
Schuß Essig
Prise Zucker
1 Eßlöffel Mehl

■ Geschnittenes Frühlingsgemüse in Brühe kochen ■ Backpflaumen und geschälte Birnen extra kochen ■ Zusammenschütten, frische gehackte Kräuter hinzugeben, mit etwas Mehl binden, salzen ■ Mit Essig und Zucker süßsauer abschmecken ■ Entgräteten Aal als Einlage in die Suppe geben.

GUTEN APPETIT !

HAMBURG EEL SOUP

To serve 4 (preparation time 30 minutes)
200g smoked eel
Assorted young vegetables, eg. celery,
parsley root, baby carrots, spring onions
1 1/4 litres meat stock
100g prunes
200g small pears
Fresh herbs, eg. marjoram, basil, sage,
rosemary, thyme, parsley
Pinch of salt
Dash of vinegar
Pinch of sugar
1 tablespoonful flour

• Cook the sliced vegetables in the meat stock
• Cook the prunes and peeled pears separately
• Mix together, add the chopped fresh herbs, thicken with flour and add salt
• Season with vinegar and sugar to give a sweet-and-sour flavour
• Bone the smoked eel and add to the soup

BON APPETIT!

The Table.

1. das Gedeck — *2.* der Teller — *3.* die Gabel — *4.* der Löffel — *5.* das Messer
6. die Serviette — *7.* das Weinglas — *8.* die Speisekarte — *9.* das Salz
10. der Pfeffer — *11.* der Senf — *12.* der Essig — *13.* das Öl — *14.* das Brot
15. die Butter — *16.* die Milch — *17.* der Kaffee — *18.* der Tee — *19.* die Cola
20. der Wein — *21.* das Mineralwasser — *22.* der Fisch — *23.* das Ei — *24.* der
Schweinebraten — *25.* das Schnitzel — *26.* die Wurst — *31.* die Möhre
32. die Kartoffeln — *33.* die Gurke — *34.* der Käse — *35.* die Kirsche
36. die Ananas — *37.* die Banane — *38.* die Weintraube — *39.* der Apfel
40. der Kuchen — *41.* das Eis mit Sahne

◉◉ LISTEN

DIE STADTBESICHTIGUNG

The following day, in Hamburg, Silke Peters and Werner Gebert meet at the Gänsemarkt (Goose Market) intending to go on a tour of the city and port of Hamburg. But a heavy shower spoils their plans.

Werner: *Mensch, was für ein Sauwetter!*

Silke: *Das ist typisch für Hamburg.*

Werner: *Na, hoffentlich hört es gleich auf!*

Silke: *Das ist nur ein Schauer. In fünf Minuten scheint die Sonne wieder.*

Werner: *Was machen wir jetzt?*

Silke: *Ich kenne ein Café hier gleich um die Ecke, den Alsterpavillon. Sollen wir dahin gehen?*

Werner: *Gute Idee! Gehen wir in den Alsterpavillon!*

....

Werner: *Überlegen wir mal: was können wir denn besichtigen?*

Silke: *Ja gleich; drehen Sie sich mal um, dann sehen Sie den Jungfernstieg und rechts das Hotel „Vier Jahreszeiten".*

Werner: *Toll, dieser Blick über die Stadt und den Hafen!*

Silke: *Nein, das ist nicht der Hafen! Das ist die Alster, der See im Zentrum von Hamburg.*

Werner: *Aha, gut. Also wohin führen Sie mich heute? Auf die Reeperbahn?*

Silke: *Später! Wir können zuerst den Hafen besichtigen. Dort hinten liegen die Schiffe für die Besichtigung.*

Werner: *Oh, nein. Ich werde seekrank.*

Silke: *In Övelgönne gibt es einen Museumshafen. Man kann ihn zu Fuß besichtigen.*

Werner: *Ist er weit weg?*

Silke: *Nein.*

Werner: *Ehrlich gesagt, ich interessiere mich nicht für Schiffe und Häfen.*

Silke: *Schade! Dann schlage ich den Stadtpark oder einen Spaziergang um die Alster vor.*

Werner: *Spaziergänge langweilen mich. Fahren wir nach St. Pauli auf die Reeperbahn.*

Silke: *Ja, da können Sie sich amüsieren. Aber das ist nichts für mich.*

Werner: *Ach kommen Sie, gehen wir!*

◉◉ LISTEN AND REPEAT

See translation on page 10 of the booklet.

Hamburg: the Alster.
Night life in St Pauli (Hamburg).

2.3 VOCABULARY

NOUNS

Mensch! — (here) heck! gosh!
Sauwetter — lousy weather
der Schauer — shower
die Sonne — sun
die Ecke — corner
die Idee — idea
der Blick — view
die Stadt — city
der Hafen — port, harbour
der See — lake
das Zentrum — centre
die Schiffe (das Schiff) — ships
die Besichtigung — tour, visit (to a place of interest)
der Museumshafen — harbour museum
der Fuß — foot
der Stadtpark — municipal park
der Spaziergang — walk, stroll

---

das Wetter — weather
der Regen — rain
der Schnee — snow
der Wind — wind
der Mond — moon
der Platz — (here) square
das Meer — sea

ADJECTIVES/ADVERBS

hoffentlich — let's hope
seekrank — seasick
toll! — super! great!
ehrlich — honest(ly), frank(ly)
schade — pity

VERBS

scheinen — to shine
überlegen — to consider, reflect
sich umdrehen — to turn round
sehen — to see
führen — to lead, guide
besichtigen — to visit, look at
liegen — to lie, be situated
werden — to become
sich interessieren für (+ acc.) — to be interested in
vorschlagen — to suggest
sich langweilen — to be bored
sich amüsieren — to amuse oneself, have a good time

---

besuchen (1) — to visit (see U1—L4)

MISCELLANEOUS

gleich — at once, straight away *(2)*
wieder (3) — again
um die Ecke — around the corner
dahin (4) — there, over there
dieser — this
im Zentrum von — in the middle of
wohin (5) — where to
später — later
zuerst — first of all
zu Fuß — on foot
weit weg — far away
nichts — nothing
ehrlich gesagt — to be frank, quite honestly

---

im Norden von — in the north of
im Süden von — in the south of
im Westen von — in the west of
im Osten von — in the east of

HOW TO SAY IT

Wir haben schönes Wetter — We've got good weather, the weather's nice
Die Sonne scheint — The sun is shining
Es ist warm/heiß — It is warm/hot
Es ist schwül/drückend — It is muggy/oppressive
Es ist herrlich draußen — It's lovely outside

Wir haben schlechtes Wetter — We've got bad weather, the weather's bad
Es regnet — It's raining *Es schneit* — It's snowing
Es ist windig — It's windy *Es friert* — It's freezing
Der Himmmel ist bedeckt — The sky is overcast

Möchtest du mitkommen? — Would you like to come (too)?
Sollen wir nach Paris fahren? — Shall we go to Paris?
Ich schlage einen Spaziergang vor — I suggest a walk
Gehen wir in die Ausstellung — Let's go to the exhibition
Das ist nichts für mich — That's not my sort of thing

Wir gehen (6) auf den Fischmarkt — We're going to the fish market
Wir gehen (6) in den Stadtpark — We're going to the park
Wir gehen (6) um den See — We're going round the lake
Wir gehen (6) über die Brücke — We're going over the bridge

REMARKS   REMARKS   REMARKS   REMARKS

(1) BESUCHEN generally means to go and see a person, eg: Ich besuche Klaus. BESICHTIGEN means to go and see a place, eg: Ich besichtige den Hamburger Hafen. The only exceptions are : die Ausstellung, die Messe, das Museum, for which BESUCHEN is used. — (2)As in English, the present tense is often used to mean the future. Usually some indication of time is given. Eg: Morgen/in drei Tagen/nächste Woche fährt er nach München (tomorrow/in three days/next week he is going to Munich). (See grammar on page 40 of the booklet.) — (3) WIEDER means "again"; it can sometimes be translated by the prefix "re—", eg: wiederverkaufen (to resell), wiederverheiraten (to remarry).— (4) DAHIN ("thither") expresses a change of place.— (5) In WOHIN and DAHIN, —hin expresses a direction away from the speaker; WOHIN? means "where to?"— (6) The verb GEHEN normally means to go on foot; FAHREN is used for travel by any kind of transport. GEHEN with the prepositions <u>auf/in/um/über</u> followed by the accusative case expresses movement from one place to another.

2.3　ORAL PRACTICE

1. WHERE IS WERNER GEBERT GOING?

🔘🔘 LISTEN

der Park / gehen in
- *er geht in den Park.*

The verb gehen with the prepositions in/auf/um/über is followed by the accusative case.
Now make some sentences using the following words, keeping er as the subject.
das Zentrum / gehen in — der Fischmarkt / gehen auf — der Hafen / gehen über — der See / gehen um — die Messe / gehen auf.

See grammar on page 42 of the booklet.

2. PRACTISING PLURALS

🔘🔘 LISTEN

Silke besucht eine Ausstellung.
- *Silke besucht Ausstellungen.*

Nouns in the indefinite plural take no article. Make the following sentences plural in the same way:
Herr Krumbach besucht eine Messe. — Udo holt ein Taxi. — Sie besichtigen einen Hafen. — Herr Hartmann hat einen Bericht. — Silke liest einen Roman. — Sie zeigt ein Buch. — Ich trinke einen Orangensaft. — Werner Gebert ißt einen Fisch. — Silke braucht einen Scheck. — Frauke von Hohen hat einen Termin. — Herr Gebert kauft eine Flasche.

See grammar on page 38 of the booklet.

3. ACCUSATIVE PRONOUNS

🔘🔘 LISTEN

Silke Peters führt Werner Gebert.
- *Silke führt ihn.*

Put the pronouns in brackets into the accusative case:
Silke trinkt (er). — Herr Gebert ißt (es). — Udo holt (du). — Sie besuchen (du). — Er braucht (ich). — Sie schreibt (es). — Peters versteht (er). — Herr Gebert findet (sie). — Silke braucht (du). — Frauke hat (er).

See grammar on page 40 of the booklet.

4. PRACTISING REFLEXIVE VERBS

🔘🔘 LISTEN

Ich interessiere mich, du interessierst dich, er/sie/es interessiert sich, wir interessieren uns, ihr interessiert euch, sie/Sie interessieren sich/Sich. Sich langweilen / er
- *Er langweilt sich.*

Your turn now
sich entscheiden / ich — sich umdrehen / sie — sich amüsieren / ihr — sich langweilen / wir — sich umdrehen / ihr — sich amüsieren / ich — sich langweilen / du.

5. PRACTISING THE IMPERATIVE

🔘🔘 LISTEN

Sie holen ein Taxi.
- *Holen Sie ein Taxi!*

Your turn now
Sie gehen dahin. — Sie hören auf. — Sie trinken Sekt. — Sie kaufen das Bier. — Sie gehen in das Museum. — Sie schreiben das Buch.

See grammar on page 46 of the booklet.

6. INTONATION

🔘🔘 LISTEN TO THESE SENTENCES AND REPEAT THEM, PAYING PARTICULAR ATTENTION TO THE INTONATION:

Mensch, was für ein Sauwetter! — Toll, dieser Blick! — Gute Idee, gehen wir! — Ach, das ist Schade! — Das ist typisch! — Das langweilt mich! — Ach, kommen Sie! — Trink das Wasser! — Hören Sie auf!

See grammar on page 36 of the booklet.

HAMBURG:
GATEWAY TO THE WORLD

Hamburg is a gateway to the world. That's what all the tour guides say, and the people of Hamburg would agree, not without pride. It owes this title to the port, der Hamburger Hafen, an evocative name to the German mind, redolent of sailors and voyages, freighters and cargoes and the smell of the open sea. In point of fact the North Sea, die Nordsee, is well out of sight, 100 kilometres to the north-west.

At present the port is experiencing severe economic problems; nevertheless, it remains central to Hamburg life. Thanks to the port, and the frenetic bustle of activity and the international trade it generates, the city has always been able to remain free and independent: Freie und Hansestadt Hamburg. Its citizens, die Hanseaten, have never paid homage to a sovereign; Hamburg has always been a city state (Stadtstaat) with its own parliament, die Bürgerschaft. It is a federal state, ein Bundesland, on a par with Bavaria or Saxony. Die Hamburger Bürgerschaft meets in the imposing City Hall next door to the Stock Exchange: no coincidence, this, for the citizens of Hamburg are dyed-in-the-wool entrepreneurs. The opening of an Airbus construction plant to offset the crisis affecting the port and the shipyards is recent proof of that spirit.

Traditionally business-minded, the Hanseaten have not baulked at demolishing historical monuments and churches in order to adapt the city's infrastructure to their commercial needs. Nevertheless, some beautiful churches have survived, among them the Michaeliskirche, one of the city's landmarks. The people fondly call it der Michel.

In the nineteenth century an entire district was razed and its inhabitants forcibly evicted to make room for the Speicherstadt, a warehouse complex completely accessible to shipping. Today not only warehousing operations abound in this area but also tourists, in growing numbers. To help put Hamburg on a healthier financial footing, the city would dearly like to sell off the whole quarter and convert it into luxury flats, boutiques, offices and penthouse apartments for yuppies. But for the moment it's business as usual in the gloomy old warehouse offices where the scents of coffee, tea, cocoa and exotic spices mingle with the pungent odours of canals and diesel fuel. In the evenings, clubs such as the

The port of Hamburg: a foretaste of the sea

Überseeclub and the Anglo-German-Club (ladies not admitted) are popular meeting places. With its rainy, foggy weather and its reserved and stolid citizens Hamburg is the most "British" of German cities. It's also a city of contrasts. Not only is it the headquarters of 10 per cent of the richest German companies: it also has one of the highest unemployment rates in the country.

The worst affected areas are near the port: places such as Kiez, where Hamburg's other famous business is centred. The Reeperbahn is notorious for its prostitution, drug trafficking and casinos, known as Spielhöllen (gambling dens). However, AIDS has cut into the sex-trade somewhat. Not far away, on the Hafenstraße (Harbour Street), Germany's most famous squatters are still holding out against the police. The municipality, which owns the buildings, has tried negotiating with the squatters, but it's a lost cause: the Hafenstraße has become a tourist attraction. Sensation-seekers come to gawp at the barricaded houses

and soak up the conspiratorial atmosphere in the local bars.

Further down the Elbe, Hamburg shows a different face: along the Elbchaussee, set amid shady trees in spacious grounds, are the sumptuous mansions and villas of the city's upper crust. This "millionaires' boulevard" stretches for a good ten kilometres. Hamburg is a green city, with numerous parks and gardens to attract joggers and walkers.

A network of canals, die Fleete, covers the city. At one time they served as sea lanes between the warehouses and the harbour, but now they've been adapted for watersports such as sailing and rowing. The Fleete flow under no less than 2,331 bridges (more than in Venice or Amsterdam), the most beautiful of which is the Köhlbrandbrücke, a suspension bridge slung 53 metres above the harbour. The pragmatic citizens of Hamburg have always had the knack of reconciling commercial needs with stylish architecture.

What is the weather like? Match the descriptions to the pictures.

1. . . . .

2. . . . .

3. . . . .

4. . . . .

5. . . . .

6. . . . .

7. . . . .

8. . . . .

9. . . . .

Where are Silke Peters and Werner Gebert going? Answer the questions!

1. Gehen sie in die Michaeliskirche?

2. Gehen sie in das Restaurant „Fischer-haus"?

3. Gehen sie in das Rathaus?

4. Gehen sie über die Elbbrücke?

5. Gehen sie auf die Reeperbahn?

6. Gehen sie in den Alsterpavillon?

7. Gehen sie auf den Fischmarkt?

8. Gehen sie in das Hanseviertel?

(See answers on page 11 of the booklet)

⊙⊙ LISTEN

EINKAUFEN

Werner Gebert wants to buy some things for his wife and children. He takes a taxi.

Werner: *Fahren Sie mich bitte in das Zentrum. Wo kann man da gut einkaufen?*

Taxifahrer: *Gehen Sie in das Hanseviertel. Da können Sie gut einkaufen.*

Werner: *Ja, dann fahren Sie mich bitte dorthin.*

Verkauferin: *Kann ich helfen?*

Werner: *Ich suche ein Geschenk für meine Kinder.*

Verkauferin: *Junge oder Mädchen?*

Werner: *Für meinen Sohn und meine Tochter.*

Verkauferin: *Wie alt sind Ihre Kinder?*

Werner: *Das Mädchen ist fünf Jahre alt und der Junge ist sieben.*

Verkauferin: *An was denken Sie denn?*

Werner: *Ach, vielleicht eine Puppe.*

Verkauferin: *Hier, diese, ist das nichts?*

Werner: *Nein, die is zu klein. Ich möchte lieber eine große Puppe.*

Verkauferin: *Da haben wir nur diesen großen Teddybär.*

Werner: *Ach nein, doch lieber keine Puppe. Was haben Sie denn noch?*

Verkauferin: *Warum nicht ein Geschenk für beide? Hier haben wir einen kleinen Spielcomputer. Der ist extra für Kinder.*

Werner: *Und was spielt man damit?*

Verkauferin: *Es gibt viele Spiele. Dieser Mann hier Muß die Prinzessin befreien.*

Werner: *Das ist gut. O.K., packen Sie mir bitte den Mini Computer als Geschenk ein. Und wieviel kostet der?*

Verkauferin: *231 Mark 90. Links ist die Kasse.*

Werner: *Wo ist bitte die Abteilung für Damenwäsche?*

Verkauferin: *Dritte Etage.*

Werner: *Ich suche einen Morgenmantel für meine Frau.*

Verkaufer: *Dieser hier, wie finden Sie den?*

Werner: *Oh nein, einen roten Morgenmantel möchte ich nicht. Haben Sie keinen weißen?*

Verkaufer: *Nein, weiße Morgenmäntel sind nicht mehr da. Aber wie finden Sie dieses schwarze Spitzenhemd?*

Werner: *Oh, das ist aber attraktiv! Ja, das nehme ich.*

⊙⊙ LISTEN AND REPEAT
See translation on page 12 of the booklet.

A pedestrian street in the old city of Rothenburg.

2.4 VOCABULARY

NOUNS

das Geschenk — gift
der Junge — boy
das Mädchen — girl
der Sohn — son
die Tochter — daughter
das Jahr, pl. die Jahre — year
die Puppe — doll
der Teddybär — teddy bear
der Computer — computer
das Spiel — game/toy
die Prinzessin — princess
die Kasse — cashier's desk, till
die Abteilung — department
die Wäsche — (here) lingerie, underwear
die Dame — lady
die Etage — floor, storey
der Morgenmantel — dressing gown
das Hemd — shirt
die Spitzen (pl.) — lace
das Spitzenhemd — lace chemise

das Unterhemd — vest
die Jacke — jacket
die Weste — waistcoat
der Mantel — coat
der Rock — skirt
die Unterhose — underpants
der Strumpf — stocking
der Schuh — shoe
der Handschuh — glove
die Hose — trousers
die Bluse — blouse
die Socke — sock
der Hut — hat
die Mütze — cap
der Büstenhalter (BH) — brassiere, bra
das Kostüm — lady's suit
der Anzug — man's suit

der Schlips — tie
das Kleid — dress

ADJECTIVES

- extra — expressly, especially
alt — old
jung — young
klein — small
groß — big
neu — new
attraktiv — attractive
weiß — white
blau — blue
gelb — yellow
grün — green
schwarz — black

VERBS

fahren — to travel, drive, go
suchen — to look for seek
denken — to think
spielen — to play
befreien — to liberate, set free
einpacken — to wrap up
kosten — to cost

MISCELLANEOUS

dorthin — to that place, thither
nicht mehr — no more
diese (-r/-s) — this, these
jede (-r/-s) each
welche (-r/-s) — which, what

HOW TO SAY IT

EXPRESSIONS

Ich mache einen Einkaufsbummel — I'm going for a stroll round the shops.
Ich suche ein Geschenk — I'm looking for a gift.
Wo finde ich Computer? — Where can I find computers?

Wieviel kostet das? — How much does that cost?
Das ist zu teuer! — That's too expensive!
Das is aber billig! — That's really cheap!
Wie alt bis du/sind Sie? — How old are you? (informal/polite).
Ich bin dreißig (Jahre alt) — I am 30 (years old).

<u>*Dieser*</u> *Blick ist schön* — This view is beautiful.
<u>*Diese*</u> *Frau heißt Silke Peters* — This woman's name is Silke Peters.
<u>*Dieses*</u> *Mädchen ist die Tochter von Gebert* — This girl is Gebert's daughter.
Packen Sie <u>*diesen*</u> *Computer ein* — Wrap up this computer.
ich möchte <u>*diese*</u> *Puppe* — I'd like this doll.
Iche finde <u>*dieses*</u> *Spitzenhemd sehr attraktiv* — I find this lace chemise very attractive.

| REMARKS | REMARKS | REMARKS | REMARKS |

Adjectives always precede nouns. Their endings can be grouped as follows:
a. definite article + adjective + noun
Note that the nominative and accusative forms of feminine and neuter nouns and adjectives are the same.
Der *billige Computer ist richtig. — Ich möchte* **den** *billigen Computer.*
Die *kleine Puppe ist schön. — Ich kaufe* **die** *kleine Puppe.*
Das *schöne Hemd is attraktiv. — Ich nehme* **das** *schöne Hemd.*
b. Indefinite article + adjective + noun
Das ist **ein** *großer Teddybär. — That's a big teddy bear.*
Wir haben **einen** *großen Teddybär. — We have a big teddy bear.*
Das ist **eine** *kleine Puppe. — That's a little doll.*
Ich möchte **eine** *kleine Puppe. — I'd like a little doll.*
Das ist **ein** *kleines Mädchen — That's a little girl.*
Ich sehe **ein** *kleines Mädchen. — I see a little girl.*
c. adjective + noun with no article preceding it
In the nominative and accusative plural of all three genders, the adjective ending for this roup is <u>*e*</u>*:*
Kleine Kinder spielen gern. — Little children like to play.
Herr Gebert hat kleine Kinder. — Mr. Gebert has small children.
Contrast with the first group (<u>*definite article + adjective + noun*</u>*) in which all plural adjective endings are* <u>en.</u>
Die *kleinen Kinder sind in München. — The small children are in Munich.*
Herr Gebert kauft ein Geschenk für **die** *kleinen Kinder. — Mr. Gebert buys a gift for the small children.*

2.4 ORAL PRACTICE

1. DEMONSTRATIVE PRONOUNS

dieser *(masculine)*, diese *(feminine)* dieses *(neuter)* diese *(plural)*.

◉◉ LISTEN

der Artikel/interessant
- *Dieser Artikel ist interessant.*

Your turn to make sentences, following the example:

die Frau/jung — das Kind/klein — die Puppe/schön — der Computer/teuer — das Spiel/spannend — die Berichte/gut.

See grammar on page 40 of the booklet

2. DEMONSTRATIVE PRONOUNS

accusative (diesen, diese, dieses, diese)

◉◉ LISTEN

lesen/das Buch
- *Ich lese dieses Buch.*
lesen/der Artikel
- *Ich lese diesen Artikel.*

Your turn:

schreiben/der Artikel — kaufen/das Hemd — nehmen/die Romane — haben/die Puppe..

See grammar on page 40 of the booklet.

3. ADJECTIVES

with the definite and indefinite article

◉◉ LISTEN

der kleine Mann
- *ein kleiner Mann*
die kleine Puppe
- *eine kleine Puppe*
das schöne Hemd
- *ein schönes Hemd*
die schönen Hemden
- *schöne Hemden*

Change the following in the same way:

die junge Frau — der alte Mann — das gute Buch — die spannenden Spiele — der billige Computer — die schwarzen Schuhe — die blaue Jacke. See grammar on page 39 of the booklet.

4. NOMINATIVE

(definite article + adjective + noun) in the nominative; watch out for the articles!

◉◉ LISTEN

das (klein) Kind spielt
- *Das kleine Kind spielt*

Supply the right adjective endings

die (deutsch) Touristin besichtigt Paris — die (französisch) Nachspeisen schmecken gut — der (grün) Salat ist für Silke — das (blau) Kleid ist für Frau Gebert — die (gut) Auskünfte sind wichtig.

5. KEIN(E) + ADJECTIVE + NOUN

In the nominative singular and plural

◉◉ LISTEN

Kein (richtig) Journalist macht das
- *Kein richtiger Journalist macht das*

Supply the right adjective endings:

Keine (attraktiv) Frau macht das — Kein (klein) Mädchen macht das — Kein (typisch) Franzose macht das — Keine (teuer) Computer machen das.

See grammar on page 40 of the booklet.

6. POSSESSIVE PRONOUN + ADJECTIVE + NOUN

in the nominative singular and plural

◉◉ LISTEN

mein Sohn/klein
- *mein kleiner Sohn*

Continue conjugating, as in the model.

deine Tochter/groß — unsere Stadt/klein — dein Spitzenhemd/schön — euer Auto/klein — eure Bücher/interessant.

See grammar on page 41 of the booklet.

7. PRONUNCIATION

◉◉ LISTEN AND REPEAT

ch sehe das Zentrum — Ich besichtige das Hanseviertel — Der Spielcomputer ist teuer — Das Mädchen hat Verspätung — sofort.

The beach on Borkum Island (East Friesland)

LEISURE

Germans were, and still are, renowned for discipline, industry and dedication to work. They themselves used to say, with some regret, that they lived to work while others worked to live. Today almost the opposite could be said. All German salaried employees are entitled to three weeks' annual holiday. There are ten to fourteen religious or national holidays (varying from region to region). Most employment contracts provide for five or six weeks' paid holiday.

According to pre-reunification statistics, a West German has about 2,130 hours of free time or Freizeit each year, ie time devoted to neither salaried work nor unpaid domestic work nor professional training nor sleep. There are many words relating to Freizeit: Freizeitgestaltung (the organisation or structuring of free time), Freizeitkleidung (leisurewear or sportswear), Freizeit- und Hobbymarkt (the leisure and hobby market), Freizeit- und Erholungspark (leisure and recreation park), Freizeitberater (leisure consultant) - all these in the context of a huge Freizeitindustrie.

On average Germans spend 6,000 DM a year each on leisure-time activities, chiefly holidays. Germany itself is their favourite holiday destination, and reunification has given them further scope for getting away from it all without stepping outside their own national boundaries. There aren't many palm trees in Germany, however, and since Germans are inveterate travellers and sun-seekers, very many of them now go abroad. Italy, Spain and Austria attract the largest numbers, closely followed by France, Switzerland, Greece and, until recently, Yugoslavia.

German literature of the Romantic period used to celebrate the solitary poet-wanderer in contrast to the stolid home-loving middle classes. Today the middle classes are on the move, often en masse in giant tour buses. But there are individualists too, particularly Rucksackturisten, backpackers who dislike nothing more than running into compatriots far from home. They call them "tourists" - a dire insult!

German intellectuals still explore museums avidly, and the adventurous take their travel seriously and try to get to know Land und Leute (country and

people) wherever they go. But like the British, the German masses tend to go for package tours on which everything is organised for them - even their amusements - and they can enjoy the illusion, at least, of a life of luxury. Sometimes they take their lifestyle with them; there are whole German holiday camps in various parts of southern Europe. Wherever they go, they are prosperous enough to be welcome vistors and consequently well catered-for. Not only are German newspapers available to well-heeled travellers in Hong Kong and New York, but German is spoken in the beach cafés of Spain and Greece.

As with the British, however, this pattern is changing and the erstwhile package tourist is becoming more independent. Nowadays, besides colonising seaside resorts on the Mediterranean, Germans also hire huge American motor-homes and tour the United States and Canada. They are drawn, like other Europeans, by the sunny beaches of Florida and the mystique of the Far West; and perhaps also by the same spirit of adventure that took flocks of German immigrants to North America in earlier generations.

No. 1

What's missing in the second drawing? Enter the names of the eight missing objects.

The man:
1. ....
2. ....
3. ....
4. ....

The woman:
1. ....
2. ....
3. ....
4. ....

BEFORE   AFTER

No. 2

Find the names of the articles of clothing. Capitalize all the words and remember ö = oe/ä = ae/ü = ue:

Example: W ——————— = WAESCHE
1. H————————
2. S————

3. ————————H————
4. ————E————————
5. ————————U——

   (See answers on page 13 of the booklet)

Figures of Speech

JEMANDEN IN DIE TASCHE STECKEN

To put someone into one's pocket
To be more than a match for someone

IHM GEHT DER HUT HOCH

His hat is rising
He sees red

ER FÜHLT SICH AUF DEN SCHLIPS GETRETEN

He feels as if his tie is being trodden on
His nose is put out of joint

PERLEN VOR DIE SÄUE WERFEN

To throw pearls before sows
To cast pearls before swine

◉◉ LISTEN

FAMILIE GEBERT IN MÜNCHEN

That evening Werner Gebert calls his wife Dagmar in Munich and tells her that he'll be back on Sunday. His son Markus answers the telephone.

Markus: *Markus Gebert!*

Werner: *Hallo Markus, hier ist Vati. Na, wie schaut's aus?*

Markus: *Vati! Wann kommst du wieder?*

Werner: *Morgen. Ich habe einen Zug um halb sieben.*

Markus: *Toll, dann holen wir dich am Bahnhof ab.*

Werner: *O.K., sag, ist die Mutti da?*

....

Dagmar: *Grüß dich Werner!*

Werner: *Hallo Schatz.*

Dagmar: *Wie geht's?*

Werner: *Du, Hamburg ist eine tolle Stadt. Man kann hier hervorragend bummeln. Leider hatten wir schlechtes Wetter. Ich habe nichts besichtigt, aber ich habe prima eingekauft.*

Dagmar: *Und was macht die Arbeit?*

Werner: *Wir haben gestern den ganzen Tag gearbeitet. Eine nette Spiegel-Redakteurin hat mich interviewt.*

Dagmar: *So so ...*

Werner: *Ja, und später waren wir zusammen essen. Ich habe die norddeutsche Küche probiert.*

Dagmar: *Da hast du ja spaß gehabt. Hier sieht es nicht so gut aus.*

Werner: *Was ist los?*

Dagmar: *Susi ist krank. Sie hat Grippe. Ihre Temperatur steigt und steigt. Und Markus ist auch erkältet. Sein Husten ist wirklich schlimm.*

Werner: *Hast du den Arzt geholt?*

Dagmar: *Natürlich! Kannst du so schnell wie möglich zurückkommen? Ich bin fix und fertig.*

Werner: *Ich bin morgen nachmittag da.*

Dagmar: *Bis dann.*

◉◉ LISTEN AND REPEAT

See translation on page 13 of the booklet.

Garmisch:
old-fashioned pharmacy façade.

NOUNS

Vati — Dad, Daddy
der Vater — father
der Zug — train
Mutti — Mum, Mummy
die Mutter — mother
der Schatz — treasure; (here) darling
die SPIEGEL (1) Redakteurin — SPIEGEL editor (f)
die Küche — kitchen
der Spaß — fun, pleasure
die Grippe — flu
die Temperatur — temperature
der Husten — cough
der Arzt — doctor

die Krankheit — illness
der/die Kranke — patient
die Erkältung — cold, chill
der Schnupfen — head cold, sniffles
der Schmerz — ache, pain
die Zahn-, Hals-, -Bauchschmerzen — toothache, sore throat, stomach ache
das Kopfweh — headache
das Fieber — fever
das Medikament — medication
die Tabletten — tablets
die Behandlung — treatment
das Rezept — prescription
die Apotheke — pharmacy
das Krankenhaus — hospital
der Krankenwagen — ambulance

ADJECTIVES

nett — nice
norddeutsch — North German
krank — ill

erkältet — ill with a cold
schlimm — grave, bad
schnell — rapid, fast, quick

langsam — slow
süddeutsch — South German
westdeutsch — West German
ostdeutsch — East German
gesund — healthy
apothekenpflichtig — (prescription drug) available only from pharmacists.

VERBS

abholen — to pick up, collect
bummeln — to stroll
interviewen — to interview
steigen — to climb, rise
zurückkommen/wiederkommen — to come back/return

sich bessern — to improve, get better
sich verschlechtern — to get worse
behandeln — to treat

MISCELLANEOUS

Grüß dich! (2) — Hello! Greetings
prima — super, great
so...wie möglich — as...as possible
zusammen — together
fix und fertig — quite ready; (here) exhausted, all in

ihr(e) — her
sein(e) — his

HOW TO SAY IT

Ich fühle mich wohl — I feel well
Wir sind in Form — We're feeling fit
Sie ist gesund — She is healthy (in good health)

Ich habe Husten/Kopfweh/Fieber (3) — I have a cough/a headache/a fever
Ich habe (einen) Schnupfen/(eine) Grippe (3) — I have a head cold, flu
Ich habe eine Erkältung (3) }
Ich bin erkältet } — I have a cold
Mein Zustand verbessert/verschlechtert sich — My condition is getting better/worse

Er ruft den Arzt/den Krankenwagen — He calls the doctor/ambulance
Sie kommt in (acc.) das Krankenhaus — She is going into hospital
Sie ist in Behandlung — She is being treated
Der Arzt behandelt die Kranke — The doctor is treating the patient *(f)*
Der Arzt verschreibt ein Rezept — The doctor writes a prescription
Das Medikament ist apothekenpflichtig — It is a prescription medicine
Sie nimmt den Hustensaft — She is taking the cough syrup

REMARKS   REMARKS   REMARKS   REMARKS

(1) DER SPIEGEL is an important weekly published in Hamburg. — (2) Grüß dich! is a common greeting in South Germany. Northerners don't use it. — (3) No article is used with the disorders HUSTEN, KOPFWEH, FIEBER, SCHMERZEN, e.g.: Sie hat Schmerzen. (She has pains). Sie hat Kopfweh. (She has a headache.) The article is always used with ERKÄLTUNG.

*In Dialogue 2.5 on page 88, you will find six forms of the past participle. All these participles end in **t** and are conjugated with **haben** as the auxiliary or helping verb to form the present perfect tense.*
*1. Er **hat** Spaß **gehabt.**/Sie **hat** den Arzt **geholt.** — This is the regular form for most verbs: the root (-**hab**, -**hol**) with the prefix **ge-** and the ending **-t: ge-hab-t.** The present perfect of most weak, or regular, verbs is conjugated in this way. e.g. **machen, suchen, führen, wählen, spielen, hoffen.***
*2. Sie **haben gearbeitet.** The usual form of the past participle (**ge**..**t**) + an **e** inserted before the final **t: ge-arbeit-e-t.** The same is true for other verbs whose stem or root ends in **t**, e.g. **warten, kosten, antworten.***
*3. Er **hat** die norddeutsche Küche **probiert.** Past participles of verbs with the suffix -**ieren** do not begin with **ge**- and end in **-iert, pro-biert,** e.g. **telefonieren, amüsieren, reservieren.***
*4. Er **hat** nichts **besichtigt.** Verbs with inseparable prefixes like **be**- keep the prefix and take no **ge**-. They end in **-t** if regular (weak), e.g. **besuchen, verkaufen.***
*5. Er **hat eingekauft.** Verbs with separable prefixes like **ein** use **ge**- and end in **-t.** The separable prefix preceeds **ge-: ein-ge-kauf-t,** e.g. **auflegen, umdrehen.***
*6. Sie **hat** ihn **interviewt. Inter-** is treated as an inseparable prefix. Verbs of foreign origin are usually conjugated like the verbs in Group 4.*

1. THE PRESENT PERFECT

(● ●) LISTEN

Herr Gebert sucht ein Geschenk.
● Herr Gebert hat ein Geschenk gesucht.

Put the following sentences into the present perfect:
Frauke arbeitet mit Silke. — Dagmar Gebert wartet auf Werner. — Sie holt den Arzt. — Herr Bosquet reserviert ein Zimmer. — Herr Krumbach verlegt Bücher. — Dieter Hartmann telefoniert mit Herrn Gebert. — Die Züge warten. — Ihr habt Grippe. Sie hören auf. — Wir besichtigen Hamburg.

See grammar on page 44 of the booklet.

2. POSSESSIVE PRONOUNS

(● ●) LISTEN

Silke schreibt den Bericht.
● Das ist ihr Bericht.
Werner kauft den Computer.
● Das ist sein Computer.

Indicate possession by using das ist/sind + possessive pronoun + noun, as in the examples:
Silke hat Spitzenhemden. — Dieter trinkt das Mineralwasser. — Markus hat Schmerzen. — Silke macht die Arbeit. — Dagmar bekommt das Geschenk. — Herr Gebert nimmt den Hut. — Frau Gebert hat eine Tochter. — Frau Gebert hat einen Sohn. — Herr Gebert hat eine Tochter. — Herr Gebert hat einen Sohn. — Udo gibt einen Tip.

See grammar on page 41 of the booklet.

3. REFLEXIVE PRONOUNS

(● ●) LISTEN

Er/sich amüsieren/auf der Reeperbahn.
● Er amüsiert sich auf der Reeperbahn.

Change the following in the same way, giving the reflexive pronoun that corresponds to the subject:
Du/sich langweilen/in Hamburg. — Wir/sich umdrehen/nach Silke. — Ich/sich interessieren/für Kriminalliteratur. — Ich/sich verbessern/in Deutsch. — Sein Zustand/sich verschlechtern/langsam. Silke und Frauke/sich amüsieren/im Café. — Ich/sich langweilen/im Verlag.

See grammar on page 41 of the booklet.

4. ARTICLE + ADJECTIVE

(● ●) LISTEN

Das rote Kleid ist attraktiv.
● Ein rotes Kleid ist attraktiv.

Replace the definite article with the indefinite and vice versa. Watch accusatives and plurals!
Er ißt die große Scholle. — Wir kaufen einen interessanten Computer. — Sie trinkt das gute Bier. — Sie kaufen die schönen Spitzenhemden. — Das ist ein norddeutscher Nachtisch. — Ihr besichtigt den ganzen Hafen. — Er hat interessante Bücher. — Sie holt einen guten Arzt. — Wir haben die schlimme Krankheit. — Er trifft die netten Schriftsteller.

See grammar on page 39 of the booklet.

5. PRONUNCIATION

(● ●) LISTEN CAREFULLY TO THE INTONATION OF THE FOLLOWING QUESTIONS AND REPEAT:

Na, wie schaut's aus? — Wie geht's? — Wann kommst du wieder? — Was macht die Arbeit? — Wie ist das Wetter? Was hast du gemacht? Was ist los? — Hast du den Arzt geholt? — Wie heißen Sie? Heißen Sie Müller? — Schreiben Sie den Bericht? — Haben Sie den Hafen besichtigt?

See grammar on page 36 of the booklet.

TOGETHERNESS - CLUBS AND SOCIETIES

How do Germans spend their free time? Most are very sociable. Once their work is done, they like to get together, preferably with a group of like-minded friends. Huge numbers of clubs and societies, Vereine, cater to all tastes and interests.

There are, for example, numerous associations of animal breeders, such as the Kaninchenzüchtervereine *(rabbit breeders' clubs)*, Taubenzüchtervereine *(pigeons)*, Hühnenzuchtvereine *(chickens)*, and the many Hundezuchtvereine *(dogs)*. These are not professional associations. Animal breeding is a true hobby, and the members meet primarily to enjoy one another's company and compare notes. From time to time they hold shows to display their treasured pets to interested connoisseurs. The best rabbits, pigeons etc win prizes, and the breeder gets a medal, but commercial considerations are secondary.

Those who are not animal fanciers can join one of the 30,000 Schützenvereine *(marksmen's clubs)*. Even though shooting is a serious sport in Germany, most of the members of the Schützenvereine *have never drawn a bead on anything. Their meetings are primarily an excuse for conviviality, ie drinking!*

Once a year the Schützenverein *may organise a parade. Originally it was held in honour of the "king", ie the champion marksman. Today, however, the "king" is elected by the members - rather a dubious honour, since both the actual parade with all its festooned, garlanded floats, and the banquet that follows, are at the king's expense.*

Breeders'clubs are mostly a male preserve, while the Schützenvereine *attract couples. The "king" has to choose his "queen" from among the female members. The carnival societies, the Lach- und Schießgesellschaften, are a regional variation found mainly in the Rhineland between Cologne and Mainz. Their sole purpose is to organise the Mardi Gras carnival with its fantastic costumes and permissive atmosphere. Politicians are favourite targets for satire, but everyone is fair game.*

The people of North Germany generally prefer peace and quiet to the rowdiness and exhibitionism of carnival time. Their excuse for togetherness is bowling, a sport in which a fair amount

The carnival in full swing in front of Düsseldorf City Hall

of alcohol can be consumed before the player's performance is much affected. The big event for the Kegelvereine *(bowling clubs) is the* Kaffeefahrt, *something of a misnomer since it's more of a pub crawl than a café tour. In the spas and tourist resorts of such areas as the Lüneberg Heath, the Harz mountains or the coast, nothing is more dreaded than the noisy weekend invasions of bars and restaurants by the* Kegelbrüder *(bowling buddies). Busloads of singing* Keglers *go rolling round the countryside, boozing and bowling at every stop. Mozart, who was not averse to a little jollity of this kind, is said to have composed his "Kegelstadt" trio in a bowling alley.*

As many club activities are seasonal, it is possible to belong to two or more quite different societies; thus a summertime supporter of the Kleingärtnerverein *(small gardeners' association) may take to bowling or card playing in the winter.*

Gardening is a hobby with a keen following in Germany. As most urban Germans live in flats without gardens, however, since early this century they've taken to renting allotments on the outskirts of towns. Green-fingers find refuge in these Laubkolonien, *where they can cultivate vegetables and coddle rose-bushes to their hearts' content. The Verein at each of these green oases organises barbecue parties in the summer and enforces strict rules about everything, from the size of the potting shed to the types of fertiliser allowed.*

Even the bars, the Kneipen, *have their clubs. Every bar has its regular customers who come to play cards. Skat, for three players, is a favourite, though it requires concentration. Anyone who has just come to talk sits at the* Stammtisch, *the table reserved exclusively for regulars. If some bar or restaurant is your favourite haunt you become a* Stammgast *there. Woe betide the unwary visitor who accidentally usurps a* Stammgast's *usual seat!*

But there are also individualists in Germany who detest Vereinsmeierei, *the relentless quest for togetherness. Some people choose to spend all their spare time on car maintenance and so are too busy to belong to a* Verein. *Others manage to find a balance between the extremes of individualism and gregariousness, and opt for activities that can be shared with just a few others - such as taking a sauna...*

TAKE-A-BREAK

What are they suffering from? Match the people in the drawings below with their respective health problems (or lack of them).

1. *Dieser Mann hat Schnupfen.*
2. *Dieser Mann hat Halsschmerzen.*
3. *Dieser Mann hat Bauchschmerzen.*
4. *Dieser Mann ist gesund.*
5. *Dieser Mann hat Kopfweh.*
6. *Dieser Mann hat Zahnschmerzen.*
7. *Dieser Mann hat Fieber.*
8. *Dieser Mann hat Husten.*

| A | | B | | C | | D | |

| E | | F | | G | | H | |

(See answers on page 14 of the booklet)

Figures of Speech

DAS IST NICHT DEIN BIER

SEINEN SENF DAZU GEBEN

To add one's mustard to something
To shove one's oar in

That is not your beer
That's none of your business

ALLES IST IN BUTTER

Everything is in butter
Everything's fine

2. *WRITTEN PRACTICE*

2.1

Replace each noun with a pronoun in the nominative or accusative: .... *ist anstrengend (die Arbeit)* .... *schreibt (Herr Gebert)* ...... *(der Bericht)* .... *sind krank (die Kinder)* ...... *sind spannend (die Bücher)* ...... *besucht die Messe (Herr Krumbach). Er tauscht* ..... *(das Geld) um.*
Translate: *I need the number of visitors, the photos, and the press report from Frankfurt. You can ask him. I'll call him tomorrow morning.*
Du darfst den Termin mit Herrn Gebert nicht vergessen. Sie soll die Reportage über die Yuppies übernehmen. Ich muß den Bericht am Freitag haben.

2.2

Use the accusative pronoun after „für" (for): *Die Aalsuppe ist für* ...... *(ich). — Die Vorspeise ist für* ...... *(du). Die Salate sind für* ...... *(wir). — Der Fisch ist für* ...... *(Herr Gebert). — Der Nachtisch ist für* ...... *(ihr). — Die Artikel sind für* ...... *(Dieter Hartmann).*
Translate: *The food is very good here (One eats very well here). What can you recommend? I don't like fish. I like (to eat) desserts.*
Leider essen wir in Süddeutschland wenig Fisch. Was nehmen Sie als Vorspeise? Ich trinke nur ein Mineralwasser.

2.3

Add a preposition to complete each sentence: *Ich kenne ein Café hier gleich* ...... *die Ecke. — Gehen wir* ...... *den Alsterpavillon? — Toll, dieser Blick* ...... *die Stadt und den Hafen. — Der See ist* ......: *Zentrum* ...... *Hamburg. Man kann den Hafen* ...... *Fuß besichtigen. — Ich interessiere mich* ...... *Schiffe.*
Translate: *What do we do now? First we can visit the port. No, I'm not interested in the port. Hoffentlich hort es gleich auf! Wohin führen Sie mich heute? Ich schlage den Stadtpark oder einen Spaziergang um die Alster vor. Kommen Sie, gehen wir!*

2.4

Supply the right endings: *Ich suche ein ... klein ... Geschenk für mein ... Kinder. — Sie hat nur dies ... groß...... Teddybär. — Hier ist ein ... modern ... Spielcomputer. — Herr Gebert möchte ein ......weiß...... Morgenmantel kaufen. — Weiß...... Morgenmäntel sind nicht mehr da. — Dies ...... schwarz ...... Spitzenhemd ist sehr attraktiv. — Welch ...... schwarz ... ... Spitzenhemd?*
Translate: *I'm looking for a gift for my children. My wife is 35 (years old). My son would like an electronic game.*
Die Verkäuferin hat keinen weißen Morgenmantel mehr. Wie finden Sie dieses rote Spitzenhemd? Ich nehme einen kleinen Spielcomputer für meine beiden Kinder.

2.5

Add the past participles: *Was hast due die ganze Woche* ......? *(machen). — Wir haben zwei Stunden* ...... *(warten). — Die Aalsupppe hat sehr gut* ...... *(schmecken). — Herr Gebert hat mit Dagmar* ...... *(telefonieren). — Die Spiegel-Redakteurin hat ihn durch Hamburg* ...... *(führen).*
Translate: *Mr. Gebert takes the train at 9:30. Dagmar is exhausted. Her son has a fever and her daughter has the flu. What is happening?*
Wir haben die ganze Woche gearbeitet. Ihr habt euch amüsiert. Wir hatten schlechtes Wetter.

 (See answers on page 31 of the booklet)

MORE VOCABULARY

THE BODY

der Kopf — head
das Gesicht — face
das Auge — eye
die Nase — nose
der Mund — mouth
das Ohr — ear
die Haare — hair
der Körper — body
die Schulter — shoulder
der Arm — arm
die Brust — chest
das Herz — heart
das Bein — leg
der Oberschenkel — thigh
die Haut — skin
die Muskeln — muscles
die Hand — hand
der Finger — finger
der Hintern — behind
der Rücken — back

OCCUPATIONS

der Chef — boss
der Leiter — director
der Verkaufsleiter — sales director
der Angestellte — employee
der Abteilungsleiter — head of section, departmental manager
der Kaufmann — salesman
der Buchhalter — accountant
der Personalchef — personnel manager
die Sekretärin — secretary (f)
der Buchhändler — bookseller
der Beamte * — official
der Lehrer — teacher
der Bäcker — baker
der Schlachter — butcher
der Elektriker — electrician
der Kfz-Schlosser — mechanic, garage man
der Maler — painter

die Krankenschwester — nurse
der Ingenieur — engineer
der Polizist * — policeman
der Landwirt — farmer
der Gehilfe — assistant
der Apotheker — pharmacist

EATING OUT

die Wirtschaft — inn, pub
das Speiselokal — restaurant
die Imbißstube — snack bar
die Kneipe — bar, pub
die Bier-/Weinstube — tavern/wine bar
der Biergarten — beer garden
der Weinkeller — wine cellar
die Kantine — canteen, cafeteria
die Mensa — university restaurant

FOOD AND DRINK

das Obst — fruit
die Aprikose — apricot
die Ananas — pineapple
die Banane — banana
die Kirsche — cherry
die Erdbeere — strawberry
die Apfelsine — orange
der Apfel — apple
die Mandarine — tangerine
die Melone — melon
die Stachelbeere — gooseberry
die Johannisbeere — currant
der Pfirsich — peach
die Pflaume — plum
die Weintraube — grape
das Gemüse — vegetables
der Knoblauch — garlic
die Möhre — carrot
der Rotkohl — red cabbage
der Weißkohl — white cabbage
der Blumenkohl — cauliflower
die Erbse — pea
die Bohne — bean
der Fenchel — fennel

die Linsen — lentils
der Porree — leek
die Paprikaschote — red pepper
die Petersilie — parsley
der Endiviensalat — endive salad
das Wild — game, venison
der Hase — rabbit, hare
die Ente — duck
das Hühnchen — chicken
das Schwein — pork
das Rind — beef
das Kalb — calf, veal
die Gans — goose
die Ziege — she - goat
der Hammel — mutton
der Krebs — crab
die Forelle — trout
die Austern — oysters
die Muscheln — mussels
die Krabben — crabs, shrimps
der Thunfisch — tuna
der Lachs — salmon
der Hummer — lobster
das Würstchen — sausage, (small)
die Wurst — sausage
der Schinken — ham
der Käse — cheese
die Butter — butter
der Quark — curd cheese
die Sahne — cream
der Kuchen — cake
die Kekse — biscuits
die Milch — milk
der Fruchtsaft — fruit juice
der Schnaps — spirits, brandy
der Weißwein — white wine
der Rotwein — red wine
der Tee — tea
der Kräutertee — herbal tea
die Nudeln — noodles
der Reis — rice

* weak masculine

2. TEST YOURSELF

1. WHAT WOULD YOU SAY IF YOU HAD TO ... ?

1. *Make a date for Monday:* ....
2. *Say that the weather is nice:* ....
3. *Ask the waiter for the menu:* ....
4. *Say that you have a headache:* ....
5. *Say how old you are:* ....
6. *Ask how much a cup of coffee costs:* ....

2. ONLY ONE OF EACH THREE SENTENCES IS CORRECT. WHICH ONE?

Tick the right box

A. *Du darfst die Termin mit Werner Gebert nicht vergessen.* .... ☐
B. *Du darfst den Termin mit Werner Gebert nicht vergessen* .... ☐
C. *Du dürfst den Termin mit Werner Gebert nicht vergessen* .... ☐

A. *Ich darf keine Eier und keinen Salat.* .... ☐
B. *Ich mag kein Eier und keinen Salat.* .... ☐
C. *Ich mag keine Eier und keinen Salat.* .... ☐

A. *Sie kennt ein Café hier gleich um die Ecke.* .... ☐
B. *Sie kennt ein Café bald gleich um die Ecke.* .... ☐
C. *Sie kennt ein Café hier gleich um den Ecke.* .... ☐

A. *Er sucht einer roten Morgenmantel für seine Frau.* .... ☐
B. *Er sucht einen roter Morgenmantel für seine Frau.* .... ☐
C. *Er sucht einen roten Morgenmantel für seine Frau.* .... ☐

A. *Man kann hier hervorragend bummeln, und ich habe prima eingekauft.* ... ☐
B. *Mann kann hier hervorragend bummeln, und ich habe prima*
   eingekauft. .... ☐
C. *Man kann hier hervorragend bummeln, und ich habe prima einkauft.* ..... ☐

3. MATCH THE QUESTIONS WITH THEIR ANSWERS

A. *Wann gibst du den Artikel ab?*
B. *Was wünschen Sie?*
C. *Was machen wir jetzt?*
D. *Wieviel kostet der große Teddybär?*
E. *Sind Sie krank?*

1. *89, - DM*
2. *Ja, ich habe Fieber.*
3. *Ein Bier bitte.*
4. *Heute nachmittag.*
5. *Ich schlage einen Spaziergang vor.*

4. TRUE OR FALSE? (RICHTIG ODER FALSCH?)

1. Silke soll die Reportage über die Yuppies übernehmen. ....
2. Ab Donnerstag ist Herr Gebert in Hamburg. ....
3. Herr Gebert mag Salat, aber keine Eier. ....
4. Silke Peters hat nur wenig Hunger. ....
5. Die Alster ist der See im Zentrum von Hamburg. ....
6. Herr Gebert interessiert sich für Schiffe. ....
7. Susanne Gebert ist drei Jahre alt. ....
8. Herr Gebert hat eine Hose für seine Frau gekauft. ....
9. Herr Gebert kommt am Sonntag nach München zurück. ....
10. Die Familie Gebert ist gesund. ....

5. SELECT THE VERB THAT FITS THE SENSE

brauche / darf / muß / treffe
1. Ich .... noch die Besucherzahlen.
möchtest / bestellt / trinkt / nehmt
2. Sie .... eine Aalsuppe und Labskaus.
besuchen / geben / besichtigen / kaufen
3. Wir können zuerst den Hafen ....
möchte /darf / kostet / muß
4. Er .... lieber einen kleinen Spielcomputer.
a. besichtigt / umgedreht / gearbeitet / geführt - b. gespielt / gewartet / telefoniert / amüsiert
5. Sie haben Hamburg a. .... und sich b. ....

6. GIVE THE PAST PARTICIPLE

1. Ich habe diese Arbeit heute nachmittag .... (machen).
2. Er hat den ganzen Tag mit Silke Peters .... (arbeiten).
3. Herr Gebert hat die Aalsuppe nicht .... (probieren).
4. Sie haben den Hafen nicht .... (besichtigen).
*   aber sie haben eine interessante Ausstellung .... (besuchen).*
5. Leider hat es die ganze Woche .... (regnen).

(See answers on page 33 of the booklet)

LONDON - BERLIN, ONE WAY

*H*e headed for home, and spent a large part of the evening composing the rest of his letter. He told her what he thought she might like to know about him: that he was 24, worked in marketing and was keen on jazz, travel and skiing. (That was safe enough - none of it revealed his sex!) Next he decided to tell her frankly that he hadn't enjoyed German much at school but was now anxious to improve his language skills because his career prospects might depend on it. He'd gladly write to her about London, and would be pleased to learn anything she could tell him about Berlin, and about Germany and German life in general, in exchange. Grinning to himself, he signed the letter *Simone Lambert.*

Her reply, which arrived one Monday, was typewritten and postmarked Vienna. She described a rainy day in that grey baroque city, the laden tramcars rumbling past the *Staatsoper (State Opera House),* the tourists queuing with umbrellas to see the famous Lippizaner horses of the *Spanische Reitschule,* the Danube murky under the lowering sky. Yet it was not a gloomy letter. *,,Die blaue Donau ist nicht blau heute - das Wasser ist grau und schmutzig! Aber Wien ist eine schöne alte Stadt. Mein Hotel ist ganz gut, und das österreichische Essen schmeckt mir. Der Himmel wird schon hell; morgen scheint sicher die Sonne."* It ended *,,Mit freundlichen Grüßen".* (How familiar was that? Perhaps not very.) And then the one word "Lore", written in a large clear hand.

Simon could understand it all quite easily, and felt pleased with himself. The same evening he sat down to write to her again. *,,Liebe Lore"* he began, thinking the time had come to be less formal, "I enjoyed your letter from Vienna. What were you doing there? Were you on holiday?" Then he told her something of his own holiday plans, trying to use a simple, clear style. Only when he had finished did it strike him that Lore hadn't given him any specific information about herself. Usually you can tell something about people from their handwriting, but Lore had typed her letter. He stared at the signature, wondering what she was like. She seemed observant and perceptive; perhaps she was a professional travel writer. He imagined her in old Vienna, a slim and well-groomed figure surely, strolling through the crowds in the Stephansplatz, tossing back long fair hair to gaze up at the great spire of the cathedral. It was a pleasing image.

He had given her his office address without really knowing why. Maybe so that Laura wouldn't have to know about her - not that he had anything to hide, of course. Laura - what a coincidence! When he first read the name "Lore" he hadn't noticed that the two women had the same name.

Ten days later he received Lore's second letter. This time she told him about some work she was doing. She was writing an article on the development of tourism in various regions of the former East Germany. (Aha! so he had been right about her job.) *,,Es ist eine ganz angenehme und interessante Aufgabe",* she wrote. *,,Ostdeutschland kenne ich persönlich nicht gut, aber es gibt dort wirklich sehr viel zu sehen."* Well, it was nice to know she enjoyed her work, but she hadn't really answered his questions about herself, her home background, age and interests. That was disappointing; he felt he wanted to get to know her better.

He was too busy at work to answer her letter for the next week or so. His boss Mark, nervous about all the political changes in Eastern Europe and the increased competition they might bring, was particularly anxious that the company should grab its share of the enlarged German market, and was trying to decide what action to take to ensure that it did so. Simon clearly foresaw the impact of this upon himself, and decided that he really must polish up his German and his knowledge of Germany as quickly as possible.

Munich: Asamkirche (first half of the 18th century).

He therefore asked a lot of questions about Germany in his next letter, and especially about Berlin. He asked Lore how the city had changed since the Wall came down, how her own life had been affected, what West Germans thought of East Germans, and much more.

Lore replied two weeks later in a long letter. This time Simon needed a dictionary, but he didn't mind because what she wrote was so interesting. She told him about West Berlin as it had been, a showcase for the West in the communist East. Creative people had long been drawn to it not only by the generous assistance given to them, but also by its atmosphere of vitality and freedom. Now the same applied to the whole reunited city. She wrote of Berliners, open-minded citizens of the world with their famous irreverent wit and distinctive style of speech. She wrote of the night in November '89 when they had heard the amazing news on the radio and rushed out to celebrate the opening of the Wall.

TO BE CONTINUED . . .

The Oktoberfest in Munich.

UNIT 3

3.1 DIALOGUE

LISTEN

DER VERLORENE SOHN

Werner Gebert arrives in Munich. His wife and children aren't at the station, as arranged. He waits for them. Finally, his wife and daughter arrive, running.

Werner: *Na endlich! Was ist denn los? Wo seid ihr denn gewesen? Ich warte schon eine halbe Stunde! Warum seid ihr nicht gekommen?*

Dagmar: *Entschuldige unsere Verspätung. Wir hatten vorhin noch eine Viertelstunde Zeit und da haben wir eingekauft.*

Werner: *Und wo habt ihr eingekauft? Die Kaufhäuser sind doch heute geschlossen.*

Dagmar: *Der Bahnhofsbasar ist geöffnet.*

Werner: *Ja, und dann, was habt ihr dann gemacht?*

Dagmar: *Wir haben Markus verloren!*

Werner: *Was? Wieso verloren?*

Dagmar: *Ja, er war plötzlich weg. Wir haben überall gesucht. Wir haben ihn nicht gefunden.*

Werner: *Wo habt ihr gesucht?*

Dagmar: *Wir sind überall gewesen, wo wir waren. Und wir haben ihn nirgends gesehen. Dann haben wir den Abteilungsleiter gefragt, und der hat eine Durchsage gemacht. Wir haben gewartet. Er ist nicht gekommen. Vielleicht ist er nach Hause gegangen.*

Werner: *Wir müssen sofort etwas tun! Hast du schon zu Hause angerufen?*

Dagmar: *Nein, das habe ich vergessen.*

Werner: *Also, ich fahre jetzt langsam den Weg nach Hause und suche ihn. Du gehst mit Susi in das nächste Polizeirevier und gibst eine Suchmeldung auf.*

LISTEN AND REPEAT

See translation on page 15 of the booklet.

*(Above) The Bonn underground.
(Below) ICE, the train of the future
and a tram stop in Frankfurt.*

3.1 VOCABULARY

NOUNS

- das Kaufhaus — department store
- die Durchsage — announcement, paging
- das Polizeirevier — police station
- die Suchmeldung — missing person report
- der Bahnhofsbasar — station department store
- der Polizeibeamte — police officer
- die Polizei — police

ADJECTIVES

- geöffnet — open
- geschlossen — closed

VERBS

- aufgeben — give/hand in, file
- verlieren — to lose

MISCELLANEOUS

- schon — already
- plötzlich — suddenly
- überall — everywhere
- nirgends — nowhere
- nach Hause — homewards
- zu Hause — at home
- nächste, -r, -s — nearest, next

- jemand — someone
- irgendjemand — anyone
- niemand — no one, nobody

REMARKS   REMARKS   REMARKS   REMARKS

(1) In ETWAS SCHÖNES, the adjective schön is used as a neuter noun. (See grammar on page 37 of the booklet.) — (2) When used in the perfect tenses, the participle never has an ending.

The past participles of irregular or strong verbs begin with ge- and end in -en. Often, but not always, the stem vowel of the infinitive changes to another vowel. Sometimes there are changes in consonants too.

Er ist gekommen (2) — He has come, he came
Wir haben Markus verloren — We (have) lost Markus
Wo seid ihr gewesen? — Where have you been? Where were you?
Wir haben ihn nicht gefunden — We haven't found him
Wir haben ihn nirgends gesehen — We haven't seen him anywhere
Er ist nach Hause gegangen — He went home, he has gone home
Hast du zu Hause angerufen? — Have you phoned home? Did you phone home?
Das habe ich vergessen — I forgot (I have forgotten) that

HOW TO SAY IT

Wir haben ihn überall gesucht — We looked for him everywhere
Überall sehe ich nur Autos — Everywhere I see only cars
Er findet das Buch nirgends — He can't find the book anywhere

Sie hat etwas gesagt — She has said something
Er interessiert sich für nichts — He is interested in nothing
Ich möchte etwas Schönes (1) sehen — I'd like to see something beautiful

Jemand hat angerufen — Somebody has telephoned
Heute war irgendjemand bei Frau Peters — Today somebody or other was visiting Mrs. Peters
Alle waren da — Everybody was there
Niemand war da — No one was there

Ich bin daheim — I am at home
Ich bin zu Hause — I am at home
Mein Zuhause ist schön — My home is beautiful
Ich gehe nach Hause — I am going home

Was ist denn los? — What is the matter?
Wo wart ihr denn? — Where were you?
Was soll das? — What's that supposed to be/mean?
Was ist passiert? — What happened? what has happened?

3.1 ORAL PRACTICE

1. IRREGULAR VERBS (+ HABEN)

using the past participle

(• •) LISTEN

finden
* *er hat gefunden*

Now give the present perfect of the following verbs:
rufen — verstehen — bekommen — geben — treffen — beginnen — helfen — lesen — vergessen — essen — sehen — liegen — empfehlen.
See grammar on page 44 of the booklet.

2. IRREGULAR VERBS (+ SEIN)

using the past participle

(• •) LISTEN

Erk kommt heute.
* *Er ist heute gekommen.*

Change the present to the present perfect.
Ich gehe in den Stadtpark. — Sie ist zu Hause. — Er fährt nach Hamburg. — Er wird alt. — Die Temperatur steigt auf 40 Grad.
See grammar on page 44 of the booklet.

3. REGULAR AND IRREGULAR VERBS

using the past participle

(• •) LISTEN

Er wartet auf ein Taxi
* *Er hat auf ein Taxi gewartet.*

Change the present to the present perfect:
Ich esse eine Suppe — Er geht in das Zentrum — Wir tauschen Geld um — Er verkauft sein Auto — Ich bekomme ein Geschenk — Sie brauchen Geld — Ich vergesse die Telefonnummer — Wir probieren den Camembert — Er zeigt die Stadt — Er richtet eine Nachricht aus — Ich hole Silke ab.
See grammar on page 44 of the booklet.

4. THE NEGATIVE IN THE PRESENT PERFECT

(• •) LISTEN

Er hat mich angerufen.
* *Er hat mich nicht angerufen.*

Er ist 50 geworden.
* *Er ist nicht 50 geworden.*

Make the following sentences negative:
Er hat Markus gefunden — Er ist bei Silke gewesen — Er hat das Buch gelesen — Er hat mich verstanden — Er hat eine Aalsuppe empfohlen — Er ist gekommen.

5. QUESTIONS IN THE PRESENT PERFECT

(• •) LISTEN

Er hat dich angerufen.
* *Hat er dich angerufen?*
Er ist 50 geworden.
* *Ist er 50 geworden?*

Turn the sentences in exercise 4 into questions:

6. SEPARABLE PREFIX

using the past participle

(• •) LISTEN

Silke anrufen.
* *Er hat Silke angerufen.*

Form sentences with a 3rd person singular subject. Be careful of the auxiliary verb (haben or sein)
in Hamburg anhalten — schnell weitergehen — gestern wiederkommen — das Telefon — abheben — darauf anstoßen — den Bericht abgeben.
See grammar on page 45 of the booklet.

7. PRONUNCIATION

(• •) LISTEN TO Ü, Ä, E, O, U, EI, AU AND REPEAT:
Fünf-fünfzig-München/Hand, Hände — Arzt, Ärzte — Glas, Gläser/nehmen - zehn-Kaffee-essen-den / vorne-Sonne- rot-Brot-Portion/tun-Husten-Suppe-du - uns/eine - zeigen-mein-sein-Frankreich / Fieber-vier - hier - lieben / aus-Auto- Haus.

Munich: the Olympic swimming pool seen from the Olympia Tower

EDUCATION

German education does not begin officially till the age of 6. Classes are numbered from 1 to 13, Class 13 being the final year of the Gymnasium (grammar school) in which students, then aged 19, take public examinations qualifying those who pass for university admission.

The day's lessons end at about 1 pm, though pupils may stay later for sports or extra-curricular activities. Usually they go home for lunch and devote part of the afternoon to homework.

After Grundschule (primary school) there is a choice, dependent upon the child's ability and inclinations, between the Hauptschule, Realschule, Gymnasium and Gesamtschule. The first three are all more or less specialised, but the fourth option is the German equivalent of a comprehensive school, created in the 1970s as an alternative to what some regard as a premature selection process.

Hauptschule students spend five years preparing for a professional apprenticeship. This then takes a further three years, during which the apprentice electricians, mechanics etc spend one day a week on an appropriate training course. Apprentices are salaried, and the state and private enterprise share the cost of their education.

The Realschule also leads directly to the world of work. Realschüler choose careers in banking, publishing, commerce or administration. If they are bright enough they can transfer to the Gymnasium to prepare for the Abitur, which is more akin to the French baccalauréat than to British Advanced Level exams. Those who pass the Abitur often serve an apprenticeship before going on to university; this is highly recommended because it provides a practical grounding for careers in business.

Private institutions of higher education are almost non-existent. The German state universities are prestigious. Heidelberg, Cologne and Tübingen are among the oldest, but the first German-language university was actually founded in Prague in 1348.

The basic philosophy behind the university system still owes much to the ideas of Wilhelm von Humboldt, who founded one of Berlin's universities in 1810. He believed that the university should be a place for independent research, freely undertaken. Even the state cannot prescribe research subjects. Collaboration between teachers and students is expected to be close and mutually enriching. The primary goal is not professional training but the acquisition of good working habits and a broad general culture. Studies tend to focus on theory, and team-work is encouraged. The final exam, der Abschluß, counts for a great deal in terms of social and professional status. It would be rude not to address the author of a doctoral thesis as Herr or Frau Doktor!

Nowadays universities increasingly emphasise collaboration with industry. Many students spend more than six years at university, structuring their own courses and collecting credits as they go along. They can also move fairly freely from one university to another. Unfortunately, the universities are overcrowded, and a centralised system now distributes vacancies in the different institutions, so that students may have to go far from home. But young Germans cherish their independence anyway. They often choose to live in a Wohngemeinschaft, a residence co-operative.

Education in Germany is not organised by the federal Ministry of Education. Instead each Bundesland (federal state) is responsible for its own. The federal Minister of Education coordinates the regional systems and ensures parity among them. Since the universities are autonomous, the degrees awarded and the content of courses vary from one Bundesland to another.

3.1   *TAKE-A-BREAK*

No. 1   🔊 LISTEN

At the station. Listen and fill in the blanks:

Am Gleis .... bitte einsteigen, Türen schließen, Vorsicht bei der Abfahrt. Auf Gleis .... fährt der Schnellzug aus Rom ein. Achtung, der Intercity aus Berlin hat .... Minuten Verspätung. Planmäßige Ankunft .... Uhr .... Der .... aus Köln fährt .... Gleis 5 ein. Vorsicht bei der .... Am .... 19 bitte einsteigen.

No. 2

Mr. Gebert's diary. Write down what he's been doing:

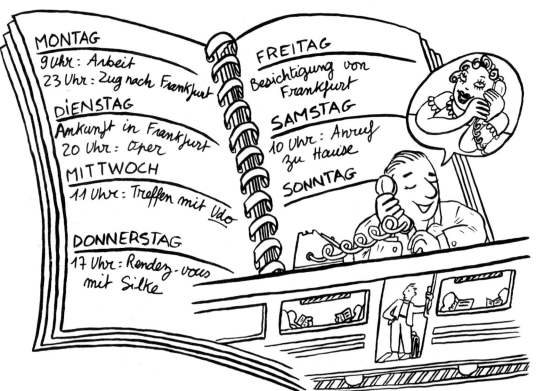

Example: Monday at 9 A.M. he was working.

Montag: Am Montag	Donnerstag: ....
Dienstag:	Freitag: ....
Mittwoch:	Samstag: ....

Look at the train timetables and fill in the blanks:

Düsseldorf

km 674	→	München	
ab	Zug	an	Bemerkungen
8.32	11	15.08	
9.21	*TEE* 15	15.44	
9.32	7	16.03	U Köln
10.33	25	17.03	
10.38	513	17.08	

Der Zug No. 11 nach München fährt um ...... Uhr ...... ab und kommt um ...... Uhr ...... an. Der Intercity No. 25 fährt ...... Stunden und ...... Minuten bis München. Der Intercity No. 7 fährt bis Köln muß man umsteigen. Er ist um ...... Uhr ...... in München. Der TEE braucht nur ...... Stunden und ...... Minuten bis München.

German adverbs never change. The following indicate place:

OBEN

LINKS

RECHTS

HINTEN

VORNE

UNTEN

(See answers on page 16 of the booklet)

LISTEN   **AUF DER SUCHE NACH MARKUS GEBERT**

While Werner Gebert returns home Dagmar and her daughter go to the police station.

Dagmar: *Kann ich hier eine Suchmeldung aufgeben?*

Polizeibeamter: *Ja, da sind Sie hier richtig. Worum geht es denn?*

Dagmar: *Mein Sohn ist verschwunden. Wir haben eingekauft, und da...*

Polizeibeamter: *Moment, eins nach dem anderen. Beruhigen Sie sich erstmal. Wo und wann ist das passiert?*

Dagmar: *Das war heute nachmittag, so gegen 17 Uhr im Bahnhofsbasar. Da war er plötzlich weg. Wir sind dann zu der Lebensmittelabteilung weitergegangen, und ich habe dem Kind*

noch gesagt, daß es schon spät ist.

Polizeibeamter: *Aber Ihr Sohn ist Ihnen nicht gefolgt?*

Dagmar: *Nein. Ist er jemandem nachgelaufen? Ich habe einen Moment nicht aufgepaßt, weil ich einer Freundin begegnet bin.*

Polizeibeamter: *Und da war es zu spät. Ist Ihnen sonst nichts aufgefallen?*

Dagmar: *Nein, nichts.*

Polizeibeamter: *Machen Sie sich keine Sorgen. Ich versichere Ihnen, daß wir Ihnen helfen. Können Sie Ihren Sohn beschreiben? Name, Alter, Größe, Haarfarbe? Was hat er an?*

Dagmar: *Also, mein Sohn heißt Markus Gebert, er ist 7 Jahre alt, eine Meter fünfzehn groß, er hat blonde, kurze Haare, und er trägt ein gelbes Hemd und eine grüne Hose und ...*

But before Mrs. Gebert can finish giving the description, the door opens suddenly and a policeman comes in with little Markus.

Polizeibeamter II: *Sieh mal, Klaus, wer hier ist. Der Kleine hat seine Eltern verloren, weil er der Schokolade im Bahnhofsbasar nicht widerstehen kann. Ein Clown hat ihm Schokolade gegeben.*

Dagmar: *Markus!*

Polizeibeamter I: *Na, dann ist ja alles in Butter.*

LISTEN AND REPEAT
See translation on page 16 of the booklet.

A demonstration for the 35-hour week

3.2 VOCABULARY

NOUNS

der Clown — clown
die Schokolade — chocolate
die Lebensmittelabteilung — food department
die Freundin — friend (f)
die Sorgen (pl.)/die Sorge — care, worry
das Alter — age
die Größe — (here) size
die Haarfarbe — hair colour
der Kleine — the little boy
die Eltern — parents

der Freund — friend (m)
die Augenfarbe — eye colour
die Kleidung — clothing
die besonderen Kennzeichen — special characteristics

ADJECTIVES

blond — blond
kurz — short

dunkel — dark
lang — long

VERBS

verschwunden (verschwinden) — disappeared (to disappear)
beruhigt (sich beruhigen) — calmed down
passiert (passieren) — happened
weg sein — to be gone

gefolgt + dat. (folgen) — followed (to follow)
nachgelaufen + dat. (nachlaufen) — ran after (to run after)
aufgepaßt (aufpassen auf) — paid attention to (to pay attention to)
begegnet + dat. (begegnen) — met (by chance) (to meet)
aufgefallen + dat (auffallen) — struck, made an impression on (to strike, make an impression)

versichern + dat. (versichert) — to assure
beschreiben (1) + acc. (beschrieben) — to describe
anhaben + acc. (angehabt)
tragen + acc. (getragen) }— to wear (clothes)
widerstehen + dat. (widerstanden) — to resist

MISCELLANEOUS

worum — about what
eins nach dem anderen — one thing at a time
erstmal — firstly
so gegen — approximately
daß — that
wahrscheinlich — probably
weil — because
sonst — otherwise

HOW TO SAY IT

PREPOSITIONS

• Verbs followed by the dative.

geben (1): *Peter gibt* **dem/einem/diesem** *Gast ein Bier* — Peter gives the/a/this guest a beer.
sagen: *Silke sagt* **der/einer/dieser** *Frau etwas.* — Silke says something to the/a/this woman.
folgen: *Markus folgt* **dem/einem/diesem** *Mädchen nicht.* — Markus doesn't follow the/a/this girl.
nachlaufen: *Susi läuft* **dem/einem/diesem** *Mädchen nicht nach* — Susie doesn't run after the/a/this girl.
begegnen: *Dagmar begegnet* **der/einer/dieser** *Freundin im Bahnhof.* — Dagmar meets the/a/this friend in the station.
auffallen: *Der Mann fällt* **der/einer/dieser** *Freundin auf.* — The man is noticed by the/a/this friend.
versichern: *Klaus versichert dies* **dem/einem/diesem** *Kind.* — Klaus assures the/a/this child of that.
helfen: *Der Polizeibeamte hilft* **dem/einem/diesem** *Kind.* — The police officer helps the/a/this child.
widerstehen: *Udo widersteht* **dem/einem/diesem** *Sekt nicht.* — Hugo can't resist the/a/this champagne.

• Prepositions with the dative:
The most common are: **aus, bei, mit, nach, seit, von, zu** — See grammar on page 42 of the booklet.

CONJUNCTIONS

• **Daß** *and* **weil** *introduce subordinate clauses. In subordinate clauses the verb is placed at the end.*
Sonntag scheint die Sonne, sagt Dieter.
Dieter sagt, **daß** *Sonntag die Sonne scheint* — Dieter says that on Sunday the sun will shine.
Markus verliert seine Eltern, er ißt Schokolade.
Markus verliert seine Eltern, **weil** *er Schokolade* **ißt.** — Markus loses his parents because he eats chocolate.

COMPLAINTS

Ich möchte Anzeige gegen jemand erstatten. — I'd like to make a complaint against someone.
Ich möchte eine Suchmeldung aufgeben. — I'd like to make a missing person report.
Ich möchte einen Verlust/Diebstahl melden — I'd like to report a loss/theft.
Der Polizeibeamte nimmt seine Personalien auf. — The police officer takes a description of him.
Der Polizeibeamte faßt ein Protokoll ab. — The police officer draws up a report.

REMARKS   REMARKS   REMARKS   REMARKS

(1) GEBEN, BESCHREIBEN, ZEIGEN can take both a direct object (accusative) and an indirect object (usually a person) in the dative, e.g. Er gibt DEM Mann DEN Apfel. He gives the man the apple.

3.2 ORAL PRACTICE

1. VERBS WITH THE DATIVE

(●●) LISTEN

Silke empfiehlt (der Gast) Labskaus.
● *Silke empfiehlt dem Gast Labskaus.*

Put the nouns in brackets into the dative case.
Pay attention to the definite and indefinite
articles and to the demonstratives (dieser):
Die Fischsuppe schmeckt (der
Unternehmensberater) sehr gut. — Die
Krankenschwester hilft (ein Kind). — Herr Gebert
antwortet (eine Journalistin). — Silke zeigt (dieser
Mann) den Hafen. — Dagmar schlägt (die Freundin)
eine Reise vor. — Dieter folgt (das Mädchen) —
Werner Gebert begegnet (ein Arzt) im Krankenhaus.
See grammar on page 37 of the booklet.

2. THE PRESENT PERFECT WITH „HABEN"
AND „SEIN"

(●●) LISTEN

Silke geht in den Stadtpark.
● *Silke ist in den Stadtpark gegangen.*

Rewrite the following sentences in the present
perfect using the correct auxiliary:
Markus verschwindet im Bahnhofsbasar. — Frau
Gebert kauft Obst. — Die Schokolade kostet 3,3 DM.
— Markus läuft dem Clown nach. — Peter
antwortet dem Chef. — Frauke begegnet einer
Freundin. — Susi folgt der Mutter. — Udo hat eine
Idee. — Frau Gebert paßt nicht auf.
See grammar on page 44 of the booklet.

3. SENTENCES WITH „DAß"

(●●) LISTEN

Frauke sagt: die Ausstellung ist
interessant.
● *Frauke sagt, daß die Ausstellung*
interessant ist.

Now change the following sentences in the same
way:
Silke glaubt: die Information ist wichtig. — Dieter
findet: der Tip ist gut. — Udo hofft: der Roman ist
spannend. — Der Gast denkt: das Essen ist schlecht.
— Herr Gebert antwortet: ich nehme ein Bier. — Der
Pressesprecher sagt: die Reportage ist toll. — Der
Verkäufer antwortet: das Buch kostet 10,-DM.
See grammar on page 47 of the booklet.

4. SENTENCES WITH „WEIL"

(●●) LISTEN

Sie besichtigen den Hafen nicht. Er
wird seekrank.
● *Sie besichtigen den Hafen nicht,*
weil er seekrank wird.

Use „weil" to connect the following sentences:
Wir essen Obst./Wir mögen keinen Fisch. — Susi
trinkt Mineralwasser./Sie ist durstig. — Herr und
Frau Gebert gehen in die Ausstellung./Sie finden
das interessant. — Wir sind im Café./Es ist schön
dort. — Herr Gebert reserviert ein Zimmer im Hotel
Plaza./Dieses Hotel liegt im Zentrum.
See grammar on page 47 of the booklet.

5. PREPOSITIONS WITH THE DATIVE

(●●) LISTEN

Frau Gebert kauft ein (der
Bahnhofsbasar)
● *Frau Gebert kauft im*
Bahnhofsbazar ein

Complete the sentences using a preposition
before each noun in brackets. Choose from
beim, in/im, nach or zu. Sometimes more than
one preposition is possible!
Silke holt das Brot (der Bäcker). — Herr Krumbach
geht (der Verlag). — Silke und Werner amüsieren
sich (das Essen). — Frau Gebert bummelt (der
Bahnhofsbasar). — Silke arbeitet (die Redaktion).
— Herr Gebert geht (die Tochter). — Dieter
Hartmann arbeitet lange (die Reise).
See grammar on page 42 of the booklet.

6. PRONUNCIATION

(●●) LISTEN AND REPEAT

Ihr habt Aale geholt. — Heute abend
haben wir Gäste. — Ihr habt hier
Telefondienst. — Da war er plötzlich weg.
— Eins nach dem anderen. — Wer war
wahrscheinlich beim Clown? — Hat er
den Mann denn gesehen?
See grammar on page 36 of the booklet.

THE CHURCHES AND THE TRADE UNIONS

The Christian church still plays quite a prominent role in German public life, though, as everywhere in the Western world, its influence on the private lives of individuals is diminishing. The population of Germany has long been divided between Catholics and Protestants, with about 85% of the population officially belonging to one group or the other. In West Germany before 1990 the two confessions were about equally divided, but unification has added many more Protestants. The term Weißwurstgrenze (a symbolic frontier represented by a white sausage popular in the South) is still heard occasionally, though population upheavals in the aftermath of World War II blurred the old distinction between Protestant North and Catholic South. For instance, many Silesian Catholics resettled in Protestant areas, and Protestant East Prussians migrated to Catholic Bavaria.

Baden-Württemberg and Nordrhein-westfalen are almost equally divided between the two confessions. This goes back to the religious wars of the 17th century, when the ruler of a region generally imposed his own faith (Catholic or Protestant) on the population. Only under the Weimar Republic after World War I was the separation of church and state finally secured, but even after that historical ties tended to persist.

Although the state's position in regard to the churches is neutral, the churches are not private organisations. They are öffentlich-rechtliche Körperschaften (public-law corporations). The salaries of the clergy are partly paid by the state, which also assumes up to 100% of the expenses of church-run hospitals, day-care centres and schools. The churches have the right to levy taxes, with the state acting as tax-collector. Every citizen is a "member of the church", and anyone wishing to renounce his or her membership must make a formal declaration at the local Town Hall. A statute concerning "blasphemy against God" still exists in the German Civil Code.

All this gives the churches political power. There is a Kirchenlobby both in the legislature and in the broadcasting networks (which are also public-law corporations with church representatives on their governing councils). The churches also influence education. This explains why frequent demands are heard for a real separation of church and state.

Cologne cathedral at sunset

The churches' rôle in public life is to hold the balance between right and left, between conservatism and liberalism, though they sometimes oppose the state on issues such as disarmament, protection of the environment, immigration policy and, of course, abortion. Public opinion listens to the churches, even if the great majority of "members" are mere Karteileichen (card index corpses, ie fully paid-up but non-practising members). Many adherents of non-Christian religions, including Buddhism and Hinduism, are still officially counted as Catholics or Protestants. Jewish groups exist in most large cities, and many mosques have been built in recent years to cater for the growing Moslem population, which consists mainly of immigrant workers.

The trade unions are traditionally left-wing, even though their rôle in society is to keep a sharp eye on the capitalist system and try to make it work more effectively. Salaries, hours, holidays and working conditions are negotiated between the Sozialpartner (social partners), ie the Arbeitnehmer (employees), members of the Gewerkschaften (unions), and the Arbeitgeber (employers) and their associations (Arbeitgeberverbände). In 1988 42% of salaried employees were union members. The largest federation of trade unions is the DGB (Deutscher Gewerkschaftsbund) which has 7.8 million members and is made up of 17 different unions.

Now the unions are facing the biggest challenge since the war. The reunification of the two Germanies has created a vast range of social problems, and West and East German unions will have to cooperate in working out new systems of medical insurance, pensions and unemployment benefits as well as in resolving tariff difficulties and restructuring whole industries.

3.2 TAKE-A-BREAK

Where is Markus? Complete the following questions using im, in, beim or zu!

1. Ist er ... Hamburg? - Nein.
2. Ist er ... Bahnhofsbasar? - Nein.
3. Ist er ... Bäcker? - Nein.
4. Ist er ... Verlag? - Nein.
5. Ist er ... Hause? - Nein.
6. Ist er ... Flugzeug? - Nein.
7. Ist er ... Arzt? - Nein, Markus ist wirklich verschwunden.

No. 2

Now describe him:

Name : ....   Kleidung : ....

Größe : ....   Haarfarbe : ....

Alter : ....   Augenfarbe : ....

Besondere Kennzeichen : Er hat ein Kanninchen.

Who is doing what?
Listen, then match
the activities
described with
the people in
the drawing!

| 1 | | 2 | | 3 | | 4 | | 5 | | 6 | | 7 | | 8 | | 9 | |

(See answers on page 17 of the booklet)

3.3 DIALOGUE

🔊 LISTEN

EIN ABEND BEI GEBERTS

The Geberts have finished eating. For the children it's time to go to bed; Werner Gebert watches the news on television, Dagmar clears the table and gets ready to receive their friends Heinz and Renate.

Dagmar: *Habt ihr euch schon die Zähne geputzt und die Hände gewaschen? Na, dann ab ins Badezimmer!*

Markus: *Mutti, dürfen wir nachher noch etwas bei euch im Wohnzimmer bleiben?*

Dagmar: *Nein, kommt nicht in Frage! Ich habe dir doch gesagt, daß wir noch Besuch bekommen. Die Jaumanns kommen. Außerdem müßt ihr morgen sehr früh aufstehen.*

Markus: *Dürfen wir noch etwas Radio hören?*

Dagmar: *Gut, aber nicht zu lange.*

Werner: *Jetzt beeilt euch ein bißchen. Ich möchte mir noch die Tagesschau ansehen.*

The doorbell rings.

Dagmar: *Ach, da sind sie schon. Werner, kannst du ihnen die Tür aufmachen?*

Ich decke schnell den Tisch ab und stelle die Weingläser und etwas zum Knabbern bereit.

Werner: *Guten Abend. Kommt herein. Ihr seht ja ganz kaputt aus. Wo seid ihr gewesen?*

Heinz: *Hallo. - Wir hatten uns gedacht, daß wir mit den Fahrrädern zu euch fahren, weil das Wetter so schön ist.*

Werner: *Ach so. Setzt euch bitte!*

Renate: *Wo sind denn Dagmar und die Kinder?*

Werner: *Die Kleinen sind schon im Bett und schlafen hoffentlich bald, Dagmar ist noch in der Küche und ich sehe mir gerade die Nachrichten im Fernsehen an.*

Heinz: *Weiß du, ob der Europarat sich endlich geeinigt hat?*

Werner: *Sie haben im Fernsehen nichts darüber berichtet. Aber ich habe heute früh in der Zeitung gelesen, daß die Abgeordneten die Verhandlungen vertagt haben.*

Heinz: *Gibt es sonst etwas Neues?*

Werner: *Nein, nichts Besonderes.*

Dagmar: *Hallo ihr zwei. - Ach, wie schön, die Blumen!*

Renate: *Gefallen sie dir? Ich habe nicht gewußt, ob du Anemonen magst.*

Dagmar: *Das war aber doch nicht nötig. Werner, kannst du jetzt bitte mal den Fernseher ausschalten und den Gästen etwas zum Trinken anbieten?*

🔊 LISTEN AND REPEAT
See translation on page 18 of the booklet.

Mountain bikes in the mountains.

3.3 VOCABULARY

NOUNS

die Zähne (der Zahn) — teeth
das Badezimmer — bathroom
das Wohnzimmer — living room
die Tagesschau — "The Daily Survey," TV news programme on Channel 1 (ARD)
die Tür — door
die Fahrräder (das Fahrrad) — bicycles
die Kleinen (1) — the little ones
die Nachrichten — news
der Europarat — Council of Europe
das Fernsehen — television
die Zeitung — newspaper
die Abgeordneten (1) — delegates
die Verhandlungen — negotiations
die Blumen (die Blume) — flowers
der Fernseher — television set

ADJECTIVES

kaputt — broken; (here) exhausted
nötig — necessary
etwas Neues (5) — something new
etwas Besonderes (5) — something special

VERBS

putzen (geputzt) — to clean, brush
sich waschen (gewaschen) — to wash oneself
bleiben (geblieben) — to stay, remain
sagen (gesagt) — to say
aufstehen (aufgestanden) — to get up, stand up
sich beeilen (beeilt) — to hurry
ansehen (angesehen) — to look at, watch
aufmachen (aufgemacht) — to open
abdecken (den Tisch abdecken) (abgedeckt) — to clear the table

bereitstellen (bereitgestellt) — to place in readiness
hereinkommen (hereingekommen) — to come in, enter
aussehen (ausgesehen) — to seem, appear
sich setzen (gesetzt) — to sit down
schlafen (geschlafen) (2) — to sleep
wissen (gewußt) (2)(3) — to sleep
sich einigen (geeinigt) — to agree
berichten über + acc. (berichtet) — to report on
vertagen (vertagt) — to adjourn
gefallen + dat. (gefallen) — to be pleasing, be liked
ausschalten (ausgeschaltet) — to switch off
anbieten (angeboten) — to offer
fernsehen (ferngesehen) — to watch television
gehören + dat (gehört) — to belong to
etwas zum Knabbern (4) — something to nibble
etwas zum Trinken (4) — something to drink

MISCELLANEOUS

nachher — later, afterwards
kommt nicht in Frage! — out of the question
außerdem — in addition, moreover
sehr früh — very early
ein bißchen — a little, a bit
es klingelt — the doorbell is ringing
gerade etwas machen (6) — to be in the process of doing something
ob (7) — whether, if (introducing indirect questions)
die Jaumanns — the Jaumanns

HOW TO SAY IT

Kommt doch herein! (8) — Come on in! (fam. plural)
Kommen Sie doch herein! — Do come in! (polite form)
Möchten Sie Ihren Mantel ablegen? — Would you like to take your coat off?
Nehmen Sie doch bitte Platz! — Do please sit down!
Das war doch nicht nötig! — That really wasn't necessary!
Fühlen Sie sich wie zu Hause! — Make yourself at home!

Ich putze mir die Zähne — I brush my teeth
Ich wasche mein Gesicht/mein Hände — I wash my face/my hands
Ich dusche mich gerne kalt — I like to take cold showers
Ich trockne mich ab — I dry myself
Ich ziehe mich an — I get dressed
Ich ziehe meine Hose/mein Hemd an — I put on my trousers/my shirt
Kannst du bitte den Fernseher einschalten? — Can you please turn on the TV?
Das Programm ist langweilig, ich schalte den Apparat aus — The programme is boring. I'll turn off the set
Der Film is nicht spannend, ich schalte um — The film isn't exciting. I'll change channels
Die SÜDDEUTSCHE ZEITUNG ist eine Tageszeitung — The SÜDDEUTSCHE ZEITUNG is a daily newspaper
Der SPIEGEL ist ein Nachrichtenmagazin — SPIEGEL is a news magazine
DIE ZEIT ist ein Wochenzeitung — DIE ZEIT is a weekly newspaper
Der STERN ist eine Zeitschrift — STERN is a magazine

REMARKS   REMARKS   REMARKS   REMARKS

(1) An adjective or a past participle can be made into a noun. All German nouns are capitalized. Adjectival nouns retain their adjectival ending e.g. der kleine Junge or der Kleine (the little boy) — die kleinen Kinder (the little children), die Kleinen (the little ones). See grammar on page 39 of the booklet. — (2) SCHLAFEN and WASCHEN are conjugated like halten and fahren in the present tense (see 1.5); ich schlafe, du schläfst, er/sie/es schläft, wir schlafen, ihr schlaft, sie/Sie schlafen. — (3) The verb WISSEN is irregular: ich weiß, du weißt, er/sie/es weiß, wir wissen, ihr wißt, sie/Sie wissen. — (4) Any German infinitive can become a noun. All are neuter, capitalized, and generally translated by —ing. e.g. das Trinken = drinking, das Tanzen = dancing. (5) After NICHTS and ETWAS neuter adjectival nouns are used. e.g. etwas (nichts) Schönes, Gutes, Neues, Besonderes — something (nothing) beautiful, good, new, special. See grammar on page 39 of the booklet. — (6) GERADE (just) used with the present tense = to be in the process of doing something. Gerade jetzt koche ich. (Just now I'm cooking) — (7) OB (if, whether) introduces an indirect question (see grammar on page 47 of the booklet). — (8) The imperative of the 2nd person plural (familiar plural) is the same as the present indicative: Ihr kommt herein (You come in) — Kommt herein! (Come in!). See grammar on page 46 of the booklet.

3.3 ORAL PRACTICE

1. SUBORDINATE CLAUSES WITH „OB"

[••] LISTEN

Ich weiß nicht: Sind die Kinder schon im Bett?
* *Ich weiß nicht, ob die Kinder schon im Bett sind.*

Your turn to construct indirect questions starting with Ich weiß nicht, ob...:
Magst du Anemonen? — Ist Markus dem Clown nachgelaufen? — Trägt er ein gelbes Hemd und eine grüne Hose? Hat der Abteilungsleiter eine Durchsage gemacht? — War der Bahnhofsbasar geöffnet? — Ist Markus schon nach Hause gegangen? — Haben sie Markus gefunden?   See grammar on page 47 of the booklet.

2. „ETWAS" AND „NICHTS" FOLLOWED BY AN ADJECTIVAL NOUN

[••] LISTEN

Ich habe... in der Zeitung gelesen. (etwas/interessant)
* *Ich habe etwas Interessantes in der Zeitung gelesen.*

Now complete the following sentences in the same way:
Sie hat... im Radio gehört. (nichts/neu) — Er hat... für seine Frau gekauft. (etwas/attraktiv) — Sie hat... ausgerichtet (etwas/wichtig) — Eine Finanzaffäre ist... (nichts/spannend) — Sie hat in Hamburg ...gegessen (nichts/hervorragend).
                    See grammar on page 39 of the booklet.

3. THE DATIVE EQUIVALENT OF „FÜR" (+ ACC.)

[••] LISTEN

Dieser Artikel is für mich zu langweilig.
* *Dieser Artikel ist mir zu langweilig.*

Now change the following in the same way, substituting the dative pronoun for für + accusative:
Er hat für mich ein Zimmer reserviert. — Sie hat für dich Geld umgetauscht. — Er hat für sie ein Taxi geholt. — Er hat für dich ein attraktives Spitzenhemd gekauft.
                    See grammar on page 40 of the booklet.

4. PRACTISING THE DATIVE

[••] LISTEN

Das ist meine Aalsuppe.
* *Die Aalsuppe gehört mir.*

Use gehören + dative as in the example:
Das sind unsere Äpfel. — Das sind eure Bücher. — Das ist dein Bericht. — Das ist unser Doppelzimmer. — Das ist Ihr Exemplar. — Das sind ihre Karten. — Das ist meine Flasche.

See grammar on page 40 of the booklet.

5. PRACTISING THE DATIVE PLURAL

[••] LISTEN

Herr Gebert macht (die Freunde) die Tür auf.
* *Herr Gebert macht den Freunden die Tür auf.*

Complete the following sentences in the same way:
Schokolade schmeckt (die Kinder) sehr gut. — Silke schlägt (die Freunde) einen Spaziergang um die Alster vor. — Der Abteilungsleiter gibt (die Angestellten) viel Arbeit. — Sie zeigt (die Besucher) die Reeperbahn.

Listen to an example of the personal pronoun in the dative plural and change the above sentences in the same way:

Herr Gebert macht den Freunden die Tür auf.
* *Herr Gebert macht ihnen die Tür auf.*

See grammar on page 39 of the booklet.

6. PRONUNCIATION

[••] LISTEN AND REPEAT

Ihr putzt euch die Zähne — ich sehe mir noch die Tagesschau an — kannst du ihnen die Tür aufmachen? — ihr seht ja ganz kaputt aus — die Kleinen schlafen hoffentlich bald — gibt es sonst etwas Neues?

The mills of East Friesland

OSTFRIESLAND

To explain the ebb and flow of the tides in Friesland, local people tell tourists that the first time a Frisian approached the sea it drew back in panic. Since then it returns every twelve hours to see if he is still there.

The Frisians are indeed still there, sheltered behind dykes and dams, resisting tides and tempests, clinging to flat lands below sea level which are always in danger of disappearing beneath the waves of the North Sea (or Blanke Hans as they call it locally). Ostfriesland, foggy, damp and wind-battered, is a unique area in Germany's extreme north-west between the Dollart and the Ems estuary to the west and the great bay of Jadebusen and the mouth of the Weser to the east.

Water is to Ostfriesland what the sun is to Italy. There is the sea, an ever-present threat to those who stay and the stuff of nostalgic dreams for those who leave. Their most famous song, das Friesenlied, tells of the gulls crying above the stormy waves of the North Sea and the yellow flowers blooming in the sand dunes. There is water every-where, falling from the sky and filling the Tiefs, the canals which criss-cross the region.

But Frisians love water, not least because they use it to make tea; they are among the world's champion tea-drinkers, consuming over three kilos per person every year. They like their tea strong, served in fine porcelain cups, with cream and a walnut-sized lump of hard sugar. Any self-respecting Frisian forgets his troubles as the sugar dissolves in the hot black tea, crackling faintly, and the cream spreads gently over the surface. The tea is not stirred and consequently gets sweeter towards the bottom of the cup. Taking tea in Ostfriesland is quite a ritual: a guest is expected to drink at least three cups! The story goes that when Napoleon occupied the area he asked the Frisians whether they pre-ferred tea or coffee. They replied in unison: Lieber Tee! (a play on "preferably tea" and "liberty"). Frisians proudly believe that "Frisian" and "free" are synonymous.

In the eyes of the rest of Germany, however, Ostfriesland is a marginal, even backward area, and its people are the butt of many jokes. There is little industry, unemployment is high and the young leave for the big cities. The main sources of income are dairy farming (thanks to the wellknown Friesian cow) and, particularly along the coast and on the seven offshore islands, tourism. But Frisians don't accept tourists readily even though they bring money to the area. After all, the "foreigners" can't understand the local dialect of Plattdeutsch (Low German), nor are they familiar with the Frisian sports of Boßeln and Krabbenpulen.

Ostfriesland's flat roads are tem-porarily turned into giant bowling lanes for the Boßeln championships. The winning team is the one whose ball (made of wood and the size of a melon) covers the set distance in the least number of throws. Krabbenpulen (shrimp peeling) started as a simple eating procedure and developed into a competitive game. It's become a tourist attraction, especially in Greetsiel, centre of the shrimp fishing industry, where each year new records are set for the number of shrimps peeled in an hour.

TAKE-A-BREAK

No. 1 ●● LISTEN

What are the people doing?

1. Florian ....

2. Angela ....

3. Herr Hart ....

4. Frau Hart ....

5. Die Heinemanns ....

Try to remember (or guess)! (Vocabulary review of Unit 3 Chapters 1, 2, 3).

1. Wo war Frau Gebert mit den Kindern?
2. Wer hat die Verhandlungen vertagt?
3. Wo putzen sich die Kinder die Zähne?
4. Wo sieht Herr Gebert fern?
5. Was gibt Frau Gebert bei der Polizei auf?
6. Was macht der Abteilungsleiter?
7. Was hat der Clown dem Markus gegeben?
8. Was bringen die Jaumanns für Frau Gebert mit?
9. Wohin geht Frau Gebert mit Susi?
10. Was hat Herr Gebert am Morgen gelesen?
11. Was sieht sich Herr Gebert im Fernsehen an?
12. Wo haben sie Markus gesucht?
13. Wie sind die Jaumanns gefahren?

Was hat Herr Gebert für seine
Kinder aus Hamburg mitgebracht?

(See answers on page 19 of the booklet)

3.4 DIALOGUE

WAS MACHEN WIR?

Werner and Dagmar Gebert discuss places to visit.

Werner: *Sag mal, Dagmar, ich hoffe, du hast nicht vergessen, daß deine Schwester Iris morgen kommt. Hast due darüber nachgedacht, was wir machen? Wir müssen deiner anspruchsvollen Schwester doch etwas bieten.*

Dagmar: *Wir machen einen Ausflug in die Berge.*

Werner: *Ach nein, sie war doch schon in den Bergen, auf der Zugspitze. Und als Künstlerin möchte sie vielleicht lieber Kunst und Architektur sehen.*

Dagmar: *War sie schon im Schloß Hohenschwangau?*

Werner: *Ich weiß nicht, aber Neuschwanstein ist doch schöner als Hohenschwangau. Und es liegt am Chiemsee, der ist auch sehr schön.*

Markus: *Ich möchte lieber an den Starnberger See. Da kann man segeln.*

Dagmar: *Nein, das ist nichts für Iris. Warum bleiben wir nicht in der Stadt? Wir können auf den Olympia-Turm gehen, da kann man die ganze Stadt sehen.*

Werner: *Und dann können wir die Alte Pinakothek und das Deutsche Museum besichtigen und anschließend im Englischen Garten picknicken.*

Dagmar: *Das ist aber so weit! Da müssen wir mit dem Auto fahren oder die Fahrräder nehmen.*

Werner: *Ach nein, mit dem Bus ist es besser als mit den Fahrrädern.*

Dagmar: *Ja, das ist bequemer und weniger gefährlich. Vom Bahnhof ist der Englische Garten so weit entfernt wie das Deutsche Museum. Wohin gehen wir zuerst?*

Markus: *Zuerst in den Englischen Garten zum Picknick auf der Wiese beim großen Teich.*

Dagmar: *Ach, ihr seid bloß zu faul und habt kein Interesse für Kunst.*

Markus: *Iris möchte sicher auch nicht in ein Museum gehen. Aber in einem Park kann ich mit ihr Fußball spielen. Und im Englischen Garten kann sie nackte Leute sehen für ihre Skulpturen.*

Werner: *Halt, so geht das nicht, das könnt ihr mit mir nicht machen. Ich habe Markus versprochen, daß ich ihm die italienische Kunst erkläre. In der Alten Pinakothek hängt ein Botticelli, er ist wunderbar.*

Dagmar: *Und Susi, hast du gesagt, daß du ihr das alte Flugzeug im Deutschen Museum zeigst.*

Werner: *Ach, lassen wir doch Iris entscheiden. Sie weiß doch immer, was sie will.*

See translation on page 19 of the booklet.

Ludwig II's Bavaria:
Neuschwanstein Castle.

3.4 *VOCABULARY*

NOUNS

der Ausflug — excursion, trip
der Berg, die Berge — mountain
das Gebirge — mountain (range)
der Künstler, die Künstlerin — artist
die Kunst —art
die Architektur — architecture
die Skulptur — sculpture
das Schloß —castle
der Turm — tower
der Garten —garden
das Picknick — picnic
die Wiese — meadow
der Teich — pond
das Interesse — interest
der Fußball — football, soccer
die Leute (always plural) — people

---

die Landschaft — landscape
die Gegend —area
das Erholungsgebiet — recreation area
die Sehenswürdigkeit —tourist attraction
der Wald — forest, woods
der Baum —tree
das Feld — field
der Fluß — river
die Burg —fortress, castle
die Aussicht —panoramic view
der Wanderweg — walking/hiking trail
der Rucksack — rucksack, backpack
die Raststätte — shelter, resting place
die Natur —nature

ADJECTIVES

anspruchsvoll — demanding
bequem — comfortable
gefährlich — dangerous
entfernt — distant, far
faul — lazy
wunderbar — marvellous
nackt — naked

---

sportlich — athletic, sporty
unternehmungslustig — enthusiastic, enterprising
bekannt — well-known

VERBS

nachdenken über etwas — to ponder, reflect on something
liegen — to lie, be situated
segeln —to sail
picknicken — to picnic
versprechen — to promise
hängen — to hang

---

sich sonnen —to sunbathe
sich erholen — to rest
sich entspannen —to relax
lachen — to laugh
klettern — to climb
schwimmen —to swim

MISCELLANEOUS

als —as, than

ADVERBS

anschließend — subsequently
bloß — only, just

HOW TO SAY IT

Ich hoffe, daß sie pünktlich kommt — I hope (that) she comes promptly.
Du hast vergessen, daß deine Schwester kommt — You've forgotten that your sister is coming.
Ich denke, daß es zu spät is — I think (that) it's too late.
Er hat gesagt, daß er kommt — He said that he's coming.
Du hast ihm versprochen, daß wir ins Museum gehen — You promised him (that) we'd go to the museum.
Sie hat gesehen, daß das Museum geöffnet ist — She saw (that) the museum was open.
Sie weiß, daß dort ein Botticelli hängt — She knows that there is a Botticelli hanging there.

Ich fahre mit dem Auto — I'm driving, going by car
Er fährt mit dem Rad — He's going by bicycle
Wir nehmen den Bus — We're taking the bus
Sie fährt mit dem Zug nach Paris — She's travelling by train to Paris
Er nimmt immer das Flugzeug — He always takes the plane

Neuschwanstein ist schöner als (1) Hohenschwangau — Neuschwanstein is more beautiful than Hohenschwangau
Die Künstlerin möchte lieber Kunst sehen (2) — The artist would rather see art
Der Englische Garten ist so weit entfernt wie das Museum — The English Garden is as far (away) as the museum.
Mit dem Bus ist es besser als mit den Fahrrädern — It's better by bus than by bike
Das ist bequemer und weniger gefährlich — That's more comfortable and less dangerous

Wir machen einen Ausflug in die Berge (3) — We're going on a trip to the mountains
Sie war schon in den Bergen — She's already been to the mountains
Wir bleiben in der Stadt — We're staying in the city
Es liegt am Chiemsee — It is situated on the Chiemsee
Ich fahre an den Starnberger See — I'm going to the Starnberger See
Wir steigen auf den Olympia-Turm — We'er going up the Olympia Tower

REMARKS   REMARKS   REMARKS   REMARKS

(1) The comparative is formed by adding -er to the basic adjective. Comparisons of equality are expressed by: so ...wie (as...as) and ebenso...wie (just as...as). See grammar on page 39 of the booklet. — (2) LIEBER is the comparative of GERN; for irregular forms of the comparative see grammar, page 39 of the booklet. — (3) The prepositions an/auf/hinter/in/neben/über/unter/vor/zwischen are used with the dative when place where is expressed. When they express place to which or a change of condition they take the accusative. See also Section 3.2 page 115 and grammar on page 42 of the booklet.

3.4   ORAL PRACTICE

1. RELATIVE CLAUSES WITH „WAS"

(• •) LISTEN

Sie weiß etwas; sie will etwas
● *Sie weiß, was sie will.*
Er hat über etwas nachgedacht; wir machen etwas.
● *Er hat darüber nachgedacht, was wir machen.*

When a verb is followed by a preposition, the object following is replaced by the prefix „da-" joined to the preposition. When the preposition begins with a vowel, an r is inserted between „da" and the preposition:
uber → darüber, auf → darauf, etc.

Now combine each pair of sentences by using a relative clause with „ ,was":
Du weißt etwas; er hat etwas gesagt. — Er sagt etwas; etwas ist nichts für Iris. — Wir können etwas sehen; etwas ist gut für Iris. — Herr Gebert erklärt etwas; etwas hängt in der Pinakothek. — Iris berichtet über etwas; sie hat etwas gesehen. — Susi lacht über etwas; Markus hat etwas gesagt.
See grammar on page 48 of the booklet.

2. WORD ORDER: DATIVE AND ACCUSATIVE

(• •) LISTEN

Der Vater gibt (das Kind/das Buch)
● *Der Vater gibt dem Kind das Buch*

Use the dative and accusative as in the example:
Der Polizist zeigt (der Tourist/der Weg) — Das Mädchen schreibt (die Eltern/der Brief) — Herr Müller bietet (die Dame/der Arm) — Der Vater schenkt (die Mutter/Blumen) — Der Mann verkauft (die Frau/das Auto). See grammar on page 37 of the booklet.

3. PREPOSITIONS + DATIVE

(• •) LISTEN

wir sind/in/das Museum.
● *Wir sind in dem Museum.*

Your turn:
sie picknicken/in/der Park — das Schloß liegt/an/der Chiemsee — ich bleibe/in/die Stadt — ich schlafe/in/das Bett.
See grammar on page 42 of the booklet.

4. PREPOSITIONS + ACCUSATIVE

(• •) LISTEN

wir fahren/in/der Park
● *Wir fahren in den Park.*

Your turn:
Er macht einen Ausflug/in/die Berge — sie geht/in/die Stadt/sie steigen/auf/der Berg — ich fahre/an/der See — wir gehen/in/das Museum/die Sonne sinkt/in/das Meer.
See grammar on page 42 of the booklet.

5. COMPARISON OF EQUALITY

(• •) LISTEN

Neuschwanstein/touristisch/Hohen-schwangau
● *Neuschwanstein ist ebenso touristisch wie Hohenschwangau.*

Make sentences using „ebenso...wie":
die Alte Pinakothek/interessant/das Deutsche Museum — der Englische Garten/groß/der Park von Schloß Nymphenburg — München/alt/Berlin.
See grammar on page 39 of the booklet.

6. COMPARISON OF INEQUALITY

(• •) LISTEN

der Englische Garten/weit/das Olympiastadion
● *der Englische Garten ist weiter als das Olympiastadion*

Make sentences using the comparative + „als":
Iris / anspruchsvoll / ihre   Schwester / die Berge/schön/der See — der Bus/bequem/das Fahrrad — das Museum/interessant/der Park.
See grammar on page 39 of the booklet.

7. PRONUNCIATION

(• •) LISTEN AND REPEAT

links — rechts — in der Mitte — vorne — hinten — unten — oben — im Englischen — Garten — auf dem Olympia-Turm — am Chiemsee.

MOTORMANIA

You might think that Germans, reputedly well-disciplined as they are, would respect the rules of the road when they're driving. Rules there must be, of course; this they would accept. But just suppose that roadworks make it necessary to impose a 60 kph (37 mph) speed limit on a stretch of Autobahn, and suppose some law-abiding driver actually observes the limit: you can guarantee that everybody else will promptly roar past, glaring at him as if he, not they, were in the wrong. If the cautious one then glimpses in his rear-view mirror the radiator of a lorry, plastered with squashed flies and apparently about to shunt him off the road, he will probably abandon the Autobahn in favour of a Bundesstraße (national highway) or Landstraße (state road).

Normally, in fact, autobahns are the safest roads of all: fewer accidents occur there than anywhere else. There were about 8,000 kilometres of autobahn in pre-unification West Germany alone, and every year the authorities spend almost 2.5 billion marks on maintaining them. The auto-bahns carry 26 per cent of all traffic. There are no tolls, and vehicles travel at an average speed of 110 kph (70 mph). On some sections there are speed limits, but few people apart from lorry drivers take much notice of them. Most accidents are caused by speeding. On the Landstraßen 100kph is the limit, but since the roads are good and cars are engineered for faster and faster driving....

Discipline? That's mainly for pedes-trians. Jay-walking is frowned upon. People grouped patiently at the kerb will rebuke an individualist who tries to cross the road when the lights are against him. And although London drivers may tolerate pedestrians nipping across through the traffic, it could be suicidal to try the same thing in Berlin, where jay-walkers are appar-ently seen as fair game!

Germans lavish loving care on their cars and keep them scrupulously clean. Regular washing is considered essential. This is accomplished either at a car wash or in the street, and

The weekly wash

generally at the week-end - though not on Sundays in the Catholic south.

By any standards Germans have some fine cars to take care of, from the humble, old-fashioned but still much loved Volkswagen "beetle" (the original and archetypal "people's car" as its name reminds us) to the state-of-the-art automotive engineering of the latest BMW and Audi models. Since the ear-liest days of motoring German cars have been famous the world over. Two Germans, Karl Benz and Gottlieb Daimler, will always be remembered for their pioneering development work on the internal combustion engine.

In Germany as elsewhere, the car has given mobility to the masses and has thus been an instrument of social change. There are signs that the old order, and the old standards, are breaking down. It has been alleged that revolution is impossible in Germany because the compulsively law-abiding Germans cannot even walk on the grass if there is a sign telling them not to. True, during the 1968 student demonstrations, students took refuge in underground stations only after first buying a ticket! Nowadays, however, more and more young people are taking a chance with the ticket inspectors and travelling on public transport in the Nulltarif category, ie without paying the fare, even though no such free rides have been officially authorised.

Crossword. Find a tourist attraction near Munich:

				1	11			12		
		2	10				3			13
○	○9	○	○	○	○	○	○			
					4					
5										
				6				15		
7			14							
		8								

Horizontal:

1. day, 2. personal pronoun, 3. tree,
4 meadow, 5. a present tense form of "to be", 6. museum, 7. personal pronoun,
8. only

Vertical:

2. egg, 3. mountains, 9. imperfect form of "to have", 10. very, 11. excursion,
12. there, 13. a present tense form of "to like", 14. personal pronoun, 15. hour

Answer: ....

(See answers on page 21 of the booklet)

Figures of Speech

IN DEN MOND
GUCKEN

To look at the moon
To be left out in the cold

EIN HAAR
IN DER SUPPE
FINDEN

To find a hair in the soup
To find fault

SICH
ZWISCHEN DIE STÜHLE
SETZEN

To sit down between two chairs
To fall between two stools

SICH ETWAS
HINTER DEN SPIEGEL
STECKEN

*To put something behind one's
mirror*
**To make a mental note,
store in one's memory**

🔊 LISTEN

IN EINEM BIERGARTEN IN MÜNCHEN

After going to the opera Dagmar and Iris rejoin Werner in a beer garden to finish the evening together.

Werner: *Na, was habt ihr denn gemacht? Seid ihr im Kino gewesen, habt ihr euch den neuen Film von Wim Wenders angesehen?*

Iris: *Nein, ich hatte keine Lust, ins Kino zu gehen. Ich gehe lieber in Berlin ins Kino. Hier muß man doch die Gelegenheit ausnutzen, in die Oper zu gehen: Strauß, Wagner, Mozart und so weiter.*

Dagmar: *Wir waren in der „Zauberflöte". Es war ganz toll!*

Werner: *Von wem ist denn diese Oper?*

Iris: *Von Mozart, das weiß doch jedes Kind!*

Werner: *Woher soll ich das denn wissen? Ich habe keine Zeit auszugehen, weil ich viel arbeiten muß.*

Dagmar: *Eigentlich hatten wir ja vor, ins Theater zu gehen. Leider haben wir keine Eintrittskarten mehr bekommen. Alle Vorstellungen waren ausverkauft.*

Iris: *Wir haben die Opernplätze noch in letzter Minute gekriegt, weil Dagmar einen Freund getroffen hat. Der hat uns Freikarten besorgt.*

Werner: *Ja, da habt ihr aber Glück gehabt. Wen hast du denn getroffen?*

Dagmar: *Den Georg Bücklinger. Er ist jetzt Schauspieler an den Kammerspielen.*

Werner: *Und wie habt ihr die Aufführung gefunden?*

Iris: *Also mir hat alles sehr gut gefallen. Vor allem hat der Solist erstklassig gesungen. Und das Bühnenbild war auch fabelhaft.*

Dagmar: *Ich glaube, daß es ein Riesenerfolg gewesen ist. Am Ende haben wir mindestens zehn Minuten Beifall geklatscht.*

Iris: *Ja, es war hinreißend. Das Publikum hat getobt.*

Werner: *Möchtet ihr noch etwas trinken? Ich lade euch ein.*

🔊 LISTEN AND REPEAT
See translation on page 21 of the booklet.

Open air concert on Berlin's Kudamm.
Goethe's Faust at a Weimar theatre.

3.5   VOCABULARY

der Film — film
das Kino — cinema
die Gelegenheit — opportunity
die Oper — opera
das Theater — theatre
die Eintrittskarten — admission tickets
die Vorstellung — performance
die Opernplätze — opera seats
die Freikarte — complimentary ticket
das Glück — happiness, luck
der Schauspieler — actor
die Aufführung — performance
der Solist — soloist (weak masculine)
das Bühnenbild — sets, decor
der Riesenerfolg — triumph, huge success
der Beifall — applause
das Publikum — public, audience

der Zuschauer — spectator
das Ende — end
die Inszenierung — mise en scène, production
die Bühne — stage
das (Theater-) Stück — stage play
das Schauspiel — drama, play
die Einladung — invitation
das Orchester — orchestra
die Musik — music
das Konzert — concert
die Veranstaltung — show, performance

ADJECTIVES

ausverkauft — sold out
erstklassig — first-class
fabelhaft — fabulous
hinreißend — delightful
begeistert — enthusiastic

meisterhaft — masterly
ausgezeichnet — excellent

VERBS

<u>aus</u>*nutzen + acc. (ausgenutzt)* — to exploit
<u>aus</u>*gehen (ausgegangen)* — to go out
<u>vor</u>*haben + acc. (vorgehabt)* — to intend, plan
kriegen + acc. (gekriegt) — to get
besorgen + acc./dat. (besorgt) — to procure; to take care of
Glück haben (gehabt) — to be lucky
singen (gesungen) — to sing
klatschen (geklatscht) — to applaud
toben (getobt) — (here) to go wild

<u>zu</u>*schauen + dat. (zugeschaut)* — to look on, look at
einladen + acc. (eingeladen) — (here) to pay for drinks for someone
<u>auf</u>*führen + acc. (aufgeführt)* — to perform
<u>vor</u>*führen + acc. (vorgeführt)* — to perform, present, display

MISCELLANEOUS

<u>und</u> <u>so</u> <u>weiter</u>/usw. — and so forth/etc.
wem — to whom
eigentlich — really
in letzter Minute — at the last minute
vor allem — especially
am Ende — at the end
mindestens — at least

HOW TO SAY IT

Wir gehen ins Theater/Kino/Konzert — We're going to the theatre/cinema/concert
Wir gehen in den Biergarten/die Oper — We're going to the beer garden/opera
Wir sind im Theater/Kino/Konzert — We are in (at) the theatre/cinema/concert
Wir sind im Biergarten/in der Oper — We are in the beer garden/the opera

Bruno Ganz spielt seine Rolle gut — B. Ganz plays his role well
Doris Dörrie dreht einen Film — D. Dörrie makes (shoots) a film
Zadek entwirft ein Bühnenbild — Zadek designs stage sets (scenery)
Mahler komponiert eine Sinfonie — Mahier composes a symphony
Peter Stein inszeniert — P. Stein stages, produces

Die Handlung ist schlüssig — the plot is logical
Die Interpretation ist originell — the interpretation is original
Ich finde, daß der Film langweilig ist — I find the film boring
Das Drehbuch hat Längen — The script is dull, tedious in places

Er hat Lust, ein Bier zu trinken (1) — He feels like drinking a beer
Sie nutzt die Gelegenheit aus, ins Kino zu gehen — She takes the opportunity to go to the cinema
Er hat keine Zeit, einen Ausflug zu machen — He has no time to make an excursion
Sie hat vor, einen Film zu drehen — She plans to shoot (make) a film

Wem gefällt der Film? (2) — Who likes the film?
Mit wem geht er ins Kozert? — With whom is he going to the concert?
Von wem hat er das Geschenk? — From whom did he get the gift?
Bei wem sind sie eingeladen? — To whose house are they invited?
Zu wem geht sie heute abend? — To whose house is she going tonight?
An wen schreibt sie? — To whom is she writing?
Für wen kauft er das Hemd? — For whom is he buying the shirt?
Über wen spricht sie? — About whom is she talking? (Who's she talking about?)

See grammar booklet, page 40.

REMARKS   REMARKS   REMARKS   REMARKS

(1) Note that ZU precedes the infinitive if the verb has an inseparable prefix — Es ist nötig, die Konferenz zu verschieben (It is necessary to postpone the conference). If the verb has a separable prefix, ZU is placed between the prefix and the verb — Ich habe Lust, heute auszugehen (I feel like going out today.)— (2) Note the similarity between the cases of the definite article DER and the interrogative pronoun WER. For both you must select the right case. WER becomes WEM in "Wem gehört das?" because the verb GEHÖREN takes a dative object. Verbs that take a direct object require the accusative: WEN trifft er?

3.5 ORAL PRACTICE

1. EXPRESSIONS WITH „ZU" + INFINITIVE

(WOZU: for what, etc.)
(● ●) LISTEN

Wozu hat Iris Lust? Sie geht ins Kino.
● *Sie hat Lust, ins Kino zu gehen.*

Combine the following pairs of sentences in the same way:
*(Wozu hat sie Lust?) Sie ißt eine rote Grütze. —
(Wozu hat Frank Gelegenheit?) Er besucht die
Messe. — (Wozu haben Susi und Markus Lust?) Sie
laufen dem Clown nach. — (Wozu hat Werner keine
Zeit?) Werner spielt Fußball. — (Wozu hat Silke
keine Lust?) Sie trinkt Bier. — (Wozu hat Iris keine
Gelegenheit?) Sie sieht fern.*
See grammar on page 40 of the booklet.

2. PRACTISING THE PRESENT PERFECT

(● ●) LISTEN

Am Ende tobt das Publikum.
● *Am Ende hat das Publikum getobt.*

Put into the present perfect:
*Werner nutzt die Gelegenheit aus. Iris und Dagmar
gehen aus. — Werner hat viel vor. — Die Zuschauer
kriegen keine Freikarten. — Iris hat Glück. —
Werner lädt die Frauen ein. — Heinz und Renate
schauen zu. — Das Theater führt das Stück nicht
auf. — Alle genießen den Abend. — Susi hat keine
Lust, zu Hause zu bleiben.*
See grammar on page 44 of the booklet.

3. EXPRESSING INTENTION

(● ●) LISTEN

Dagmar möchte nach Berlin fahren.
● *Dagmar hat vor, nach Berlin zu
fahren.*

Change the following sentences in the same way:
*Iris möchte in die Oper gehen. — Werner möchte
Bier trinken. — Renate möchte fernsehen. — Familie
Gebert möchte einen Ausflug machen. — Werner
möchte ausgehen. — Iris möchte nicht ins Kino
gehen. — Georg möchte ein Stück inszenieren. —
Iris möchte sich die „Zauberflöte" ansehen. —
Werner möchte Sekt ausgeben.*
See grammar on page 45 of the booklet.

4. PRACTISING QUESTIONS

with „wem" and „wen"
(● ●) LISTEN

Er geht mit seiner Frau ins Kino.
● *Mit wem geht er ins Kino?*

**Now ask similar questions based on the
following sentences. Distinguish carefully
between accusative and dative!**
*Markus bekommt von seinem Vater einen
Spielcomputer. — Der Reporter dreht einen Film
über den Schriftsteller Günter Grass. — Silke
schreibt einen Brief an ihre Freundin. — Frau Gebert
kauft Äpfel für ihre Kinder. — Die Oper ist von
Mozart. — Werner Herzog dreht einen Film mit Klaus
Kinski. — Herr Gebert geht mit Heinz und Renate
essen. — Das Fernsehen berichtet über den
Europarat. — Iris und Dagmar kriegen die
Opernplätze in letzter Minute. — Das Stück gefällt
Heinz sehr.* See grammar on page 40 of the booklet.

5. ACCUSATIVE OR DATIVE?

(● ●) LISTEN

Der Solist singt mit Peter.
● *Der Solist singt mit ihm.*

**Now replace the underlined words with a
pronoun in the accusative or dative:**
*Georg besorgt die Freikarte — Herr Gebert lädt seine
Frau ein. — Heinz dreht den Film. — Die Zuschauer
sehen das Schauspiel an. — Alle pfeifen die
Inszenierung. — Die Zauberflöte gefällt Iris und
Dagmar. — Heinz und Renate gehen zu Werner. —
Georg besorgt Iris eine Eintrittskarte — Herr Gebert
genießt den Abend. — Dagmar hat die Plätze von
Georg. — Werner gibt Dagmar und Iris ein Bier aus.*
See grammar on page 40 of the booklet.

6. INTONATION

(● ●) LISTEN CLOSELY TO THE INTONATION OF THE
SENTENCES AND REPEAT
*Na, was habt ihr denn gemacht? — Ich habe keine
Lust, ins Kino zu gehen. — Das weiß doch jedes
Kind! — Also mir hat es sehr gut gefallen. — Das
Stück war hinreißend. — Fabelhaft! — Großartig!*

MÜNCHEN

Why deny it? Munich is Beer City, and it lives up to its reputation. Müncheners drink beer by the Maß (one-litre mug) under the chestnut trees of the Biergärten (tree-shaded outdoor taverns), in the streets and in innumerable Kneipen (bars). Beer is drunk both with lunch and after work during Brotzeit (snack time) around 6 o'clock. Later on in the evening it comes accompanied by a Brezel (pretzel) or a plateful of Leberkäs (meat loaf) with potato salad. People drink with friends, colleagues, families, or even alone, and they have many beers to choose from, including local brews like Löwenbräu, the extra-strong Starkbier, and Weißbier, a mild beer brewed from wheat.

Beer consumption reaches its peak during the Oktoberfest, a festival dedicated to eating and drinking. München is an old form of Mönche (monks); the people of Munich, being good Catholics (more or less), justify their love of beer by pointing out that as far back as the Middle Ages monks extolled its nutritive properties and looked on it as an essential part of their daily diet. But it would be an injustice to Munich to think of it as Beer City and nothing more. Unlike some smaller towns in Freistaat Bayern (Bavaria), of which it is the capital, Munich is far from being a sleepy place full of stolid burghers. Schwabing, a Bohemian quarter populated by artists and students, bubbles with life. There is plenty of activity on the streets. Straßenfeste (street parties) are organised and pub crawling is a popular pastime.

Life is good, if costly, in Munich. It is Germany's most expensive city. Rents and property prices are sky-high. In fashionable areas such as Haidhausen yuppies abound and art galleries ply a thriving trade. Munich has several important art collections, notably the old and new Pinakothek. There is also the Deutsches Museum, a museum of technology where almost everything the human race has invented, from the nail to the loco-motive, can be seen and admired.

Munich is also an industrial city. BMW (Bayerische Motorenwerke)

The Oktoberfest in Munich

builds its famous cars there. Recently film producers such as Wolfgang Petersen and Steven Spielberg have made notable films (The Never-Ending Story, for example) in Munich's sophisticated Bavaria Studios. A large proportion of films made for television and German language films are also shot in Munich. The city has become an important centre for communications and the media.

Besides beer, Müncheners have another passion: football, represented by two major clubs, Bayern München and 1860 München. In 1990 the German team, under the direction of Munich's famous Franz Beckenbauer

(known as the Kaiser) won the World Cup. Munich offers a wide range of excellent sports facilities. In the Olympiapark, the former Olympic village, there are countless gymnasiums, stadiums and tracks suitable for everything from international sporting events to ordinary keep-fit activities.

At times the Alpine wind called the Föhn sweeps down on Munich and makes people feel edgy, but generally it's la dolce vita in this beautiful city at the foot of the Alps. Indeed, according to its inhabitants, it is really the most northerly town in Italy....

3.5 TAKE-A-BREAK

Match the descriptions to the photos:

1. *Gustaf Gründgens als Mephisto in Goethes «Faust».*

2. *Bruno Ganz als guter Engel in Wim Wenders Film «Der Himmell über Berlin».*

3. *Wagner*

A

B

C

Culture Quiz:

1. Wer hat den Film „Paris/Texas" gedreht?
a. Werner Herzog - b. Wim Wenders - c. Volker Schlöndorff

2. Von wem ist die Oper „Tannhäuser"?
a. Mozart - b. Strauß - c. Wagner

3. Welchen Film hat Fritz Lang 1927 gedreht?
a. Mephisto - b. Metropolis - c. Moderne Zeiten

4. Woher kommt Nastassja Kinski?
a. München - b. New York - c. Hollywood

5. Wer ist Bertolt Brecht?
a. Ein Dramatiker - b. Ein Schauspieler - c. Ein Verleger

6. Wann ist Rainer Werner Fassbinder gestorben?
a. 1989 - b. 1962 - c. 1982

7. Wo finden die Wagner-Festspiele statt?
a. In München - b. In Bayreuth - c. In Baden-Baden

(See answers on page 22 of the booklet)

3. WRITTEN PRACTICE

3.1

Supply the missing past participles: *Warum bist du gestern nicht .... (kommen)? — Wir haben Markus .... (verlieren). — Wir haben ihn überall .... (suchen), aber nirgendwo .... (finden). Vielleicht ist er nach Hause .... (gehen)? — Habt ihr schon zu Hause .... (anrufen)?*

Translate: *I am (have been) waiting for half an hour. The department stores are closed today. Perhaps he has returned home.*

Wir hatten vorhin noch eine Viertelstunde Zeit, und da haben wir eingekauft. Wir müssen etwas tun. Ihr geht in das nächste Polizeirevier und gebt eine Suchmeldung auf.

3.2

Supply the dative case of the words in brackets: *Der Clown hat .... (Markus) Schokolade gegeben. — Ich habe .... (das Kind) gesagt, daß es schon spät ist. — Die Polizei hilft .... (die Familie Gebert). — Herr Hartmann antwortet .... (die Journalistin). — Silke zeigt .... (der Mann) den Hafen. — Sie schlagt .... (der Freund) einen Spaziergang vor.*

Translate: *What is it all about? My son has disappeared. Calm down! Didn't your son follow you? Wir sind zu der Lebensmittelabteilung weitergegangen. Ich habe einen Moment nicht aufgepaßt, weil ich einer Freundin begegnet bin. Können Sie Ihren Sohn beschreiben? Jetzt ist alles in Butter!*

3.3

Supply the dative case of the words in brackets: *Kannst du .... (sie/pl.) bitte die Tür aufmachen? — Wir wollen mit .... (die Fahrräder) zu euch fahren. — Gefallen .... (du) Anemonen? — Diese Fotos gehören .... (wir). — Herr Gebert bringt .... (die Gäste) etwas zum Trinken, und seine Frau holt .... (sie/pl.) etwas zum Knabbern.*

Translate: *Hurry up a bit! I'd like to watch the news on television. You seem tired. The little ones are already asleep. Sit down please. What's new? Nothing particular.*

Ich decke schnell den Tisch ab und stelle die Weingläser bereit. Sie haben im Fernsehen nichts darüber berichtet. Kannst du den Gästen bitte etwas zum Trinken anbieten?

3.4

Supply the comparative of the words in brackets: *Neuschwanstein ist (schön) als Hohenschwanstein. — Das Deutsche Museum ist (groß) als die Alte Pinakothek. — Der Chiemsee ist (klein) als der Starnberger. — Mit dem Bus ist es (gut) als mit den Fahrrädern. — Mit dem Flugzeug ist es (schnell) als mit dem Auto.*

Translate: *Why don't we stay in town? We can visit the Alte Pinakothek and then the Deutsches Museum. It's more comfortable and less dangerous!*

Hast du nachgedacht, was wir machen? Sie möchte vielleicht lieber Kunst und Architektur sehen? Ihr seid bloß zu faul und habt kein Interesse. Im Park kann ich mit ihr Fußball spielen. Lassen wir sie entscheiden. Sie weiß doch immer, was sie will.

3.5

Supply the interrogative pronoun: *Von w .... ist diese Oper? — W .... hast du getroffen? — W .... habt ihr die Aufführung gefunden? — W .... haben sie keine Eintrittskarten mehr bekommen? — W .... hat der Freund für Dagmar und Iris besorgt? — W .... ist George Bücklinger jetzt Schauspieler? — W ... hat erstklassig gesungen?*

Translate: *I don't feel like going to the cinema. I don't have time to go out because I always have too much work. Unfortunately there were no more seats.*

Hier muß man die Gelegenheit ausnutzen, in die Oper zu gehen. Wir haben die Opernplätze in letzter Minute gekriegt. Da habt ihr aber Glück gehabt! Ich glaube, daß es ein Riesenerfolg gewesen ist.

(See answers on page 32 of the booklet)

MORE VOCABULARY

THE HOUSE

der Eingang — entry
der Gang — corridor
der Flur — entrance hall
der Raum — room
das Schlafzimmer — bedroom
das Eßzimmer — dining room
das Kinderzimmer — children's room
der Abstellraum — storeroom
die Toilette (WC) — toilet
der Boden — floor
die Decke — ceiling
das Fenster — window
das Gebäude — building
die Treppe — stairs
das Treppenhaus — staircase
das Erdgeschoß — ground floor
die Heizung — heating
der Strom — electricity
die Miete — rent
der Mieter — tenant
der Vermieter — landlord
die Wohnung — flat
die 4-Zimmer-Wohnung — 4-room flat

FURNITURE

der Stuhl — chair
der Sessel — armchair
der Schrank — cupboard
das Sofa — couch, sofa
das Regal — shelf
der Schreibtisch — desk
der Teppich — rug, carpet
der Kühlschrank — refrigerator
der Herd — stove
die Waschmaschine — washing machine
die Spüle — sink
die Lampe — lamp

THE BATHROOM

das Waschbecken — wash basin
die Badewanne — bathtub
der Bademantel — dressing gown
das Handtuch — hand towel
der Waschlappen — face flannel
die Seife — soap
der Kamm — comb
die Zahnbürste — toothbrush
die Zahnpasta — toothpaste
der Föhn — hairdryer
der Rasierer — razor

THE FAMILY

die Großmutter — grandmother
die Oma — granny
der Großvater — grandfather
der Opa — grandad
der Bruder — brother
die Schwester — sister
der Onkel — uncle
die Tante — aunt
der Cousin — cousin
die Cousine — cousin
die Nichte — niece
der Neffe — nephew
der Schwager — brother-in-law
die Schwägerin — sister-in-law
die Schwiegereltern — in-laws
die Schwiegermutter — mother-in-law
der Schwiegervater — father-in-law
die Schwiegertochter — daughter-in-law
der Schwiegersohn — son-in-law
das Adoptivkind — adopted child
die Adoptiveltern — adoptive parents

MARITAL STATUS

verheiratet sein — to be married
sich scheiden lassen — to divorce
geschieden sein — to be divorced
der Ehemann }
der Gatte   } — husband, spouse
die Ehefrau }
die Gattin   } — wife, spouse
ledig sein — to be single
der Witwer — widower
die Witwe — widow
eine Familie haben — to have a family
aufwachsen — to grow up
die Kindheit — childhood
die Jugend — youth
die Jugendlichen — young people
der Erwachsene — adult
der Teenager — adolescent, teenager

SPORTS AND RECREATION

der Sport — sport
die Sporthalle — gymnasium
der Tennisplatz — tennis court
der Ball — ball
das Fußballspiel — football game
das Schwimmen — swimming
das Reiten — riding
das Pferderennen — horse racing
(das) Wasserski — water skiing
(das) Windsurfing — windsurfing
(das) Golf — golf
(das) Judo — judo
die Gymnastik — gymnastics
rudern — to row
skilaufen — to ski
wandern — to go hiking
tanzen — to dance
der Tanz — dance
(das) Bergsteigen — mountain climbing
das Kartenspiel — card game
Karten spielen — to play cards
das Schachbrett — chess board
Schach spielen — to play chess
das Damespiel — draughts
Dame spielen — to play draughts
(das) Bridge — bridge
das Kreuzworträtsel — crossword puzzle
angeln — to fish
basteln — to do craft work
jagen — to hunt
malen — to paint
zeichnen — to draw
die Zeichnung — drawing
töpfern — to do pottery, throw pots
die Musik — music
ein Instrument spielen — to play an instrument
die Geige — violin
das Klavier — piano
die Gitarre — guitar
das Saxophon — saxophone
die Flöte — flute

3. *TEST YOURSELF*

1. FILL IN „OB", „WEIL" OR „DAS"

1. *Es tut mir leid, ... ich eine halbe Stunde Verspätung habe.*
2. *Ich weiß nicht, ... er schon nach Hause gegangen ist.*
3. *Er kann heute abend nicht ins Kino gehen, ... er krank ist.*
4. *Weißt du, ... der Bahnhofsbasar schon geschlossen ist?*
5. *Sie glaubt, ... diese Ausstellung sehr interessant ist.*
6. *Er geht in den Biergarten .... er Durst hat.*

2. ARRANGE THE FOLLOWING WORDS INTO SENTENCES

(be careful of word order)

1. *nach Hause / ich / langsam / und / fahre / ihn / suche.*
2. *gesagt / daß / sie / schon / dem Kind / ist / spät / sehr / hat / es.*
3. *Silke / abends / ist / arbeitet / den Pressebericht / weil / für / verantwortlich / sie.*
4. *die Kleinen / in der Küche / sind / noch / schon / ist / im Bett / Dagmar / und.*
5. *wir / weil / können / man / auf den Olympia-Turm / da / gehen / die ganze Stadt / kann / sehen.*
6. *Wir / hat / haben / getroffen / die Opernplätze / einen Freund / in letzter Minute / weil / gekriegt / Dagmar.*

3. FIND THE OPPOSITE OF ...

1.	*etwas*	11	*billig*
2.	*jemand*	12.	*schlecht*
3.	*offen*	13.	*immer*
4.	*schnell*	14.	*alt*
5.	*klein*	15.	*gesund*
6.	*lang*	16.	*links*
7.	*anschalten*	17.	*ohne*
8.	*zumachen*	18.	*steigen*
9.	*faul*	19.	*viel*
10.	*fragen*	20.	*überall*

4. WHAT WOULD YOU SAY IF YOU HAD TO ...

1. Ask what's happening: ....

2. Ask someone to come in: ....

3. Say that it's easier and less dangerous to take the bus: ....

4. Ask about what to do tonight: ....

5. Make comments on a show: ....

5. ASK QUESTIONS ABOUT THE UNDERLINED PHRASES

1. Sie haben <u>im Bahnhofsbasar</u> eingekauft.

2. Herr Gebert ist <u>langsam nach Hause</u> gefahren.

3. Frau Gebert ist <u>in das nächste Polizeirevier</u> gegangen.

4. Markus ist wahrscheinlich <u>diesem Clown</u> nachgelaufen.

5. <u>Die Jaumanns</u> kommen mit den Fahrrädern.

6. Sie haben <u>für Dagmar schöne Blumen</u> mitgebracht.

7. Herr Gebert hat <u>heute früh</u> <u>in der Zeitung</u> gelesen, daß die Abgeordneten <u>die Verhandlungen</u> vertagt haben.

8. Neuschwanstein is <u>schöner</u> als Hohenschwangau.

9. Wir machen einen Ausflug <u>in die Berge.</u>

10. Der Freund hat <u>ihnen</u> Freikarten besorgt.

11. <u>Iris</u> hat alles <u>sehr gut</u> gefallen.

6. COMPLETE:

Ich wart. schon ei.. halbe St..de! — Wa. um sei. ihr n..t ge...men? — Wo ha.t ihr ein..kauf.? — Plötz..ch wa.er weg. — Hast du sch.n zu ..use an..ru.en? — Kan.ich ei.. Su..mel..ng auf..b.n? — Ich habe ein.. Moment ni..t auf..pa.t, weil ich ein.. Fr..ndin bege..et bin. — Ihr mü..t mor.en se.. fr.h auf ..ehen. — Je.zt be..lt euch ein biß..en. — Hat der Eur..ar.t sich end.ich ge..nigt? — Gibt es so.st et..s N..es? — Wir mü..en dein.. ansp.uchsv..len Schwe.ter etwas b..ten. — Wa.um bl..ben wir nicht in d.. Sta.t? H..r muß ma.die Ge..gen.eit ausnutzen, in d.. Oper zu gehen. — We.. hast du ge.ro..en? Ich glaube, d..es ein Rie.ener.olg ge.esen ist. — M.chtet ihr noch et.as t.in.en?

(See answers on page 33 of the booklet)

LONDON - BERLIN, ONE WAY

As the weeks went by Simon's long-forgotten German revived and improved and he began to feel quite knowledgeable about Germany. The mysterious Lore, while still telling him next to nothing about herself, supplied plenty of interesting information about her country. Simon's boss Mark, who knew that he was trying to brush up his German, asked whether he were making progress. ,,Ja, es geht ausgezeichnet, ich bin schon viel weitergekommen" said Simon rapidly, hoping to impress. Mark raised an eyebrow. ,,Ich gratuliere" he said drily, "and how are you getting on with that German girl who writes to you?" Simon was irritated. How had Mark guessed his correspondent was female? A natural assumption, perhaps; it was no secret that Simon liked girls. All the same, he had no wish to discuss this particular friendship with anyone, and he wished Mark had not noticed it. He was also beginning to wish that he had not pretended to be a female penfriend.

It was August now, and holiday time. Simon spent nine days in a gîte in Brittany with Laura and two other couples. Although he enjoyed the sun, sand and sea, he found that the local night life did not have much appeal for him, nor could he join wholeheartedly in the usual noisy revelries with his young friends. More than once he noticed Laura looking puzzled and disappointed, but he could not explain.

When Mark got in touch with him and summoned him back to London he was secretly almost relieved, though of course he grumbled, as one is supposed to when work interferes with pleasure.

The next day he arrived back at the office and was handed the file on Germany. A large pile of completed market research questionnaires had arrived and needed to be analysed and evaluated immediately. ,,Es tut mir leid" said Mark, who now sometimes liked to practise his German on Simon, ,,aber du mußt es sofort machen: es kann nicht warten". If he hurried, of course, he might still rejoin the party in Brittany before the fortnight was up; but he decided he wouldn't. That afternoon he telephoned Laura to tell her his holiday was over because he had urgent work to do that would take him at least a week.

At last he was alone in his flat again. He poured himself a whisky and began to read the questionnaires. The product was evidently quite popular with older people in Germany but didn't appeal much to the 18-24 year olds. Lore might be able to explain that, he thought, and once again he began to speculate about her. He knew so little of her life, yet somehow she fascinated him. Her letters made absorbing reading, but very little of the information they contained seemed to relate to her own experience. Often she described people and places as if she were trying to put herself in his shoes, so that it was almost as if they were exploring Berlin together.

He put the questionnaires aside and sat down at his computer. Two hours later he finished a long letter. His previous letters to Lore had been rather short, but now he suddenly wanted her to be able to visualise him in his daily surroundings. He described his office, his favourite haunts, even the parties he went to at weekends; but he still, though with growing reluctance, kept up the pretence that he was a girl.

At the end of the letter, on an impulse, he asked Lore to send him a photograph of herself.

A week later Mark tossed him a letter with a Berlin postmark. Simon took it coolly and opened it when Mark had gone. It seemed rather short. ,,Ich danke für die schöne Beschreibung. London ist eine faszinierende Stadt.... England ein wunderbares Land..... Sie erzählen so gut, daß ich noch viele Briefe von Ihnen bekommen möchte.... Bitte schreiben Sie

Moritz von Schwind: "Schubert evening at Joseph von Spaun" (1868).

bald wieder.... " As he pushed it back into the envelope a photo fell out. His eyes widened as he picked it up. It showed the face of a young woman with ash-blonde hair and blue eyes. Her smile was gentle but humorous, her gaze very direct.

It took Simon two days to persuade Mark that the results of the questionnaire needed to be verified and amplified through on-the-spot interviews in Germany. At last Mark agreed and suggested, with a wink, that he might as well go to Berlin. Simon lost no time in getting a plane ticket. He didn't even think of telling Laura.

On arrival in Berlin he took a taxi to his hotel and left his luggage there. His business appointments were arranged for the next day, but that evening he was free. Her address was Mommsenstraße 10. The street turned out to be within walking distance of his hotel, so he set out at a brisk pace. It was only six o'clock, which he felt was an entirely suitable time for visiting.

But would she be pleased to see him if he turned up unannounced? She would get a shock, and he would have some explaining to do. And after all he still didn't even know whether she was married... though he hoped she wasn't.....

Continued ....

1989: the fall of the Berlin Wall.

UNIT 4

◄●●► LISTEN

NACHRICHTE AUF DEM ANRUFBEANTWORTER

Speech bubble: *Hallo Iris Hier ist Karin*

Iris has returned to Berlin. She listens to the messages on her answering machine.

Männerstimme: *Hallo Iris! Hier ist Wolfgang. Nichts Besonderes. Wenn du Zeit und Lust hast, ruf mich doch zurück. Tschüß!*

Frauenstimme: *Ja hallo, ich bin's, Ingrid; Monika hat mir gesagt, daß du für ein paar Tage nach München gefahren bist. Du verreist einfach, ohne etwas zu sagen... Wir wollten uns doch treffen, um das Projekt zu besprechen. Wenn du wieder da bist, ruf mich an. Ciao!*

Männerstimme: *Ich bin's, Manfred. Ich habe die Einladung für die Fete angenommen, ohne dich zu fragen. Hoffentlich paßt dir das.*

Iris: *Manni, das ist nett von dir!*

Frauenstimme: *Hallo Iris, hier ist Karin. Die Entwürfe sind fertig. Wenn nichts dazwischen kommt, kann ich sie dir morgen bringen.*

Männerstimme: *Guten Abend, Joachim am Apparat. Ich rufe nur an, um dir zu sagen, daß ich Donnerstag nicht zur Versammmmlung kommen konnte. Ich mußte bis zehn Uhr arbeiten. Bist du da gewesen?*

Iris: *Ach du lieber Himmel, das habe ich total vergessen!*

Männerstimme: *Guten Tag, Wagner, Düsseldorf; als wir uns auf der „Documenta" gesehen haben, haben Sie mir fest versprochen, die Entwürfe bis spätestens zum fünfzehnten fertigzumachen. Wir haben heute den achtundzwanzigsten! Bitte rufen Sie mich umgehend in der Düsseldorfer Galerie an. Es ist wirklich sehr dringend!*

Frauenstimme: *Hier ist Karin. Nachdem ich dreimal bei dir war und du nie da warst, habe ich die fertigen Entwürfe bei deinen Nachbarn abgegeben. Hoffentlich bekommst due sie rechtzeitig.*

Iris: *Danke Karin, du bist ein Schatz!*

Frauenstimme: *Iris, hier ist deine Mutter. Bevor dein Vater und ich zur Kur nach Spiekroog fahren, wollte ich mich noch einmal bei dir melden. Du bist wohl noch bei Dagmar in München. Paß gut auf dich auf, mein Herz. Wir kommen in vier Wochen wieder.*

◄●●► LISTEN AND REPEAT

See translation on page 23 of the booklet.

Düsseldorf:
Berlin Avenue and Church of St. John

NOUNS

der Anrufbeantworter — answering machine
das Projekt — project
die Einladung — invitation
die Fete — party
die Entwürfe (sing.: der Entwurf) — sketches, drafts, plans
die Versammlung — assembly, meeting
die Nachbarn (sing.: der Nachbar) — neighbours (weak masculine)
die Kur — medical treatment, rest, baths etc. at a spa/health resort
die Mitteilung — message, communication
das Seebad Spiekeroog — the Spiekeroog seaside resort
der Kurort — spa, health resort
die Erholung — rest, relaxation
die Besprechung — discussion

VERBS

<u>zurück</u>rufen *(zurückgerufen)* — to call back
verreisen (verreist) — to set off on a journey
besprechen (besprochen) — to discuss
passen (gepaßt) — to fit, be suitable
<u>dazwischen</u>kommen
(dazwischengekommen) — to intervene
<u>fertig</u>machen *(fertiggemacht) — to finish*
sich melden (gemeldet) — to contact; report for, show up

<u>auf</u>passen *(aufgepaßt)* — to watch out for

<u>mit</u>teilen *(mitgeteilt)* — to communicate, inform, tell

ADVERBS

einfach — simple, simply
total — total(ly)
fest — firm(ly)
umgehend — immediate(ly)
dringend — urgent(ly)
rechtzeitig — on time
spätestens — at the latest

MISCELLANEOUS

ein paar — a few
ohne...zu + infinitive — without
um...zu + inf. — in order to
ach du lieber Himmel! — Good heavens! Ye gods!
nachdem — after
bevor — before
wenn — if (see booklet page 48)
als — when (see booklet page 48)
wenn — when (see booklet page 48)

anstatt...zu + inf. — instead of

EXPRESSIONS

Ich möchte für Iris eine Nachricht hinterlassen — I'd like to leave a message for Iris.
Richten Sie bitte aus, daß (+ subordinate clause) — Please pass on the message that ....
Sie können mich bei XY erreichen — You can contact me at XY.
Ich möchte Ihnen mitteilen, daß (+ subordinate clause) — I should like to inform you that

HOW TO SAY IT

• The imperfect of modal auxiliaries.

Wollen: *(wollt + -e, -est, -e -en, -et, -en)*
Joachim wollte nicht zur Versammlung kommen — Joachim didn't want to come to the meeting.

Können: *(konnt- +* **regular endings as in wollen above***)*
Er konnte nicht kommen. — He couldn't come.

Müssen: *(mußt- +* **regular endings***)*
Herr Berger mußte eine Kur machen. — Mr. Berger had to take a course of treatment (at a health resort).

Sollen: *(sollt- +* **regular endings***)*
Iris sollte am fünfzehnten ihre Entwürfe abgeben. — Iris was supposed to submit her sketches on the 15th.

Dürfen: *(durft- +* **regular endings***)*
Susi durfte keine Schokolade essen — Sue wasn't allowed to eat any chocolate.

Mögen: *(mocht- +* **regular endings***)*
Iris mochte den Film nicht. — Iris didn't like the film.

Als (1) *wir das letzte Mal im Kino waren, haben wir einen langweiligen Film gesehen.* — When we were last at the cinema, we saw a boring film.

Wenn (1) *ich wieder in Berlin bin, rufe ich meine Freundin an.* — When I'm in Berlin again I'll call my friend.

Wenn (1) *du dich für Kunst interessierst, mußt du in die Pinakothek gehen.* — If you're interested in art you must go to the Pinakothek.

Bevor (2) *die Kinder ins Bett gehen, putzen sie sich die Zähne.* — Before the children go to bed, they brush their teeth.

Nachdem (2) *Iris und Dagmar in der Oper waren, gingen sie in den Biergarten.* — After Iris and Dagmar had been to the opera, they went to the beer garden.

um...zu + inf.: *Ich rufe nur an, um dir guten Tag zu sagen* — Just phoning to say hello.

ohne...zu + inf.: *Sie sieht einen Film, ohne ihn zu verstehen.* — She sees a film without understanding it.

Wolfgang geht ins Bett, ohne gute Nacht zu sagen. — Wolfgang goes to bed without saying good night.

anstatt...zu + inf.: *Anstatt zu Hause zu bleiben, fährt Iris nach München.* — Instead of staying at home, Iris goes to Munich.

REMARKS   REMARKS   REMARKS   REMARKS

(1) Distinguish between WENN and ALS. WENN means "if" or "if ever" or "whenever". ALS (when) expresses a single, particular time in the past. (See grammar on page 48 of the booklet.) (If a sentence starts with a subordinate clause, the main clause must begin with the verb immediately followed by the subject. e.g. Als Klaus klein war, hatte er einen Teddy. When (not whenever) Klaus was little, he (subject) had (verb) a teddy bear. — (2) After BEVOR and NACHDEM a personal subject and verb are used, not an infinitive or gerund. e.g. Bevor (Nachdem) er nach Hause kam, rief er uns an. Before (After) coming home, he telephoned us.

4.1 ORAL PRACTICE

1. THE IMPERFECT OF „WOLLEN"

See grammar on page 45 of the booklet.

🔊 LISTEN

Iris will nach München fahren.
● *Iris wollte nach München fahren.*

Put the following sentences into the imperfect:
Susi will keine Schokolade essen. — Wir wollen mit dem Bus fahren. — Werner will nicht in die Oper gehen. — Iris will die Entwürfe fertig machen. — Du willst nicht zu spät kommen.

See grammar on page 45 of the booklet.

2. „WENN" OR „ALS"

🔊 LISTEN

... sie in München war, ist sie in die Oper gegangen.
● *Als sie in München war, ist sie in die Oper gegangen.*
... sie einkauft, geht sie in die Stadt.
● *Wenn sie einkauft, geht sie in die Stadt.*

Fill in the blanks with wenn or als:
.... Iris nach Hause kommt, hört sie die Nachrichten auf dem Anrufbeantworter. ...Iris wieder da ist, ruft sie Ingrid an. ...Dagmar ihren Mann abgeholt hat, ist Markus verschwunden. ...die Oper zu Ende war, sind Iris und Dagmar in den Biergarten gegangen. ...das Wetter morgen schön ist, machen wir einen Ausflug.

See grammar on page 48 of the booklet.

3. „UM/OHNE/ANSTATT ...ZU" — + INFINITIVE

🔊 LISTEN

Iris verreist einfach, ... etwas zu sagen.
● *Iris verreist einfach, ohne etwas zu sagen.*

Fill in the blanks with um, ohne or anstatt:
Iris und karin treffen sich, ... ins Kino zu gehen. Dagmar geht in den Bahnhofsbasar, ... Lebensmittel einzukaufen. Herr Gebert besucht eine Austellung, ... ins Büro zu gehen. — Manfred reserviert Karten für die Oper, ... Iris etwas zu sagen.

See grammar on page 48 of the booklet.

4. EXPRESSIONS WITH „ZU" + INFINITIVE

🔊 LISTEN

Herr Gebert hat keine Zeit, jeden Tag (ausgehen)
● *Herr Gebert hat keine Zeit, jeden Tag (auszugehen).*

Put zu in the right position:
Karin und Ingrid treffen sich, um das Projekt (besprechen). — Susi geht ins Bett, ohne (sich waschen). — Werner hat keine Lust, das Fernsehen (ausschalten). — Markus verschwindet, ohne (auffallen). — Iris hat vergessen, ihre Freundin (anrufen). — Dagmar trinkt ein Glas Wasser, ohne (sich beruhigen).
See grammar on page 48 of the booklet.

5. „BEVOR" AND „NACHDEM"

🔊 LISTEN

Iris ist nach Hause gekommen./Sie hört die Nachrichten auf ihrem Anrufbeantworter.
● *Nachrichten Iris nach Hause gekommen ist, hört sie die Nachrichten auf ihrem Anrufbeantworter.*
Herr Gebert geht ins Büro./Er frühstückt.
● *Bevor Herr Gebert ins Büro geht, frühstückt er.*

Connect the two sentences with bevor or nachdem:
Iris fährt nach München./Sie geht zur Versammlung. — Dagmar hat eine Freundin getroffen./Markus ist verschwunden. — Herr und Frau Berger sind in der Ausstellung gewesen./Sie gehen in ein Café. — Markus hat viel Schokolade gegessen./Er ist krank geworden.
See grammar on page 48 of the booklet.

6. INTONATION

🔊 LISTEN CLOSELY TO THE INTONATION OF THE SENTENCES AND REPEAT

Hallo, ich bin's, Wolfgang. — Due verreist einfach, ohne etwas zu sagen! — Wir wollten uns doch treffen! — Hoffentlich paßt dir das! — Ach du lieber Himmel, das habe ich total vergessen! — Es ist wirklich sehr dringend. — Danke Karin, du bist ein Schatz! — Paß gut auf dich auf!

BERLIN - FROM WEST TO EAST

Berlin today, post-reunification, is a fast-changing place, unpredictable and hard to describe.

Once it was Germany's capital city, and in all likelihood its former status will be restored to it. But what kind of capital will it be? Will it be full of bureaucrats, loyal servants of the state? Will it again attract artists and writers from all over the world? In size (883 square kilometres) and population (about 3.2 million in 1989) Berlin is the largest city in Germany. Indeed, the erstwhile western sector alone, with its 480 square kilometres (only slightly smaller than Hamburg) was more populous than any other German city.

The present sharp contrast between the western and eastern sectors of Berlin is likely to persist for some time to come because of Berlin's dominant role in the West German economy. Statistics published a few years ago showed that half the light-bulbs, half the lifts and one-third of the cigarettes and air conditioners used in West Germany were all manufactured in West Berlin.

Advertisers have calculated that West Berlin's rivers and lakes add up to a longer coastline than the French Riviera, and that Berlin has more bridges than Venice.

And what about former East Berlin? It is ready to welcome tourists, and has numerous attractions to offer them. One of the best known and most beautiful recreation areas is the Müggelsee, Berlin's largest lake. On its shores you can visit Neu Venedig (New Venice) or Hessenwinkel, idyllic spots that still retain some of their pre-war charm. You can stop for coffee or lunch at the Rübezahl or Müggelseeperle restaurants. You can swim, sunbathe or take a river trip in one of the pleasure boats of the Weiße Flotte (White Fleet).

An excursion on the Spree (the little river that flows through Berlin) will take you from the old residential district of Treptow to Köpenick Castle and Friedrichshafen, then into the Gössen canal to Schmöckwitz and finally, via the Dahme (another little river) to Grünau, before returning to Köpenick. Historic Köpenick, built on an island where the Dahme joins the Spree, still has an old city centre with a gothic town hall.

Almost as well-known an entry point

November 1989: joyful reunions

as Checkpoint Charlie was East Berlin's central station, Bahnhof Friedrichsstraße. Near the station is the Friedrichstadt-palast, long famous for a variety of theatrical offerings. One of East Berlin's best known theatres is the Theater am Schiffbauerdamm where the Berliner Ensemble still performs Bertolt Brecht in echt (authentic) Brechtian style. Brecht himself was director there for many years. Other famous theatres include the Deutsches Theater, the Kleine Komödie, the Komische Oper and the Maxim Gorki Theater.

The Fernsehturm (television tower), 365 metres high, became the symbol of East Berlin. Its observation platform offers magnificent panoramic views of Berlin, and the visitor can also survey the city from east to west while enjoying a leisurely meal in the revolving restaurant. When the skies are clear, the dome of the Fernsehturm reflects the sun in a pattern resembling a cross. Berliners call it "the revenge of the Marienkirche" (church of St Mary) because the simple but beautiful old church is dwarfed by the mammoth tower.

Das Rote Rathaus (Red City Hall) is so called not in honour of the Communists who ruled there but because it is built of red bricks. Wander

round the former Gendarmenmarkt, today Platz der Akademie, and you will discover one of Europe's most beautiful squares with its French and German cathedrals and the Schauspielhaus, an imposing theatre rebuilt in classical style after a fire in 1817.

Berlin's historic centre is in former East Berlin. The old neighbourhood around the Nikolaikirche, with its restau-rants and cafés, has been restored. Not far away, on the famed and once ultra-fashionable avenue Unter den Linden (Under the Linden Trees) are the Deutsche Staatsoper (opera house) and the university. The Schloß, once the Kaiser's residence, was slightly damaged in the war and razed afterwards to make room for the administrative pile known as the Palast der Republik (which the Saxons fittingly nicknamed Ballast der Republik). Reflected in its glass walls is the Dom (cathedral) facing it. Nearby is the Museumsinsel (Museum Island), site of the Pergamonmuseum and its awe-inspiring second century B.C. Pergamon Altar. Many treasures of ancient Troy, brought back by Heinrich Schliemann from his excavations in Turkey, disap-peared from Berlin after World War II. Museum officials are still hoping to get them back.

4.1 TAKE-A-BREAK

No. 1

Link each main clause (A - K) with a subordinate clause (1 - 11) so as to make complete sentences.

A. Bevor Herr und Frau Berger zur Kur fahren,
B. Iris nimmt den Zug,
C. Iris fährt nach München,
D. Nachdem Iris angekommen ist,
E. Als Iris das letzte Mal in der Oper war,
F. Werner findet,
G. Wolfgang möchte kein Bier trinken,
H. Wenn Iris ausgeht,
I. Heinz und Renate essen Schokolade,
J. Iris konnte nicht zur Versammlung kommen,
K. Dagmar hat keine Lust,

1. um nach München zu fahren.
2. daß der Film langweilig war.
3. und sehen fern.
4. weil sie in München war.
5. geht sie ins Kino.
6. um ihre Schwester Dagmar zu sehen.
7. einen Ausflug zu machen.
8. hört sie die Nachrichten auf ihrem Anrufbeantworter.
9. telefonieren sie mit Iris.
10. hat sie die Zauberföte gesehen.
11. weil er lieber Wein trinkt.

A	B	C	D	E	F	G	H	I	J	K
9										

Cross out the incorrect statistics

1. Die deutschen Verlage haben 1987 | 87 630 / 65 680 / 45 325 | Bücher veröffentlicht.

2. In Westdeutschland hat es 1988 | 65 643 / 15 715 / 23 530 | Sportclubs gegeben.

3. Die Museen haben in einem Jahr | 45 287 / 12 436 / 66 337 | Eintrittskarten verkauft.

4. Die Theater hatten | 13 Millionen / 16 Millionen / 9 Millionen | Zuschauer.

5. Die Deutschen sind | 108 Millionen / 75 Millionen / 90 Millionen | Mal ins Kino gegangen.

6. Ein Deutscher trinkt in einem Jahr | 94 Liter / 234 Liter / 144 Liter | Bier.

(See answers on page 24 of the booklet)

🔊 LISTEN

AUF DEM WOCHENMARKT AM WINTERFELDTPLATZ

Iris and her friend Manfred go to the market

Iris: *Komm, wir gehen zuerst zum Türkenstand.*

Manfred: *Zu dem Türken, der immer biologisch angebaute Erdbeeren hat?*

Iris: *Ja, den meine ich. Der hat das beste Obst.*

Manfred: *Hast du den Zettel, auf dem wir alles aufgeschrieben haben?*

Iris: *Ja, hier: Obst, Gurken, Brot, Eier, Müsli, Schafskäse und Wurst.*

Manfred: *Die Wurst ist auf dem Markt doch nicht gut. Die ist beim Schlachter besser als hier.*

Iris: *Och, weißt du, alle Metzger in Berlin verkaufen nur Wurst mit Phosphat, und Fleisch, das aus der Massentierhaltung kommt.*

Manfred: *Warum denn Phosphat?*

Iris: *Phosphat bindet das Wasser im Fleisch und dann ist das Einfrieren leichter. Hast du noch nie Schnitzel gesehen, die beim Braten zusammenschrumpfen?*

Manfred: *Ja, aber ich wußte nicht, daß das am Phosphat liegt.*

Iris: *Hier auf dem Markt vom Winterfeldtplatz findest du immer noch gesündere Nahrung als im Supermarkt.*

Manfred: *Da hinten ist der Stand vom Bioladen. Da kaufen wir die Gurken, die du einlegen willst.*

Iris: *Ja, und da gibt es auch das Frischkornmüsli, das du so gern magst.*

Manfred: *Das Brotangebot der Bäcker ist aber größer als das Angebot hier auf dem Markt.*

Iris: *Aber hier ist es auch gesünder. Das Vollkornbrot hier ist am schmackhaftesten und bleibt am längsten frisch.*

Manfred: *Und wo kaufst du die Eier? Gibt es hier etwa wirklich Eier von Freilandhühnern?*

Iris: *Über 80 Prozent der Eier und die meisten Hühner, die man ißt, sind aus Legehennen-Betrieben. Aber ich kenne hier einen Händler, der wirklich Frischeier verkauft.*

Manfred: *Wahrscheinlich bezahlst du aber dafür mehr als für die anderen Eier.*

Iris: *Na ja, wenn man umweltbewußt ist, lebt man zwar länger, aber auch teurer! Und trotzdem kaufe ich lieber den leckersten Schafskäse, den ich nur hier kriege, da drüben, am Stand der Jugoslawin.*

🔊 LISTEN AND REPEAT
See translation on page 24 of the booklet.

Tübingen:
the market on the Rathausplatz

4.2 VOCABULARY

NOUNS

der Wochenmarkt — weekly market
der Türkenstand — the Turk's stall
der Zettel — slip of paper, list
der Einkaufszettel — shopping list
der Metzger — butcher
die Massentierhaltung — factory farming
das Schnitzel — cutlet, chop
der Bioladen — health food shop
die Nahrung — food, nourishment
der Händler — dealer
das Frischkornmüsli — fresh grain muesli
das Angebot — offer; selection
das Brotangebot — selection of bread
das Vollkombrot — whole grain bread
das Korn — grain
das Freilandhuhn — free-range chicken
das Huhn — chicken
der Legehennen-Betrieb — lit. "laying-hen business", i.e. battery chicken farm
die Frischeier — fresh eggs
der Schafskäse — sheep's (ewe's) milk cheese
die Jugoslawin — Yugoslav *(f.)*

---

der Fleischer — butcher
der Schlachter — butcher
der Konditor — pastry cook
der Obst- und Gemüsehändler — greengrocer
die Umwelt — environment
der Umweltschutz — environmental protection
die Umweltverschmutzung — pollution
das Ozonloch — hole in the ozone layer
der Triebhauseffekt — greenhouse effect
das Recycling — recycling
der saure Regen — acid rain
der Klimaschutz — protection of the climate
die Kost — food, meals
die Frischkost — fresh produce

der Lebensmittelzusatz — food additive
der biologische Anbau — organic farming
der Sondermüll — special (toxic waste)

ADJECTIVES

biologisch — biological, organic
leicht — easy
schmackhaft — tasty
frisch — fresh
lecker — delicious

ökologisch
umweltfreundlich } — ecological, evironmentally friendly
umweltbewußt — environmentally aware

VERBS

anbauen (angebaut) — to cultivate, grow
meinen — (here) to mean, think
aufschreiben (aufgeschrieben) — to write down
an etwas liegen (gelegen) — to be due to, the result of
braten (gebraten) — to grill, fry, roast
zusammenschrumpfen (zusammengeschrumptft) — to shrivel
einlegen (eingelegt) — to pickle
einfrieren (eingefroren) — to freeze

MISCELLANEOUS

trotzdem — nevertheless, despite

HOW TO SAY IT

Welchen Bäcker wählen wir? — Which baker shall we choose?

Die Eier sind von Freilandhühnern — The eggs are from free-range chickens.
Das Huhn ist aus einer Legehennenbatterie — The chicken is from a battery farm.

Sie verkaufen Fleisch, das aus der Massentierhaltung kommt (1) — They sell meat that comes from factory-farmed animals.
Wir kaufen die Gurken, die du einlegen willst. — We buy the cucumbers (gherkins) that you want to pickle.

Das Angebot des Bäckers ist groß (2) — The baker has a large selection.
Die Politik der Bundesrepublik is pluralistisch — The political system in the Federal Republic is pluralistic.
Die Teilung Deutschlands war nicht definitiv — The division of Germany was not definitive (final).
Das Angebot auf dem Markt ist groß (3) — There is a wide choice at the market.
Beim Bäcker is das Angebot großer als auf dem Mark — There's a bigger selection at the baker's than at the market.
Im Supermarkt ist das Angebot am größten ⎫
Das größte Angebot gibt es im Supermarkt ⎭ — The widest choice is at the supermarket.
Die Wurst schmeckt in Deutschland gut — Sausage tastes good in Germany
Die Wurst vom Schlachter schmeckt besser als die Wurst vom Markt — Sausage from the butcher tastes better than sausage from the market.
Dieses Müsli mag ich am liebsten — I like this muesli best (See 2.2 remark 5).
Da gibt es die beste Wurst — That's where the best sausage is.

REMARKS   REMARKS   REMARKS   REMARKS

(1) Relative pronouns resemble the definite article, with the exception of the genitive, singular and plural, and the dative plural (see grammar on page 41 of the booklet). — (2) The ending -(e)s indicates the genitive singular masculine and neuter. The genitive of the definite article masculine and neuter is des. Most masculine and neuter nouns end in -(e)s in the genitive. e.g. des Kleides, des Mannes, des Monats. Their indefinite article is eines. e.g. eines Mannes, eines Kleides, eines Monats. The ending -er indicates the feminine genitive singular: der Frau, einer Frau. For all three genders -er is the sign of the genitive plural. e.g. der Männer, der Frauen, der Kinder. Proper nouns, whether masculine or feminine, take an -s in the genitive singular. e.g. Karls Freund. Lulus Apfelstrudel. (See grammar on page 38 of booklet.) — (3) The comparative of the adjective: Die Rose ist eine schönere Blume als die Nelke (carnation); or you can say Die Rose ist schöner als die Nelke. The superlative of the adjective: Die Rose ist die schönste Blume; or Die Rose ist am schönsten. The comparative of the adverb: Hans arbeitet schneller als Max. The superlative of the adverb: Hans arbeitet am schnellsten. For irregular comparatives and superlatives, see grammar on page 39 of the booklet.

4.2 ORAL PRACTICE

1. PAST PARTICIPLES AS ADJECTIVES

(• •) LISTEN

Das Fleisch ist eingefroren.
● *Das ist eingefrorenes Fleisch.*

Change the past participles into adjectives as in the example:
Die Erdbeeren sind biologisch angebaut. — Das Obst ist gewaschen. — Das Müsli ist gut zubereitet. — Die Gurken sind eingelegt. — Der Käse ist geschnitten. See grammar on page 44 of the booklet.

2. ADJECTIVES IN THE SUPERLATIVE

(• •) LISTEN

das gute Obst
● *das beste Obst*

Give the superlatives:
Diese Nahrung ist gesund. — Diese Wurst schmeckt gut. — Dieses Schnitzel ist klein. — Dieses Auto fährt schnell — Diese Kinder spielen gern. See grammar on page 39 of the booklet.

3. IRREGULAR SUPERLATIVE

(• •) LISTEN

Dieses Brot bleibt lange frisch.
● *Dieses Brot bleibt am längsten frisch.*

Give the superlatives:
Diese Nahrung ist gesund. — Diese Wurst schmeckt gut. — Dieses Schnitzel ist klein. — Dieses Auto fährt schnell — Diese Kinder spielen gern. See grammar on page 39 of the booklet.

4. RELATIVE CLAUSES

(• •) LISTEN

Wir gehen zu dem Türken. Er hat Erdbeeren.
● *Wir gehen zu dem Türken, der Erdbeeren hat.*

Substitute relative pronouns for the underlined words and link the pairs of sentences as in the example:
Er kauft nur Eier. Sie sind von Freilandhühnem. — Wir kaufen die Gurken. Du willst sie einlegen. — An dem Türkenstand gibt es Gemüse. Wir kaufen es gerne. See grammar on page 41 of the booklet.

5. RELATIVE CLAUSE + PREPOSITION

(• •) LISTEN

Du hast den Zettel. Auf dem Zettel haben wir alles aufgeschrieben.
● *Du hast den Zettel, auf dem wir alles aufgeschrieben haben.*

Substitute relative pronouns for the underlined words and link the pairs of sentences:
Ich treffe die Kinder. Ich habe für sie Bonbons gekauft. — Ich esse gern Schafskäse. Für den Schafskäse muß ich mehr bezahlen. — Iris trifft Manfred. Mit ihm geht sie auf den Markt. — Die straße heißt Motzsraße. In der Straße ist das schönste Café. See grammar on page 42 of the booklet.

6. THE GENITIVE

(• •) LISTEN

der Türkenstand
● *der Stand des Türken.*

Change the following in the same way:
der Metzgerladen — das Eigelb — die Kinderspiele — die Küchengeräte — das Marktangebot — das Bäckerbrot. See grammar on page 38 of the booklet.

7. GENITIVE OF PROPER NAMES

(• •) LISTEN

Herr Müller hat eine Frau.
● *Das ist Herrn Müllers Frau.*

Use the genitive as in the example:
Otto hat ein neues Auto. — Silke hat einen sympathischen Chef. — Manfred hat eine Freundin. — Helga hat kleine Kinder. — Herr Gebert hat eine Fahrkarte. See grammar on page 38 of the booklet.

8. PRONUNCIATION

(• •) LISTEN AND REPEAT

das Spiegelei — der Baum — die Bäume — das Auge — die Leute — das Jackett — die Angst — der Arzt — die Straße — der Metzger — die Legehenne — die Ozonschicht — das Ozonloch — das Frischkornmüsli — das Freilandhuhn.

VISITING WEST BERLIN

- The Brandenburg Gate *(das Brandenburger Tor)*:
Situated in East Berlin but very close to the Wall, the Brandenburg Gate was a symbol of the divided city as well as a favourite meeting place between East and West. Graffiti-covered fragments of the Wall from the area around it are now much prized. On top of the Gate stands the Quadriga *(a chariot drawn by four bronze horses), which was carried off by Napoleon in 1806. It was subsequently restored, but East and West Berlin had great difficulty in agreeing which way the horses should face. On December 31st 1989 revellers drunk with new-found freedom - and perhaps not only with freedom - made a determined attempt to climb it.*
- Christstraße
A block of houses nostalgically restored in 19th-century style. Typical Berlin cafés and bars (Kneipen), *together with many "alternative" shops abound here.*
- Dahlem
Museums and art galleries offer insight into European art from the 13th to the 18th centuries. In 1968 student riots took place at the Free University here.
- Deutschlandhalle:
This huge hall, capable of accommodating 12,000 spectators, contains the velo-drome, site of the famous Sechstagerennen, *a six-day bicycle race which has its own theme tune, the* Sechstagerennen *waltz. (The race used to be held in the* Sportpalast, *the place where Goebbels once asked a select audience of loyal Nazis, "Do you want total war?") The* Deutschlandhalle *is also a venue for rock concerts and circuses. Its motto is :,,Menschen, Tiere, Sensationen" (people, animals, thrills).*
- Europa-Center
This complex is described as a "city within a city". There are stylish shops, supermarkets, restaurants, nightclubs, cabarets, a casino (roulette) and the famous Wasseruhr *(water clock), a globe-shaped fountain disrespectfully referred to by Berliners as the "aquatic dumpling". From the top of the Europa-Center's tower there is a superb view of the whole city.*
- Funkturm
The radio tower (138 metres high) dates from the Weimar Republic and has become the emblem of West Berlin. Berliners call it Langer Lulatsch, *a nickname for someone tall and skinny - the Beanpole, perhaps. It is like a miniature Eiffel Tower, with a restaurant and an open-air observation platform.*
- Kaiser Wilhelm Gedächtniskirche (Memorial Church)
The old ruin with the modern church alongside have become the main tourist

Modern sculpture and the Kaiser Wilhelm Gedächtniskirche (Memorial Church)

centre and the starting point for bus tours. Like the Bahnhof Zoo, *however (West Berlin's main railway station at the zoological gardens), it has also become a meeting place for junkies.*
- Hansaviertel
This quarter was built after the war in a then revolutionary style. The Akademie der Künste *(Academy of Arts), scene of many cultural events, is situated here.*
- ICC (International Congress Centre)
Berliners have dubbed this building der Kongreßdampfer *(Congress Steamboat) because of its distinctive shape. It can accommodate 20,000 people for conven-tions and international congresses. It also hosts major theatrical productions and other events such as the annual press ball.*
- Der Kurfürstendamm *(popularly known as ,,der Ku-damm")*
Although East Berlin's Unter den Linden *and* Friedrichstraße *may well regain some of their prewar elegance and animation, the ,,Ku-damm" is likely to remain Berlin's most fashionable street for a while. A pro-fusion of boutiques, restaurants, cafés, cinemas and theatres line its 3.5 kilo-metres. Hurrying pedestrians, dawdling tourists, elegant jetsetters and colourful street entertainers are all part of the scene here.*
- Philharmoniehalle
Its architecture inspired the nickname ,,die schwangere Auster" (the pregnant oyster). However, the building has excellent acoustics and world-famous concerts take place here. Claudio Abbado

has succeeded Herbert von Karajan as conductor of the resident Berlin Philharmonic Orchestra.
- Schloß Charlottenburg
This castle, an example of German Baroque architecture, was originally built in 1695-99 for Queen Sophie Charlotte and later became the summer residence of Prussian kings. It was destroyed by an air raid in 1943 but restored to all its former glory, at vast expense, after the war. In the grounds are statues of the Great Elector Frederick William I and of numerous other members of the Hohenzollern dynasty.
- Teufelsberg
This little mountain is popular with Berliners for Sunday outings. It is a good place for skiing and sledging in winter and for flying kites and hang-gliding in the autumn. In the spring its "lovers' lanes" attract courting couples, and in the summer there is swimming in its little lake.
- Tiergarten
Once the imperial hunting grounds, today a park with lakes (boat rentals), picnic areas and expanses of meadow for playing volleyball or sunbathing. In short, it is one of the city's green lungs.
- Zoologischer Garten
In the zoo Berliners can admire their heraldic animal, the bear, as well as many rarer and more exotic animals (such as pandas). The zoo is home to about 14,600 animals belonging to 1,712 dif-ferent species.

4.2 TAKE-A-BREAK

No. 1

Match the words with their definitions. Enter the correct numbers in the boxes below.

Example: Wasserverbindung: → die Verbindung mit dem Wasser

A. der Einkaufszettel
B. das Frischkornmüsli
C. das Brotangebot
D. das Vollkornbrot
E. das Freilandhuhn
F. der Körnerfresser
G. der Schafskäse
H. das Frischei
I. die Legehenne

1. das Brot aus Vollkorn
2. die Henne, die Eier legen muß
3. das Brot, das man in einem Laden anbietet
4. jemand, der Körner ißt
5. der Käse aus Schafsmilch
6. ein frisches Ei
7. das Müsli aus frischen Körnern
8. das Huhn, das frei lebt
9. der Zettel zum Einkaufen

A	B	C	D	E	F	G	H	I

No. 2

Use the genitive after the percentages as in the example:
Example: Die Deutschen sind älter als 65. (15%)
→ 15% der Deutschen sind älter als 65.   *Your turn!*

1. Die Eier sind von Freilandhühnern. (20%)

....

2. Die deutsche Bevölkerung hat einen Farbfernseher. (94%)

....

3. Die Frauen in Deutschland sind nicht verheiratet. (53%)

....

4. Die Deutschen haben einen Fotoapparat. (100%)

....

5. Die Ausländer in Deutschland sind Türken. (ein Drittel)

....

(See answers on page 26 of the booklet)

Figures of Speech

HAHN IM KORB SEIN

To be the rooster in the basket
To be cock o' the walk

MIT DEN HÜHNERN SCHLAFEN GEHEN

To go to bed with the chickens
To go to bed very early

MIT JEMANDEM EIN HÜHNCHEN RUPFEN

To pluck a chicken with someone
To have a bone to pick with someone

4.3 DIALOGUE

IM AUTO

Iris and her brother Günter, who is visiting Berlin, take the car to visit a friend. Günter has just got his driving licence and is behind the wheel.

Iris: *Hier die Wagenschlüssel.*

Günter: *Was, ich soll fahren?*

Iris: *Natürlich! Du hast doch jetzt deinen Führerschein. - Steig ein! Mach das Radio an, damit wir die Nachrichten hören können.*

Günter: *Na, das wird etwas werden!*

....

Iris: *Hast du den Sitz und den Rückspiegel eingestellt? Vergiß nicht dich anzuschnallen!*

Günter: *Na, so was! Warum springt er nicht an?*

Iris: *Das ist ein Diesel, du mußt warten. - So, fahr jetzt gleich links.*

Günter: *Ich hoffe, du hast getankt?*

Iris: *Ja, ja, nur keine Angst. - Hier habe ich einen Stadtplan, damit wir uns nicht verfahren.*

Günter: *Kennst du dich in Berlin nicht aus?*

Iris: *Doch, aber sicherheitshalber! - Fahr zuerst geradeaus bis zur nächsten Kreuzung. Warum bremst du? Den Käfer kannst du noch überholen.*

Günter: *Ich fahre lieber langsam. - Es ist kaum zu glauben, die Berliner scheinen, die Geschwindig-keitsbegrenzung nicht zu beachten.*

Iris: *Bieg bei der nächsten Ampel links ab! - So, jetzt fahr bis zu dem großen Marktplatz.*

Günter: *Warum sind da so viele Leute? Der Platz ist ja gesperrt!*

Iris: *Ach so, das ist die Demo, von der sie heute früh im Radio berichtet haben. Wir müssen die Umleitung nehmen. Halt mal an, da ist ein Automat, ich möchte Zigaretten holen.*

Günter: *Wo soll ich anhalten? Das ist viel zu gefährlich.*

Iris: *Sei nicht so ängstlich. Warte einen Augenblick, ich bin gleich zurück.*

Günter: *Beeil dich aber!*

....

Iris: *Weiter geht's! - Bieg nach der dritten Ampel rechts ab; links siehst du die Kirche, jetzt fahr über diese Brücke. Das ist der kürzeste Weg.*

Günter: *Um wieviel Uhr hast du dich mit Manfred verabredet?*

Iris: *Um halb drei. Das schaffen wir schon! - Nach der U-Bahnstation, hundert Meter weiter sind einige freie Parkplätze. Zeig mal, ob du rückwärts einparken kannst!*

Günter: *Liebes Schwesterchen, nachher fährst du nach Hause. Ich habe die Nase voll, durch Berlin zu fahren.*

Iris: *Das war doch gar nicht so schlimm! Aller Anfang ist eben schwer!*

●●) LISTEN AND REPEAT
See translation on page 26 of the booklet.

Tyrol: the village of Gries and the autobahn.
Berlin: Breitscheidplatz and the Memorial Church

4.3 VOCABULARY

NOUNS

der Wagen — car
die Wagenschlüssel — car keys
der Führerschein — driving licence
die Haustür — front door (of house)
der Sitz — seat
der Rückspiegel — rear-view mirror
ein Diesel — diesel car
die Angst — fear
die Stadt — city
der Stadtplan — city map
die Kreuzung — intersection
eine Vorfahrtsstraße — major road
die Berliner (1) — Berliners
die Geschwindigkeitsbegrenzung — speed limit
die Ampel — traffic light
der Marktplatz — market place
die Leute — people
die Demo — protest demonstration
die Umleitung — detour
der Automat — vending machine
die Zigarette — cigarette
der Motor — motor, engine
die Kirche — church
die Brücke — bridge
der Weg — way
die U-Bahnstation — underground station
der Parkplatz — parking space
das Schwesterchen (2) — little sister
der Anfang — beginning

der Strafzettel — parking ticket
das Rathaus — city hall
die Autobahngebühr — motorway toll
die Ausfahrt — exit (for vehicles)
der Unfall — accident

ADJECTIVES

gesperrt — blocked
lieb — kind, dear
ängstlich — fearful, timid
schwer — difficult

VERBS

abschließen (abgeschlossen) — to lock
einsteigen (eingestiegen) — to get in
einstellen (eingestellt) — regulate; turn on
sich anschnallen (sich angeschnallt) — to buckle up, fasten seatbelt
anspringen (angesprungen) — to start
tanken (getankt) — to fill up with petrol
sich verfahren (verfahren) — to take the wrong road
sich auskennen (ausgekannt) — to know one's way around
bremsen (gebremst) — to brake
überholen (überholt) — to overtake
scheinen (geschienen) — (here) to seem
beachten (beachtet) — to respect, observe
abbiegen (abgebogen) — to turn off
berichten von (berichtet) — to report on
sich verabreden mit (verabredet) — to make an appointment with
(es) schaffen (geschafft) — to succeed in doing, manage to do something
einparken (eingeparkt) — to park

MISCELLANEOUS

vorher — before
sicherheitshalber — for safety's sake
geradeaus — straight ahead
rückwärts — backwards
damit (3) — so that, in order to
kaum — hardly
nachher — afterwards

HOW TO SAY IT

Fahr geradeaus bis zur nächsten Kreuzung — Drive straight ahead to the next intersection.
Sie müssen die Umleitung nehmen — You must take the detour.
Nehmen Sie die erste Straße links — Take the first street to the left.
Fahren Sie über die Brücke — Drive over the bridge.
Hundert Meter weiter sehen Sie die U-Bahnstation — A hundred metres further on you'll see the underground station.
Das ist der kürzeste Weg — That is the shortest way.

Wie komme ich zum Bahnhof bitte? — How do I get to the station, please?
Ist das weit? — Is that far?

Na so was! — Really, you don't say!
Ich habe die Nase voll! } __ (lit. I've got a nose full.)
Ich bin es leid! } I'm sick of it. I've had enough.
Ach so! — Oh, I see!
Unglaublich! — Unbelievable!
Das gibt es ja nicht! — That is impossible!
Ach, du lieber Himmel! **(see Unit 4.1)** — Great heavens! Ye gods!

Nur keine Angst! — Don't be afraid now!
Sei nicht so ängstlich! — Don't be so timid!
Das war doch gar nicht so schlimm! — That really wasn't so bad.
Das schaffen wir schon! — We'll manage/make it!

Steig ins Auto ein! **(4)** — Get into the car!
Halte bitte hier an! — Please stop here!

REMARKS   REMARKS   REMARKS   REMARKS

(1) The suffix -er is added to the names of cities to designate their inhabitants, e.g. der Berliner (the Berliner), die Berliner (the Berliners), der Londoner (the Londoner), die Londoner (the Londoners). For women, the suffix -in (plural -innen) is further added: die Berlinerin (the Berliner [f]), die Berlinerinnen (the Berliners [f]), die Londonerin (the Londoner [f], die Londonerinnen (the Londoners [f]) (see 1.1). — (2) The suffixes -chen and -lein form diminutives. All are neuter. Die Schwester →das Schwesterchen, das Schwesterlein (little sister), der Bruder → das Brüderchen, das Brüderlein. In northern Germany, -chen is preferred. In the south dialect forms of -lein (-le, -l -li) are widely used. — (3) DAMIT (so that): If the subject in the main clause is the same as the subject in the subordinate clause um...zu + infinitive (see 4.1) may be used. e.g. Ich rufe dich an, um dir guten Tag zu sagen (I'm calling to say hello.) If the subjects in the two clauses are different, it is necessary to use DAMIT which introduces a subordinate clause. e.g. Du ziehst die Antenne 'raus, damit wir Radio hören können. (You pull out the antenna so that we can listen to the radio). — (4) The imperative of the second person singular (see grammar on page 46 of the booklet).

4.3 ORAL PRACTICE

1. IMPERATIVE

2nd person singular

(••) LISTEN

Du sollst ins Auto einsteigen.
* *Steig ins Auto ein.*

Put the following sentences into the imperative:

Du sollst nicht vergessen, dich anzuschnallen. — Du sollst zuerst geradeaus fahren. — Du sollst bei der nächsten Ampel links abbiegen. — Du sollst mal kurz anhalten. — Du sollst nicht so ängstlich sein. — Du sollst den Motor abstellen. — Du sollst dich beeilen. — Du sollst mal zeigen, ob du rückwärts einparken kannst.

See grammar on page 46 of the booklet.

2. IMPERATIVE

Summary

(••) LISTEN

Zuerst zum Türkenstand gehen
* *Geh zuerst zum Türkenstand!* (2nd person singular, familiar)
Geht zuerst zum Türkenstand! (2nd person plural, familiar)
Gehen Sie zuerst zum Türkenstand! (polite form, singular and plural).

Now make the same changes in the following:

mich umgehend in der Düsseldorfer Galerie anrufen. — bitte für uns Eintrittskarten besorgen. — sich die Zähne putzen. — den Gästen etwas zum Trinken anbieten. — den Fernseher ausschalten. — dieses Bild beschreiben. — auf meine Frage antworten. — die Tür zumachen. — nicht so anspruchsvoll sein. — sich ein bißchen beeilen. — nicht so schnell fahren. — der alten Dame helfen. — den Roman lesen, der sehr spannend ist. — bitte pünktlich sein. — ein Hotelzimmer für eine Nacht reservieren. — die Auskunft anrufen. — auf mich warten.

See grammar on page 46 of the booklet.

3. „UM...ZU" OR „DAMIT"

(••) LISTEN

Ich rufe dich an. Ich sage dir guten Tag.
* *Ich rufe dich an, um dir guten Tag zu sagen.*
Du ziehst die Antenne raus. Wir können Radio hören.
* *Du ziehst die Antenne raus, damit wir Radio hören können.*

Connect the two sentences with um...zu or damit:

Wir nehmen ein Taxi. Wir fahren ins Theater. — Ich nehme den Stadtplan mit. Wir verfahren uns nicht. — Due hältst an. Ich hole Zigaretten. — Sie ruft bei der Firma an. Sie bekommt die neuesten Informationen. — Er fährt nach Hamburg. Er trifft die Journalistin. — Ich gebe dir den Bericht. Du kannst ihn heute noch lesen. — Du leihst mir dein Auto. Ich kann in die Stadt fahren. — Wir nehmen ein Taxi. Wir sind pünktlich.

See grammar on page 48 of the booklet.

4. INTONATION

(••) LISTEN AND REPEAT

Was, ich soll fahren? — Natürlich! — Na, das wird was werden! — Na, so was! — Kennst du dich in Berlin nicht aus? — Doch, aber sicherheitshalber! — Sei nicht so ängstlich! — Beeil dich aber! — Weiter geht's! — Das schaffen wir schon! — Das war doch gar nicht so schlimm!

BERLIN'S BACKGROUND AND INTELLECTUAL TRADITIONS

Berlin is a relatively young city. It was founded early in the thirteenth century at a time when much of Western Europe was, by medieval standards, overpopulated. The lands east of the Elbe beckoned to all those seeking a new and better life. The first "Berliners" were merchants from the Rhineland, Holland and Flanders. They developed the two settlements of "Berlin" and "Cölln" on the banks of the Spree (a borough of present-day Berlin is called Neukölln) into an important trading centre. Then in the 15th century the Hohenzollerns chose Berlin as their place of residence. In the following centuries the growing city offered refuge to a long stream of persecuted minorities from all over Europe.

1685 saw the revocation of the Edict of Nantes, which had guaranteed freedom of worship to French Protestants; in the same year, however, religious toleration was proclaimed in Prussia. Frederick William I, Der Große Kurfürst, the Great Elector (of the Holy Roman Empire of the German Nation) invited persecuted French Huguenots to make their home in Brandenburg. Within a few years, one Berliner in four was French. Prussian kings later granted refuge to Austrian Protestants, Bohemian Hussites, Dutch Catholics, East European Jews and many more. These refugees played an important part in Berlin's affairs and made it comparable in style and character to the great cities of Western Europe.

Although the Prussian Brandenburg state was known for its authoritarian character, it imposed no intellectual yoke on the mixed and mutually tolerant population of Berlin. Der Preußische Geist (the Prussian spirit) is a rare combination of strict discipline and absolute tolerance. Around the year 1700 English and French scholars mingled at the court of Queen Sophie Charlotte, consort of the first King of Prussia. He, prompted by the German philosopher Leibniz, founded the Deutsche Akademie der Künste (German Academy of Arts and Sciences), where theologians argued with atheists, philosophers expounded their ideas, and German language and culture flowered. The cultural life of Berlin was soon equal to that of London and Paris. With the accession in 1740 of Friedrich der Große (Frederick the Great), known as der Soldatenkönig (the Soldier King), Berlin gained a sovereign capable of combining intellectual interests with the exercise of power. From then on it attracted famous architects and scholars as well as minorities in distress. Voltaire

Das ist der Lauf der Welt: ein Kapital ist des andern Feind ...!

Das Kapital crushing a capitalist

was for several years the star of the court; also present were other French intellectuals belonging to the rationalist movement which in Germany came to be called die Aufklärung (the Enlightenment).

Young German intellectuals soon began to rebel against the French spirit of the court. Lessing, who was known as das Licht der deutschen Aufklärung (the leading light of the German Enlightenment) wrote brilliant plays on the classical model and founded the German tradition of literary criticism. Many of the great names of German philosophy and literature - Tieck, the Schlegel brothers, Brentano, Arnim and Novalis, among others - met in Berlin salons. This was the beginning of the Romantic movement in Berlin. It seems astonishing that Romanticism, with its mysticism, sentimentality and nostalgia could have gained acceptance in liberal, progressive Berlin. But the young adherents of the Sturm und Drang (Storm and Stress), as the early phase of the Romantic movement was called in

Germany, were anything but backward-looking. Opposing the rigid conventions of the Aufklärung, they fought for ideals of universal justice and liberty, including freedom for the Jews and even the emancipation of women. They succeeded in enlisting King Frederick William III in the Wars of Liberation against Napoleon. A surge of nationalist feeling after two years of French occupation went hand in hand with the emergence of more liberal ideas.

In 1810 the Humboldt University (Humboldt-Universität) was founded. It subsequently played an important rôle in scholarly research and teaching, and in establishing the liberal approach to education which came to be adopted throughout most of Europe. Numerous eminent scholars taught there: Hegel, Dilthey and Schleiermacher (philosophy), Ranke and Mommsen (history), the physicists Einstein and Planck, the Grimm brothers (Germanic studies); these and a host of others all helped to lay the foundations of our present technological age.

No. 1   ⊙⊙ LISTEN

Listen to the person giving directions and find the streets on the map:

A. *Wie komme ich zur St. Matthias Kirche?*
B. *Wo ist der Nollendorfplatz bitte?*
C. *Wo finde ich die Post?*
D. *Wie komme ich zur Luitpoldstraße?*

The car:

1. der Rückspiegel — 2. die Windschutzscheibe — 3. die Motorhaube — 4. der Kotflügel — 5. der Scheinwerfer — 6. die Stoßstange — 7. der Blinker — 8. das Nummernschild — 9. die Felge — 10. der Autoreifen — 11. das Lenkrad — 12. der Türgriff — 13. die Autotür — 14. der Außenspiegel — 15. der Auspuff — 16. der Kofferraum — 17. die Heckscheibe — 18. der Rücksitz — 19. der Sicherheitsgurt — 20. die Antenne — 21. das Autodach

(See answers on page 27 of the booklet)

◖•• LISTEN   **IRIS BEKOMMT POST**

Liebes Mäuschen!

Trotz des schlechten Wetters machen Vati und ich jeden Tag einen langen Spaziergang. Die Gegend ist ja so herrlich! Wir haben auch schon viele nette Leute kennengelernt. Könntest Du bitte Günter nochmal sagen, daß er regelmäßig Pussi füttern, die Blumen gießen und den Briefkasten leeren soll. Du weißt, er ist ja so vergeßlich! Es würde uns sehr freuen, wenn Du uns am nächsten Dienstag vom Bahnhof abholen könntest. — Wie geht es Dir? Arbeite nicht zu viel, schone Dich ein wenig. Viele liebe Grüße aus Spiekeroog.

Bis bald
Mutti

Wenn das Wetter doch besser wäre! — Ich hätte nie gedacht, daß es hier so schön sein kann. Heute abend gehen wir in ein Konzert.

Kuß
Vati

die Postkarte / SPIEKEROOG

Frau

Iris Berger

Kienitzerstraße 114

1000 BERLIN 44

Hamburg, den 1.5.1990

Hallo Iris,

Na, wie geht's? Wie war Deine letzte Ausstellung? Sicherlich ein Riesenerfolg! Ich hätte sie auch gerne gesehen, aber Du kennst ja meinen überlasteten Terminkalender. Hier in der Redaktion gibt es — wie immer — viel zu tun. Ich muß nächste Woche wegen einer Reportage für einige Tage nach Berlin. Es wäre schön, wenn wir uns vielleicht mal an einem Abend treffen könnten. Ich ruf Dich aber vorher nochmal an. Weißt Du, daß Peter Ende des Monats seine Doktorprüfung feiern will? Das wäre während der Pfingstferien, wahrscheinlich das Wochenende vom 26./27. Du könntest natürlich bei mir hier übernachten. Vielleicht sollten wir ihm gemeinsam etwas schenken? Ich hätte an ein Buch über Kunst gedacht. Was würdest Du dazu sagen? Für heute Schluß.

Mach's gut

Silke

Holzgroßhandel GmbH
FEUERSÄNGER
Postfach 2305   BONN

Frau Iris Berger
Kienitzerstraße 114
1000 BERLIN 44

Bonn, den 15.05.1990

Sehr geehrte Frau Berger,

Vielen Dank für Ihren Brief vom 25.04.1990. Gerne schicken wir Ihnen unseren neuen Katalog mit Preisliste. Im Augenblick haben wir nur europäische Hölzer auf Lager. Leider bekommen wir derzeit keine exotischen Hölzer aus Kuba (Exportstopp). Die Lieferzeit dauert bei europäischen Hölzern 2 Wochen, bei exotischen Hölzern etwa 3 Monate. Unsere Preise können Sie unserer Preisliste entnehmen. Wir gewähren bei Bezahlung innerhalb von 8 Tagen nach Rechnungsdatum 2 Prozent Rabatt.
Für weitere Auskünfte stehen wir Ihnen jederzeit zur Verfügung.
Mit freundlichen Grüßen...

Rhine at Lorch

4.4 VOCABULARY

die Maus — mouse
das Mäuschen — little mouse; darling
der Briefkasten — mailbox
die Postkarte — postcard
der Terminkalender — appointment book, diary
die Prüfung — exam
die Doktorprüfung — doctoral exam
(das) Pfingsten — Whitsun
die Ferien — holiday
der Schluß — conclusion, finish
das Holz — wood
der Großhandel — wholesale trade
*GmbH (Gesellschaft mit beschränkter
Haftung)* — limited liability company
das Postfach — post office box
der Betreff (Betr.) — reference
die Anfrage — demand
der Katalog — catalogue
der Preis — price
die Preisliste — price list
der Lagerbestand — stock, inventory
der Exportstopp — embargo
die Lieferungen (die Lieferung) — deliveries
die Lieferzeit — delivery time
die Bezahlung — payment
das Rechnungsdatum — billing date
das Prozentsatz — percentage
der Rabatt — reduction, discount
die Bestellung — order
die Auskünfte (die Auskunft) — information
(see *1.4*).
die Verfügung — (here) disposition
(zur Verfügung stehen) — to be at someone's
service
die Anlagen (die Anlage) — (here) enclosures

ADJECTIVES

herrlich — splendid, marvellous
vergeßlich — forgetful

überlastet — overburdened
europäisch — European
exotisch — exotic
inbegriffen — included
weiter — further: (here) other

VERBS

kennenlernen (kennengelernt) — to get to
know someone
füttern (gefüttert) — to feed
gießen (gegossen) — to pour; water
leeren (geleert) — to empty
sich freuen (gefreut) — to be glad
sich schonen (geschont) — to spare oneself
feiern (gefeiert) — to celebrate
übernachten (übernachtet) — to spend the
night
schenken (geschenkt) — to give a present
entnehmen (entnommen) — to gather from,
perceive
gewähren (gewährt) — to grant

MISCELLANEOUS

trotz(1) — despite
nochmal — again, once more
regelmäßig — regularly
sicherlich — certainly
wegen(1) — because of
während — during
gemeinsam — together
derzeit — at the moment
bis — until
innerhalb (1) — within
jederzeit — any time

HOW TO SAY IT

Liebes Mäuschen, Lieber Schatz — Darling, Sweetheart
Liebe Iris, Lieber Günter — Dear Iris, Dear Gunter

Sehr verehrte Frau Berger (2) — Dear Mrs. Berger
Sehr geehrter Herr Gebert — Dear Mr. Gebert
Sehr geehrter Herr Direktor — Dear Director

Bis bald (3) — See you soon!
Für heute Schluß — Enough for today
Mach's gut! — All the best!
Viele liebe Grüße — Affectionately
Herzliche Grüße — Very best wishes
Kuß — kiss(es)

Hochachtungsvoll — (formal, less used today) With great respect
Mit freundlichen Grüßen (MfG) }
Mit freundlichem Gruß } — With best wishes (friendly greetings)

Wenn das Wetter schön wäre! (4) — If only the weather were nice!
Es wäre schön, wenn... — It'd be nice if...
Könntest du bitte Günter nochmal sagen, daß (5) — Could you please tell Gunter again that
Du könntest natürlich bei mir übernachten — Of course you could spend the night at my place
Vielleicht sollten wir gemeinsam etwas schenken? — Perhaps we should give a joint present?

Es würde uns sehr freuen (6) — We should be very glad
Ich hätte sie auch gerne gesehen — I, too, should have liked to see her
Ich hätte nie gedacht, daß (7) — I never should have thought that

See grammar on page 46 of the booklet.

REMARKS   REMARKS   REMARKS   REMARKS

(1) These prepositions are followed by the genitive. (See grammar on page 43 of the booklet.) — *(2)* Whether <u>Lieb</u>- (friendly), <u>Sehr geehrt</u>-, or <u>Sehr verehrt</u>- (formal) is used for "Dear", remember to add the correct adjective ending. Courtesy requires the use of professional titles in formal letters; e.g. Ing. Jaumann (Engineer Jaumann), Dr. Wolf, used after <u>Sehr</u> geehrter Herr ... — *(3)* Other informal complimentary closes are: Mit vielen guten Wünschen/Mit vielen lieben Grüßen und Wünschen. Mit freundlichen Empfehlungen is a formal complimentary close more favoured today than Hochachtungsvoll — *(4)* Subjunctive II (past subjunctive) of HABEN and SEIN is formed from the imperfect (past) (ich hatte, du hattest, etc. and ich war, du warst etc.) (see *1.5*) The <u>a</u> is umlauted to <u>ä</u>, Subjunctive II endings are -e, -est, -e, -et, -en. — *(5)* Modal auxiliaries with an umlaut in the infinitive (dürfen, können, mögen, müssen) take an umlaut in all forms of subjunctive II. Modals with no umlaut (sollen, wollen) in the infinitive are not umlauted in subjunctive II, which is therefore the same as the imperfect. — *(6)* In the conditional (would) and the future (shall, will) the infinitive is placed at the end of the sentence or clause. — *(7)* The subjunctive II (for past or hypothetical conditions) uses the subjunctive II of HABEN or SEIN + the past participle. (See grammar on page 46 of the booklet).

4.4   *ORAL PRACTICE*

1. SUBJUNCTIVE II OF „HABEN" AND „SEIN"

hypothetical or conditional

(● ●) LISTEN AND REPEAT

haben

Ich hätt_e_, du hätt_est_, er/sie/es hätt_e,_
wir hätt_en_. ihr hätt_et,_ sie hätt_en_.

sein

ich wär_e_, du wär_est_, er/sie/es wär_e_,
wir wär_en_, ihr wär_et_, sie wär_en_.

See grammar on page 46 of the booklet.

2. SUBJUNCTIVE II: „WÜRDE" + INFINITIVE

(● ●) LISTEN AND REPEAT

ich würde, du würdest, er/sie/es
würde, wir würden, ihr würdet, sie
würden.

*(viel Geld haben) - ich fahre nach
Amerika.*

● *Wenn ich viel Geld hätte, würde ich
nach Amerika fahren.*

**Use (viel Geld haben) in the first clause and
change the rest of the sentence as in the
example:**

*Er kauft ein Haus. — Sie macht Urlaub. — Wir
leben gut. — Ich studiere nochmal. — Er schläft
nur. — Wir kaufen einen neuen Computer.*

See grammar on page 46 of the booklet.

3. SUBJUNCTIVE II (PAST OR HYPOTHETICAL)

(● ●) LISTEN

*(viel Geld gehabt haben) — ich fahre
nach Amerika*

● *Wenn ich viel Geld gehabt hätte,
wäre ich nach Amerika gefahren.*

**Now put the sentences in Exercise 2 into the
past subjunctive:**

4. SUBJUNCTIVE II OF MODAL VERBS

(● ●) LISTEN AND REPEAT

*könne_n:_ ich könnte, du könntest,
er/sie/es könnte, wir könnten, ihr
könntet, sie könnten.*

*müsse_n:_ ich müßte, du müßtest,
er/sie/es müßte, wir müßten, ihr
müßtet, sie müßten.*

*dürfe_n:_ ich dürfte, du dürftest, er/sie/es
dürfte, wir dürften, ihr dürftet, sie
dürften.*

*möge_n:_ ich möchte, du möchtest,
er/sie/es möchte, wir möchten, ihr
möchtet, sie möchten.*

*wolle_n:_ ich wollte, du wolltest,
er/sie/es wollte, wir wollten, ihr
wolltet, sie wollten.*

*solle_n:_ ich sollte, du solltest, er/sie/es
sollte, wir sollten, ihr solltet, sie sollten.*

See grammar on page 46 of the booklet.

5. CONDITIONAL

können; sollen

(● ●) LISTEN

*a) Hätte sie doch Geld! Dann könnte sie
einen Anrufbeantworter kaufen!*

● *Wenn sie Geld hätte, könnte sie einen
Anrufbeantworter kaufen!*

b) Er raucht zu viel.

● *Er sollte nicht zu viel rauchen!*

Now change the following as in the examples:

a. *Hätten wir doch Zeit! Dann könnten wir einen
Spaziergang machen. — Hätte ich doch eine
Kreditkarte! Dann könnte ich sofort bezahlen. —
Wäre er doch nicht krank! Dann müßte er nicht
zum Arzt gehen. — Hätte ich doch mehr Platz! Dann
könntet ihr bei mir übernachten.*

b. *Sie trinken zu viel Bier. — Wir essen zu viel
Wurst. — Die Kinder sehen zu viel fern. — Ihr
kommt zu spät. — Frau Gebert kauft zu viel ein.*

See grammar on page 46 of the booklet.

THE SPIRIT OF BERLIN

Opposition to authority is said to be the essence of the Berlin spirit. The revolution of 1848 erupted in Berlin, proving that liberal and democratic ideas were still alive and well. In 1871 Berlin became the capital of the second Reich (Empire) of which Bismarck was the architect. The city then had a population of 80,000, and rapid and uncoordinated industrialisation were giving rise to enormous social problems, with which the Social Democratic government wrestled manfully. The struggle had a literary side too. The novelist Fontane and the playwright Hauptmann, both realist writers, flourished in Berlin at that time. In the 1920s the theatre reached great heights with names like Piscator and Brecht, and theatrical life is still very vigorous today.

But let us return to the roaring Twenties. The casting-off of social restraints and the change in moral attitudes were even more evident in post World War I Berlin than in other European capitals. Avant-garde artists from East and West were drawn to Berlin by the city's receptivity to anything new and different. The press entered a new age as mass circulation newspapers were born, while the film industry gave Hollywood some keen competition. Modern architects, such as those of the Bauhaus movement, built innovative buildings. The political upheavals at the end of World War I did not destroy intellectual life in Berlin, though it was already threatened. Only when Berlin became capital of the Third Reich was its freedom of expression violently repressed for a while. Since 1945, despite its eventful history, Berlin has again become a centre of German political and cultural life. Even now, though, it is a city apart, not strictly comparable to any other large German city such as Munich, Hamburg, Frankfurt or Cologne.

A few important dates show the significance of Berlin even during the Cold War years when Germany was divided. For eleven months in 1948 West Berlin endured the Soviet food blockade. The solidarity of the Western allies, especially the Americans, created a

President Kennedy at the Brandenburg Gate in 1963

Frontstadtgeist (front-line-city mentality) that made Berliners feel proudly different from other Germans. In June 1953 East Berliners rebelled against their harsh working conditions, which led to a general insurrection throughout East Germany. The uprising was put down by Soviet tanks. When the Wall was built through the heart of the city on August 13, 1961, Berliners felt abandoned by their "American big brother". Two years later in West Berlin, John F Kennedy made his famous statement „Ich bin ein Berliner!", which in fact occasioned some hilarity, because a Berliner is a jam doughnut as well as a citizen of Berlin. (More idiomatic would have been: Ich bin Berliner.)

The student movement of 1968 spread from Berlin through West Germany. Groups such as the SDS (Sozialistischer Deutscher Studentenbund), expelled from the Social Democratic party for being too radical, organised demonstrations against the Vietnam war and protests against the educational system. It was also in Berlin that the first terrorist cells were formed.

Until the Wall came down, through all the long process of rapprochement between East and West, Berliners on both sides always felt themselves to be different from other Germans and tried to draw what advantage they could from their peculiar situation. Their fabled resourcefulness and Berliner Schnauze (Berlin Big Mouth, ie quick-thinking wit and humour) are today once again much in evidence in this difficult period of post-unification.

4.4 TAKE-A-BREAK

ABBREVIATIONS

abk. *(die Abkürzung)* — abbreviation
abs. *(der Absender)* — sender
ADAC *(der Allgemeine Deutsche Automobilclub)* — German Automobile Club
AG *(die Aktiengesellschaft)* — public limited company
BLZ *(die Bankleitzahl)* — bank identification number
b.w. *(bitte wenden)* — please turn over (p.t.o.)
bzw. *(beziehungsweise)* — respectively
DB *(die Deutsche Bundesbahn)* — German Railways
DGB *(der Deutsche Gewerkschaftsbund)* — Federation of German Trade Unions
d.h. *(das heißt)* — i.e., that is
einschl. *(einschließlich)* — including
EG *(Europäische Gemeinschaft)* — European Community (E.C.)
EWG *(die Europäische Wirtschaftsgemeinschaft)* — European Economic Community (E.E.C.)
Emp. *(der Empfänger)* — addressee
Fa. *(die Firma)* — enterprise firm
Fr. *(die Frau)* — Mrs.
frz. *(französisch)* — French
Hbf. *(der Hauptbahnhof)* — main railway station
hg. *(herausgegeben)* — published
i.A. *(im Auftrag)* — on behalf of
i.V. *(in Vertretung)* — acting for
kfm. *(kaufmännisch)* — commercial
Kfz. *(das Kraftfahrzeug)* — motor vehicle
led. *(ledig)* — single, unmarried
lks. *(links)* — to (on) the left
LKW. *(der Lastkraftwagen)* — lorry
Mwst. *(die Mehrwertsteuer)* — VAT*
Mitgl. *(das Mitglied)* — member
od. *(oder)* — or
p.A. *(per Adresse)* — care of
Pf *(der Pfennig)* — pfennig
PKW. *(der Personenkraftwagen)* — motor car
r. *(rechts)* — to (on) the right
s.o. *(siehe oben)* — see above
Std. *(die Stunde)* — hour
Str. *(die Straße)* — street
s.u. *(siehe unten)* — see below
TÜV *(der Technische Überwachungsverein)* — Technical Control Board (mines)
U *(die Untergrundbahn)* — underground railway
u. *(und)* — and
u.a. *(unter anderem)* — inter alia, among others
u.s.w. *(und so weiter)* — etc.
vgl. *(vergleiche)* — compare
z.B. *(zum Beispiel)* — for example
z.H. *(zu Händen)* — for the attention of
z.T. *(zum Teil)* — in part
z.Z. *(zur Zeit)* — at present

*VAT = Valued Added Tax, a kind of government sales tax

True (R) or False (F)?

The Bergers' letter

1. Herr und Frau Berger schreiben aus Hamburg .... [R] [F]

2. Iris Berger wohnt in der Kienitzerstraße 113 .... [R] [F]

3. Das Wetter in Spiekeroog ist sehr schön .... [R] [F]

4. Günter soll seine Eltern vom Bahnhof abholen .... [R] [F]

5. Günter vergißt alles .... [R] [F]

6. Die Eltern kommen am nächsten Mittwoch zurück .... [R] [F]

7. Den Eltern geht es gut .... [R] [F]

8. Die Eltern schreiben einen Brief an Iris .... [R] [F]

Silke's letter

1. Silke hat wenig Arbeit .... [R] [F]

2. Silke macht eine Kur in Berlin .... [R] [F]

3. Peter will seine Doktorprüfung feiern .... [R] [F]

4. Er will seine Doktorprüfung während der Sommerferien feiern .... [R] [F]

5. Silke möchte Peter ein Buch über Architektur schenken ..... [R] [F]

6. Silke schreibt eine Postkarte aus München .... [R] [F]

The timber merchant's letter

1. Die Firma FEUERSÄNGER schickt Iris nur einen Katalog .... [R] [F]

2. Im Sonderangebot haben sie Olivenholz aus Kuba .... [R] [F]

3. Iris muß das bestellte Holz abholen .... [R] [F]

4. Die Lieferzeit für alle Hölzer beträgt 2 Monate .... [R] [F]

5. Die Firma FEUERSÄNGER gewährt keinen Rabatt .... [R] [F]

(See answers on page 29 of the booklet)

(••) LISTEN

STELLENANGEBOTE

Iris: *Das wird nicht gesagt. Aber hier steht: zur Unterstützung unserer Geschäftsleitung. Ich bin davon überzeugt, daß du da als Marketing-Direktor eingestellt wirst.*

Monika: *Nun übertreibe nicht gleich. Was wird von der Firma hergestellt?*

Iris: *Sie produzieren Recycling-Anlagen.*

Monika: *Und was bieten sie?*

Iris: *Na ja, das ist so vage wie immer: leistungsgerechte Bezahlung, eine zukunftssichere Position, eine vielseitiges und interessantes Aufgabengebiet.*

Monika: *Wie wird man als Marketing-Manager bezahlt, wie hoch is das Gehalt?*

Iris: *Frag Jürgen! Der kann dir auch sagen, wie du das Bewerbungsschreiben aufsetzen mußt und wie du dich bei dem Einstellungsgespräch verhalten mußt.*

Monika: *Aber bevor ich mich bewerbe, möchte ich doch gerne wissen, was von dem Betrieb an Sozialleistungen geboten wird, wie die Arbeits- und Urlaubszeiten geregelt sind, und was von mir erwartet wird.*

Iris: *Schick ihnen auf alle Fälle deine Bewerbungsunterlagen. Englische und französische Sprachkenntnisse werden vorausgesetzt. Du kannst doch Englisch und Französisch. Ich nehme an, daß du viel im Ausland zu tun haben wirst.*

Monika: *Du has wohl recht. Und die Einzelheiten werden mir sicher von der Personalabteilung mitgeteilt.*

Monika, a friend of Iris, is looking for work. Monika and Iris read the job adverts.

Iris: *Guck mal, hier, diese Anzeige: Marketing- und Verkaufs-Manager mit technischer Ausbildung und praktischer Erfahrung.*

Monika: *Ich habe doch noch nie im Vertrieb gearbeitet.*

Iris: *Aber in einem Marketing-Büro. Und außerdem kennst due die Arbeit eines Verkaufs-Managers sehr gut durch deinen alten Freund Jürgen. Er kann dir sicher sagen, was man da wissen muß.*

Monika: *Ja, das stimmt. Und mit meinem Ingenieurstudium, den Kenntnissen in Informatik und der Diplomarbeit über Werkstoffe hätte ich ganz gute Chancen.*

Iris: *Die machen Daten- und Umweltschutz im zukünftigen europäischen Binnenmarkt, das ist doch auch sehr interessant.*

Monika: *Zeig mal, was soll man denn da genau tun?*

(••) LISTEN AND REPEAT
See translation on page 29 of the booklet.

An employment agency.

NOUNS

Die Anzeige — advertisement; announcement
der Marketing-Manager — marketing manager
der Verkaufsmanager — sales manager
die Ausbildung — training
die Erfahrung — experience
der Vertrieb — distribution, sales
die Kenntnis — knowledge
die Informatik — computer science
die Diplomarbeit — dissertation
der Werkstoff — raw materials
der Datenschutz — data protection
der Binnenmarkt — domestic market
die Unterstützung — support, aid
die Geschäftsleitung — management
die Anlage — equipment/installation/facility
das Aufgabengebiet — job specification, duties
das Gehalt — salary
das Bewerbungsschreiben — letter of (job) application
das Einstellungsgespräch — job interview
die Sozialleistung — fringe benefits
die Arbeitszeit — hours of work
die Bewerbungsunterlagen — résumé, CV
die Sprachkenntnisse — knowledge of (foreign) languages
die Einzelheit — detail
die Personalabteilung — personnel department

---

die Bewerbung — application
der Lebenslauf — curriculum vitae
das Zeugnis — certificate
das Lichtbild — photo
die Aufstiegschance — promotion prospects
die Karriere — career

das Personal — personnel
der Betrieb — enterprise, firm
der Kunde (weak masculine) — client, customer

ADJECTIVES/PARTICIPLES

vorausgesetzt — required; presupposed
überzeugt — convinced
leistungsgerecht — commensurate with competence
zukunftssicher — with a secure future
vielseitig — many-sided, varied

VERBS

einstellen (eingestellt) — to engage, employ
übertreiben (übertrieben) — to exaggerate
herstellen (hergestellt) — to manufacture
produzieren (produziert) — to produce
aufsetzen (aufgesetzt) — to draw up, write
sich verhalten (verhalten) — to behave
sich bewerben (beworben) — to apply
regeln (geregelt) — to regulate
erwarten (erwartet) — to await, expect
annehmen (angenommen) — to suppose, assume
recht haben — to be right

---

kündigen (gekündigt) — to resign
entlassen (entlassen) — to dismiss, discharge

HOW TO SAY IT

Vermutlich is das ein interessanter Posten — That is probably an interesting job.
Ich stelle mir vor, daß das interessant ist — I imagine that that is interesting.
Ich bin davon überzeugt — I'm convinced of that (it).
Ich bin der Meinung, daß... — I am of the opinion that...

Hiermit möchte ich mich bewerben um den Posten als Sekretärin — I should (hereby) like to apply for the post of secretary
Mein Schreiben betrifft Ihre Anzeige aus der ZEIT — My letter is in reference to your advertisement in DIE ZEIT.
Die Stelle als Abteilungsleiter interessiert mich — I am interested in the position of head of department/departmental manager.
Meine Qualifikationen entsprechen ihren Anforderungen — My qualifications meet your requirements.

Die Beherrschung der französischen Sprache wird vorausgesetzt (1) — (Good) command of French is required
Du wirst als Marketing-Direktor eingestellt — You will be engaged as marketing director

Der Marketing- und Verkaufs-Manager (2) — The marketing and sales manager
Der Daten- und Umweltschutz — data and environment protection
Die Arbeits- und Urlaubszeiten — hours of work and holidays

Du wirst viel im Ausland zu tun haben (3) — You will have much to do abroad.
Du wirst ein gutes Gehalt bekommen — You will receive a good salary
Er wird bald kommen — He will come soon.

REMARKS   REMARKS   REMARKS   REMARKS

(1) The passive is formed using the auxiliary WERDEN + the past participle of the verb. The past participle GEWORDEN becomes WORDEN in the perfect passives: sie wird gelobt (she is praised), sie ist gelobt worden (she has been praised). Only active verbs can be made passive. Der Mann schließt die Türe (The man closes the door) → Die Tür wird von dem Mann geschlossen. (The door is closed by the man). "Door," direct object in the active sentence, is the subject in the passive. Passive subjects do not act but are acted upon. The agent that performs the action is expressed by von + dative *for people or by* durch + acc. *when the agent is not a human but an instrument or means. An idiomatic, impersonal passive also exists: Heute wird nicht mehr gearbeitet (No more work today). The auxiliary SEIN is used for the so-called "false" or "adjectival" passive which describes the results of an action rather than the process of the action itself. Die Tür ist geschlossen. (The door is closed) contrasts with: Die Tür wird geschlossen. (The door is [being] closed). If you can insert "being", it is a true passive. (See grammar on page 47 of the booklet). — (2) A hyphen at the end of a word indicates its connection with a word following: Ein- und Ausgang (entry and exit). — (3) For the use of the future, see 2.3, page 85 and 3.4, page 131.*

4.5 ORAL PRACTICE

1. PRESENT PASSIVE

Er stellt jemanden ein
● *Jemand wird eingestellt.*

Change from active to passive as in the example:
er überzeugt jemanden — er zeigt etwas — er regelt etwas — er nimmt etwas an — er bezahlt etwas — er erwartet etwas — er entläßt jemanden..
See grammar on page 47 of the booklet.

2. PRESENT PASSIVE + AGENT

Die Firma stellt dich ein.
● *Du wirst von der Firma eingestellt.*

Change from active to passive as in the example:
Der Direktor stellt das Personal vor — Der Verkaufsmanager überzeugt den Kunden. — Der Direktor zeigt die Produktion. — Der Betrieb produziert eine technische Anlage. — Die Buchhaltung bezahlt die Arbeit.
See grammar on page 47 of the booklet.

3. PASSIVE OF THE PRESENT PERFECT

Der Personalchef hat Iris eingestellt.
● *Iris ist vom Personalchef eingestellt worden.*

Change from active to passive as in the example:
Der Verkaufsmanager hat die Waren gezeigt. — Das Unternehmen hat den VW produziert. — Iris hat den Wagen eingeparkt — Manfred hat ein neues Auto bestellt. — Die Firma hat ein gutes Gehalt geboten.
See grammar on page 47 of the booklet.

4. PASSIVE

Die Tür wird geschlossen.
● *Die Tür ist geschlossen.*

Make the same change in the following:
Der Binnenmarkt wird gemacht. — Das Haus wird gebaut. — Das Gehalt wird ausgezahlt. — Das Buch wird gelesen.
See grammar on page 47 of the booklet.

5. FEMININE NOUNS

with the suffix -„ung"

meinen → die Meinung
The suffix -<u>ung</u> forms feminine nouns based on verbs.

Form nouns from the following verbs:
steigen — schalten — besichtigen — behandeln — entschuldigen — beschreiben — kleiden — versichern.

6. FUTURE

Du kommst nach Hause
Du wirst nach Hause kommen

Change the following from the present to the future:
Wir fahren nach München. — Sie verkauft Skulpturen. — Ich kaufe auf dem Markt ein. — Er stellt das Personal vor. — Sie stellen dich als Direktorin ein.
See grammar on page 44 of the booklet.

7. PRONUNCIATION

Fischers Fritze fischt frische Fische. — In drei Streichholzschächtelchen sind hundertdreiunddreißig Streichhölzer. — Chinesen speisen mit chinesischen Stäbchen.

BERLIN TODAY - A LOST LEGEND?

Most things that people used to associate with Berlin (though they really pertained only to West Berlin) are no longer relevant today. Gone are the Durchhalteparolen (morale-boosting "stick-it-out" slogans) with which politicians used to season their speeches, gone is the city's identity as a Frontstadt (front-line city between the two power blocks) and even its Sonderstatus (special status). Monuments such as the Freiheitsglocke (Liberty Bell) that Kennedy gave to the Berlin-Schöneberg city hall are meaningless now.

Before 1989 Berlin was notorious for its political anecdotes and nicknames. Take the 1948 blockade and airlift, for example. People called the monument erected to commemorate it die Hungerharke (the hunger rake). Planes bringing food supplies were dubbed Rosinenbomber (raisin bombers). Civil aircraft were used to transport coal. Chocolate and foodstuffs were often dropped on Tempelhof cemetery because the air traffic at nearby Tempelhof airport was so heavy that some planes had to dump their cargoes rather than land.... These are a few of the stories Berliners love to tell.

Because Berlin's special status exempted its young men from military service, many went there to avoid being called up. That was one reason why West Berlin attracted seekers after an "alternative" life-style. The 1968 student movement, which was particularly turbulent in Berlin, was partly attributable to a feeling of being caged in behind the Wall. The Wall! Monstrous though it was, some Berliners will miss it. Now it has vanished so completely - broken up, its graffiti-covered fragments carried off by souvenir-hunters - that today's tourist can hardly tell where it stood. Films such as Wim Wenders'The Wings of Desire are memorials to a vanished way of life. Young Berliners used to rejoice to be living in a city that offered them a modern lifestyle as well as a sense of history, green areas as well as concrete, museums as well as recreation areas, a sophisticated bus and underground transport system and enough canals to earn Berlin the nickname "Little Venice". Nowadays, of course, they can visit not only the other half of the city, but the surrounding country. There is the Spreewald, for instance, a beautiful lowland forest crisscrossed by canals and rivers. The old town of Potsdam and Frederick the Great's Sanssouci palace can be reached via the

A glimpse of Berlin night-life

Brücke der Einheit, the famous "unity bridge" on which spies and political prisoners used to be exchanged.

But above all they can explore the former East Berlin, where the Prenzlauer Berg district is now a more attractive artists' quarter to some than Kreuzberg in the West. A wide range of night-clubs and bars cater to all tastes from traditional to anarchist. There is the Café-WC and the Restauration 1900 in the Kollwitzplatz, the Café Schliemannstraße, the Prenzlbohne with its almost all-black décor, the punk-style Rat-Pub in the Kastanienallee, the ZK (the initials stand for "central committee"!), Im Eimer ("in the bucket", signifying "down the drain") in the Rosenthaler Platz, and many more. Some

of these café-bars are in houses occupied by squatters and thus have precarious tenure; but the young squatters have made long-term plans and mean to resist any pressure to evict them.

Before the monetary reform of July 1990, when there was still an East German mark, even Westerners were obliged to pay in Ostmarks to get into the JoJo club in Wilhelm-Pieck-Straße - a demonstration of East German pride, in marked contrast to the government-run East German tourist facilities, where payment had to be made in West German marks and other hard western currencies. Could it be that the legendary proud spirit of Berlin is still alive and well - but in the East?

4.5 TAKE-A-BREAK

The two Germanies before 1990. Listen and tick the right answer:

1. Einwohner : DDR ☐ 60,3 Mio   BRD ☐ 40,7 Mio
                         ☐ 20,2 Mio   ☐ 62,4 Mio
                         ☐ 16,4 Mio   ☐ 50,3 Mio

2. Monatslohn : DDR ☐ 730 Mark   BRD ☐ 3500 D-Mark
                          ☐ 1280 Mark   ☐ 7200 D-Mark
                          ☐ 925 Mark   ☐ 2198 D-Mark

3. Länge der Autobahn : DDR ☐ 1855 km   BRD ☐ 7534 km
                                  ☐ 2345 km   ☐ 8168 km
                                  ☐ 2730 km   ☐ 5423 km

4. Zahl der Autos : DDR ☐ 2,8 Mio   BRD ☐ 67,2 Mio
                              ☐ 3,9 Mio   ☐ 39,3 Mio
                              ☐ 3,7 Mio   ☐ 28,9 Mio

No. 2

A game of definitions. Find the true meaning of each compound noun:

1. Ein Kundenberatungsschalter ist...
a. ein Schalter, in dem Kunden sich beraten
b. ein Kunde, der eine Beratung schaltet
c. ein Ort, wo Kunden beraten werden

2. Ein Umweltschutzprogramm ist...
a. eine Umwelt, die ein Programm schützt
b. eine Programme zumm Schutz der Umwelt
c. eine programmatische Idee für einen
    Schutz um die Welt

3. Eine Unterwäscheverkaufsabteilung ist...
a. ein Ort, wo Unterwäsche verkauft wird
b. ein Verkäufer, der unter Wäsche etwas abteilt
c. ein Teil des Verkaufs von Unterwäsche

1		2		3	

Who are these people? Match the descriptions with the pictures and write down the names:

1. . . . .

2. . . . .

3. . . . .

4. . . . .

(See answers on page 31 of the booklet)

4. WRITTEN PRACTICE

4.1

Complete with „als", „wenn", „bevor", „nachdem": ...... *Iris in München war, hat Herr Wagner angerufen.* — ..... *sie verreist, schaltet Iris den Anrufbeantworter ein.* .... *Iris in Berlin ist, arbeitet sie viel.* — .... *Karin die Entwürfe fertiggemacht hat, gibt sie sie Iris.*
Translate: *Iris konnte nicht zur Versammlung kommen. Wolfgang konnte kein Französisch sprechen. Susi durfte Schokolade essen. Ach du lieber Himmel, das habe ich total vergessen! Before going to the office, Mr. Gebert drinks coffee. When she goes goes shopping she forgets nothing. After having been in Munich, Iris works in Berlin. Come, if you want to! (fam. sing.)*

4.2

Complete with the superlative of the adjectives „groß", „wichtig", „schön", „gut": *Der ..... Anruf ist von Herrn Wagner aus Düsseldorf.* — *Die .... Tomaten hat der Türke.* — *Der .... Bäcker ist neben dem Markt.* — *Die .... Apfel gibt es auf dem Winterfeldtmarkt.*
Translate: *Der Mann, der beim Türken kauft, heißt Wolfgang. Die Wurst, die der Schlachter Müller verkauft, ist am besten. Das Gemüse, das Iris ißt, ist biologisch angebaut.*
Mr. Müller's wife is a saleslady (salesperson). Karin's car is very old. Wolfgang's flat is in Berlin. Günter's friends go shopping at the market.

4.3

Complete with the imperative of the verb „vergessen", schließen", „beeilen", zeigen", „fahren": ..... *nicht so schnell!* — ...... *nicht, dich anzuschnallen!* — ...... *bitte die Tür!* — ..... *dich!* — ...... *mal, ob du rückwärts einparken kannst?*
Translate: *Geht bis zum Bahnhof! Nehmt den Bus! Seht euch den Film an! Lest den Roman von Goethe! Kauft auf dem Winterfeldtmarkt!*
He telephones Mr. Wagner to make an appointment. He stops to buy cigarettes. We take a taxi to go to the theatre. I give him the map of the city so that he can find my flat.

4.4

Complete with the subjunctive of „haben" or „sein": *Wenn er aufgepaßt ..... würde er jetzt alles wissen.* — *Wenn Iris nicht nach München gefahren .... Karin sie erreicht.* — *Wenn Wolfgang Iris rechtzeitig angerufen .... sie gekommen.* — *Wenn das Gemüse nicht so teuer .... Iris mehr gekauft.*
Translate: *Stefan würde lieber Franösisch als Spanisch lernen. Iris ist nicht sicher, ob ihn das interessieren würde. Iris fragt Karin, ob sie die Entwürfe fertigmachen würde.*
If he had taken the car, he would already be there. If Karin had known that she wouldn't have bought it. if Wolfgang were here, we'd be less bored.

4.5

Complete the verb in the following passive sentences: *Karin .... bei Siemens eingestellt.* — *Bei Volkswagen ..... viele Autos produziert.* — *Die Einzelheiten ..... ihr von der Verkaufsleitung gesagt. Gute technische Kenntnisse .... erwartet.* — *Die Beherrschung der englischen Sprache .... vorausgesetzt.*
Translate: *Auf dem Markt wird Gemüse verkauft. In Berlin werden Marketingspezialisten gesucht. Wolfgang wird entlassen.*
Marketing specialists are much in demand (sought after). The applicant is not hired. A thousand copies have already been sold.

See answers on page 32 of the booklet

MORE VOCABULARY

ANIMALS

das Tier — animal
der Hund — dog
die Katze — cat
das Pferd — horse
die Kuh — cow
der Hahn — rooster
das Schaf — sheep
der Esel — donkey
das Kaninchen — rabbit
die Ratte — rat
das Eichhörnchen — squirrel
das Wildschwein — boar
der Hirsch — stag
das Reh — roe deer
der Adler — eagle
der Falke* — falcon
der Bussard — buzzard
die Schwalbe — swallow
der Mauersegler — swift
die Meise — titmouse
die Amsel — blackbird
der Spatz* — sparrow
der Star — starling
die Möwe — gull
der Reiher — heron
der Schmetterling — butterfly
die Ameise — ant
der Käfer — beetle
der Wurm — worm
die Mücke — gnat
die Biene — bee
die Wespe — wasp
die Hummel — bumblebee
der Maikäfer — cockchafer
der Marienkäfer — ladybird
der Wal — whale
das Krokodil — crocodile
der Elefant* — elephant
das Zebra — zebra

PLANTS

die Birke — birch
die Tanne — fir
die Kiefer — pine
der Kastanienbaum — chestnut tree
die Pappel — poplar
der Stamm — trunk; stem
der Ast — branch
das Kraut — herb

das Blatt — leaf
die Nadel — needle
der Pilz — mushroom
die Sonnenblume — sunflower
die Tulpe — tulip
die Nelke — carnation
die Rose — rose
der Flieder — lilac
der Krokus — crocus

HOLIDAYS

Neujahr (1.1) — New Year
Karfreitag — Good Friday
Ostern — Easter
Tag der Einheit (13.10) — Unity
(Unification) Day
Tag der Arbeit (1.5) — Labour Day
Himmelfahrt — Ascension
Pfingstmontag — Whit Monday
Buß-und Bettag — Day of Prayer and
Repentance
Allerheiligen — All Saints Day
Erster Weihnachtstag (25.12) —
1st day of Christmas
Zweiter Weihnachtstag (26.12)
— Boxing Day
Heiligabend (24.12) — Christmas
Eve

EDUCATION

der Kindergarten — kindergarten
die Vorschule — nursery school
die Grundschule — primary school
die Hauptschule — grammar school
die Realschule — secondary school
das Gymnasium — grammar school,
academic secondary school preparing for
university
das Fachgymnasium — technical
high school
die Berufsschule — technical school
die Hochschule — college of higher
education
die Universität — university
die Fachhochschule — technical
college
der Abschluß — final exam
das Abitur — qualifying exam for
university entry
studieren — to study

das Diplom — diploma
der Magister — MA degree
das Staatsexamen — public
examination
die Dissertation — dissertation, thesis
die Lehre — apprenticeship
das Praktikum — practical work
der Praktikant — trainee
eine Prüfung bestehen — to pass an
exam
durch die Prüfung fallen — to fail
the exam
die Note — mark

WEIGHTS AND MEASURES

Seemeile — nautical mile
Meile — mile
Kilometer (km) — kilometre
Meter (m) — metre
Zentimeter (cm) — centimetre
Millimeter (mm) — millimetre
Quadratkilometer (km²) — square
kilometre
Hektar (ha) — hectare
Ar (a) — 100 square metres
Quadratmeter (km²) — square metre
Quadratzentimeter (cm²) — square
centimetre
Quadratmillimeter (mm²) —
square millimetre
Kubikmeter (m³) — cubic metre
Hektoliter (hl) — hectolitre
Kubikdezimeter (dm³) — cubic
decimetre
Liter (L) — litre
Deziliter (dl) — decilitre
Zentiliter (cl) — centilitre
Kubikzentimeter (cm³) — cubic
centimetre
Milliliter (ml) — millilitre
Kubikmillimeter (mm³) — cubic
millimetre
Tonne (t) — tonne, metric ton
Doppelzentner (q) — 100 kilogrammes
Kilogramm (kg) — kilogramme
Pfund — pound
Gramm (g) — gramme
Karat — carat
Milligramm (mg) — milligramme

* weak masculine

4. TEST YOURSELF

1. COMPLETE WITH „ANSTATT", „OHNE", OR „UM"

1. Sie ist nach Hause gefahren, ... auf ihn zu warten.
2. Er schreibt eine Bewerbung, ... als Manager zu arbeiten.
3. Sie bestellt Olivenholz, ... eine Skulptur herzustellen.
4. Wir gehen ins Kino, ... für die Prüfung zu arbeiten.
5. Sie kaufen das Gemüse, ... nach dem Preis zu fragen.
6. Er will nach Spanien fahren, ... nach Griechenland.
7. Er schaltet das Fernsehen an, ... die Nachrichten zu sehen.

2. PUT INTO THE PASSIVE

1. Hoechst stellt drei Chemiker ein. ....
2. Die Jugoslawin verkauft zehn Kilo Tomaten. ....
3. Die Verkaufsleitung bespricht das Projekt. ....
4. Karin macht die Entwürfe fertig. ....
5. Der Chef teilt die Resultate mit. ....
6. In Deutschland baut man Gemüse biologisch an. ....
7. Frau Berger legt Obst ein. ....
8. Iris brät ein Stück Rindfleisch. ....
9. Günter überholt den BMW. ....
10. In Deutschland beachtet man die Verkehrsregeln. ....

3. USE „WENN" TO LINK THE FOLLOWING PAIRS OF SENTENCES

1. Nichts kommt dazwischen. Iris fährt nach Düsseldorf.
   → Wenn nichts dazwischen kommt, fährt Iris nach Düsseldorf.
2. Iris' Eltern machen eine Kur. Sie fahren nach Spiekeroog.
. . . .
3. Karin ist mit ihrer Arbeit fertig. Sie verreist.
. . . .
4. Man ißt biologisch angebautes Gemüse. Man lebt gesunder.
. . . .
5. Martin ist groß. Er will Architektur studieren.
. . . .
6. Monika bekommt die Stelle bei Siemens. Sie verdient viel Geld.
. . . .

4. COMPLETE THE SENTENCES WITH „UM...ZU", „ZU", „DAMIT"

1. ... als Verkaufsmanager ... arbeiten, muß man eine technische Ausbildung und praktische Erfahrung haben.
2. Iris hat vergessen, ... die Entwürfe nach Düsseldorf ...... schicken.
3. Wolfgang bestellt fünf Kubikmeter Holz, ... er eine Skulptur machen .... kann.
4. Monika lernt Spanisch und Französisch, ... bessere Chancen auf dem Arbeitsmarkt .... haben.
5. Iris schreibt eine Einkaufszettel, ... sie nichts .... vergißt.
6. Karin und Walter versprechen, ... so schnell wie möglich .... kommen.

5. PUT THE FOLLOWING SENTENCES INTO THE IMPERATIVE

1. Ihr kauft das Obst auf dem Markt. ....
2. Ihr schließt das Fenster. ....
3. Du vergißt nicht zu kommen. ....
4. Du fährst langsam. ....
5. Ihr hört die Nachrichten im Radio. ....
6. Ihr lernt Deutsch. ....
7. Du rauchst weniger Zigaretten. ....
8. Ihr folgt dem Polizisten. ....

6. GIVE THE COMPARATIVE AND SUPERLATIVE FORMS

gut *besser; am besten*   **schmackhaft** ....
nett ....   **umweltfreundlich** ....
toll ....   **gern** ....
einfach ....   **praktisch** ....

7. PUT IN SUBJUNCTIVE II

1. Wie hoch ist das Gehalt? ....
2. Wieviel verdient er bei Siemens? ....
3. Wann nimmt er seinen Urlaub? ....
4. Was machst du am liebsten? ....
5. Wohin fährst du gerne? ....

(See answers on page 30 of the booklet)

LONDON - BERLIN, ONE WAY

*H*e arrived at Mommsenstraße 10 feeling rather uneasy. It was a four-storey block of flats with two courtyards and several staircases, and in the main hallway were several large letter-boxes marked *Vorderhaus... Hinterhaus... Seitenflügel...* and several smaller boxes. Ah, there was her name on one of them, *Lore Brinkmann.* But there was nothing to indicate whereabouts she lived. He felt a bit lost.

Then he saw a woman with a pram crossing the courtyard. Hesitantly, he approached her and said *,,Entschuldigen Sie bitte, wo wohnt Fräulein Brinkmann?"* She looked at him doubtfully. *,,Wie bitte? Wer?"* she asked. Simon repeated *,,Fräulein Brinkmann, Lore Brinkmann. Sie wohnt doch in diesem Haus?"* *,,Oh, das weiß ich leider nicht. Aber fragen Sie den Hausmeister. Im Vorderhaus, zweite Treppe."* Simon thanked her and hurried up the stairs.

It had worked - he had made himself understood! Now he had to talk to the janitor on the second floor. When he rang the bell the door opened to reveal an elderly man in carpet slippers. *,, Guten Tag, ich suche Lore Brinkmann"* Simon began, holding out an envelope with her address on the back. The man glanced at it and shook his head. *,,Lore Brinkmann, kenn ick nich!"* *,,Doch, der Briefkasten!"* insisted Simon. *,,Ach ja, dat is' een Briefkasten nur für Geschäftspost! Ick weeß nich, wer dat is'. Holt die Post alle zwee Wochen!"* And he closed the door. If Simon had understood the Berlin dialect correctly, the letter box was only an accommodation address and Lore collected the post every two weeks. Would she be expecting a reply to her last letter within the next couple of days? He would have to trust to luck.

He kept his business appointments the following morning, then hurried back to Mommsenstraße. Just opposite the flats was a little café, where he ordered lunch and took a table by the window. However, he watched in vain, and it was late afternoon the following day before he was able to return to his vantage point. He sat near the window again, drinking coffee.

Almost at once he saw someone coming out of the block of flats opposite holding the sheet of yellow paper he had left in the letter box with the message *,,Hallo! Ich bin in Berlin und möchte Sie treffen - Simon Lambert".* It was a little white-haired old lady. Glancing around her with an air of uncertainty, she slowly made her way along the pavement and round the corner into the next street.

Simon got over his initial shock, gulped down his coffee and went after her. Having followed her discreetly for a few minutes he saw her disappear up the steps of a private house. Strolling past, he managed to read the name on the letter box: Hannelore Seiffert. He stood baffled and indecisive for a moment. Then he wandered along to the bar on the next corner and had a whisky while he thought about it. The old lady must presumably be some friend or relation of Lore's; but why had she picked up his message? At length he summoned the courage to go back and ring the door bell. The old lady looked even older at close quarters, but her fine-boned face had clearly once been beautiful, and a pair of bright intelligent eyes searched his face as he stumbled through his carefully-rehearsed opening question:*,,Entschuldigen Sie, aber darf ich fragen, ob Sie Lore Brinkmann kennen?"* She gave a slight gasp. *,,Sie sind also....?"* *,,Ich heiße Lambert, Simon Lambert. Ich bin Lores Brieffreund aus London."* The old lady looked bewildered. *,,Wieso denn? Simone - das ist doch ein Mädchenname, nicht?"* *,,Ja"* agreed Simon lamely, *,, aber ich bin es trotzdem. Lore wollte nämlich eine Brieffreundin haben, deshalb habe ich als Simone geschrieben. Es tut mir leid, es war sehr dumm, aber..."* His voice trailed away as the old lady suddenly clapped her hands and crowed with laughter. *,,Und Sie glaubten natürlich, daß ich ein schönes junges Mädchen wäre!"* Now it was Simon's turn to gasp. *,,Sie sind Lore Brinkmann? Aber das Foto... ?"* The old lady shook her head. *,,Kommen Sie nur herein"* she invited. *,,Ich werde es Ihnen gleich erklären."*

Over coffee and cakes the old lady told the whole story in an entertaining mixture of German and English -

Ludwig van der Rohe: Bauhaus chair (1927).

for, like most educated Germans, she spoke English quite well. She had placed the advertisement, she explained, because she wanted to learn about England through the eyes of an English person, and she had used an accommodation address to conceal the correspondence from her daughter, who shared her house and tended to try to organise her life for her. She had been married, but in her career as a journalist, which she still pursued intermittently, she had always used her maiden name, Brinkmann, with her first name shortened to Lore. No, she hadn't intended to mislead him about her age. That had come about because she had realised from the tone of his letters that he thought she was young, and then - well, she hadn't wanted to disappoint him.

„Aber das Foto?" persisted Simon, feeling a little mortified now as well as puzzled. The old lady chuckled. „Ach, das ist meine Enkelin - my granddaughter. Sie wohnt übrigens auch bei mir. Normalerweise kommt sie gegen sechs Uhr nach Hause. You like perhaps to meet her?"

Ten minutes later a key turned in the front door and a slim girl in a pale blue suit entered the room. „Ach, Lore, da bist du schon" said the old lady. „Darf ich vorstellen: das ist Herr Lambert aus London."

„Angenehm" said the girl as she shook Simon's hand. She gazed up at him, tossing back her long fair hair, and a smile not unlike the old lady's lit her face. „Aus London? Sie sehen aber genau aus wie der Nazioffizier im Kriegsfilm, den ich letzte Woche gesehen habe!"

Simon smiled back at her. He thought it was the most charming compliment he had ever received.

A traveller forewarned is a traveller forearmed!
As a supplement to EXPRESS TRACK,
we offer the following miniguide containing
a map of Germany, some general information,
and tips for getting to know Germany better.

PRACTICAL INFORMATION

DÄNEMARK

NORDSEE

OSTSEE

Rügen

Kiel

SCHLESWIG-
HOLSTEIN

Stralsund

Rostock

Lübeck

VORPOMMERN-
MECKLENBURG

Stade

HAMBURG

NIEDER-
LANDE

POLEN

BREMEN

BERLIN

NIEDERSACHSEN

Oder

Hannover

Potsdam

Frankfurt
an der Oder

Magdeburg

BRANDENBURG

NORDRHEIN-
WESTFALEN

Göttingen

SACHSEN-
ANHALT

Oder

Rhein

Dessau

Neiße

Dortmund

Düsseldorf

Leipzig

Elbe

Köln

Marburg

Erfurt

Weimar

Dresden

BONN

HESSEN

THÜRINGEN

SACHSEN

BELG

Wiesbaden

LUX

RHEINLAND-
PFALZ

Mainz

TSCHECHOSLOWAKEI

SAARLAND

BAYERN

Saarbrücken

Heidelberg

BADEN-
WÜRTTEMBERG

Nürnberg

FRANKREICH

Stuttgart

Donau

Tübingen

Linz

Freiburg

Augsburg

WIEN

München

Basel

Zürich

Salzburg

ÖSTERREICH

BERN

Innsbruck

Graz

SCHWEIZ

ITALIEN

JUGOSLAWIEN

0   100 km   200 km

MAP OF GERMANY

Germany is a federation of 15 states, the *Bundesländer*. The former West Germany comprised Schleswig-Holstein, Hamburg, Bremen Niedersachsen (Lower Saxony), Nordrhein-Westfalen (North Rhine-Westphalia), Hessen, Rheinland-Pfalz (Rhenish Palatinate), Saarland, Baden-Württemberg, and Bayern (Bavaria).

Since 1990 the preceding ten have been joined by: Mecklenburg, Brandenburg, Sachsen-Anhalt (Saxony-Anhalt), Sachsen (Saxony), and Thüringen (Thuringia), the *Bundesländer* of former East Germany.

The powers of the individual states are considerable. There is little conflict between the states and the federal government since the government is decentralized. Large cities are important cultural centres.

Hannover (Hanover) is well known for its big industrial fair. The Händel Festival takes place in the splendid baroque ensemble of the castle and gardens of Herrenhausen, former residence of the kings of Hanover (and, for a time, of England). Today Hanover is the capital of Lower Saxony.

Düsseldorf, an art and fashion centre, is an elegant Rhineland metropolis. The old town has been called "Europe's biggest bar" because so many houses have a bar or street-front café.

Köln (Cologne), known especially for its cathedral, the *Kölner Dom*, has also preserved numerous traces of its founders, the Romans, who called it *Colonia Agrippina*. The city's pre-Lenten carnival celebrations are famous.

Stuttgart is the home of Mercedes Benz. You can also find splendid parks and castles in and around the city, the residence of the former kings of Württemberg. In the suburbs vineyards abound.

Bremen, like Hamburg and other great port cities, was a member of the Hanseatic League. Bremen's armorial emblem is a key, Hamburg's the Holsten Gate. *Hamburg das Tor, Bremen der Schlüßel zur Welt* (Hamburg the gate, Bremen the key to the world) goes the saying referring to the worldwide trade of the two famous ports. Rich merchants built numerous sumptuous Gothic brick buildings. Also like Hamburg, Bremen is a free city and federal state.

Heidelberg has become a symbol of German romanticism for the whole world, especially Americans. The huge ruined castle towers over this university town in the narrow valley of the Neckar, a tributary of the Rhine.

Dortmund, a Ruhr valley mining town, actually brews more beer than Munich. Dortmunder Union beer is sold widely.

Nürnberg (Nuremberg) is one of Germany's most beautiful medieval cities - in appearance anyway. It was in fact heavily restored after World War II. The city looks back on a long and distinguished tradition of arts and crafts. Among the latter is toy manufacture. The *Christkindlmarkt* (Christmas Market) is one of the biggest and best known of the many festive open air markets set up in German cities at Yuletide. Crowds flock to them and enjoy eating *Nürnberger Lebkuchen*, an aromatic honey cake.

Göttingen, Marburg, and **Tübingen** are famed university towns. Although Göttingen University was founded as late as 1736, a local joke had it that because Hanoverian kings (the "German Georges") reigned in England, Oxford University was thus a branch of Göttingen. Marburg University was founded in 1527, Tübingen in 1477. All three continue to enjoy great prestige.

The opening of the Berlin Wall and the fall of the Communist regime changed boundaries and political structures. But cities in the former German Democratic Republic still bear the stamp of years of drab "socialist realism" and emphasis on industrial production.

Leipzig was the scene of the street demonstrations where thousands of courageous people accelerated the process that toppled the Communist regime. Famous for centuries for trade (the Leipzig Fair) and industry, the city also has a rich musical tradition as home of the *Gewandhaus* (Textile Hall) orchestra, headquarters of the music publishing house Breitkopf & Härtel, birthplace of Richard Wagner and scene of J.S. Bach's varied musical activities.

Weimar was a citadel of German classical literature. It is associated with Wieland, Herder, the composer Franz Liszt and above all with Goethe and his friend Schiller. Both *Dichterfürsten* (Princes of Poetry) are buried in Weimar. The city is rich in museums, theatres and castles.

Dresden was almost annihilated by Allied bombing in February 1945. Nevertheless, many splendid Baroque buildings have been restored, justifying Dresden's old reputation as the "Pearl of German Baroque," and "Florence on the Elbe." Dresden was the residence of the Kings of Saxony (and Poland for a time). Famous for porcelain, in recent years it has become a computer technology centre. Its museums are world famous.

Rostock is a port city that was also a member of the powerful Hanseatic League, as its architecture testifies. Like Hamburg and Bremen, Rostock proudly prefixes its automobile license plate identification with an *H* for *Hansestadt*. (See *ABBREVIATIONS p.203*). Rostock University was founded in 1419.

FORMALITIES

Residents of EEC countries need only a simple identity card. Others must have a valid passport. Rabies vaccination (performed 12 to 30 days before entry) is required for domestic animals. Don't forget to obtain an international certificate of vaccination.

For further information contact the German National Tourist Office, Nightingale House, 65 Curzon Street, London, W1Y 7PE. Tel: (071) 4956129.

HIGHWAY TRAFFIC

Road signs correspond to international conventions. Driving with parking lights is strictly forbidden. Acceptable alcohol level is: 0.8g per 1,000. Germany is honey-combed with highways. There are no tolls and speed limits are rare. Nevertheless it is advisable not to exceed 130 km (80 miles) per hour. On state roads outside towns, speed is limited to 100 km (62 miles) per hour and in populated areas to 50 km (31 miles) an hour. The rules of the road are observed and subject to frequent checks.

MONEY

The monetary unit is the Deutsche Mark (D-Mark or simply Mark). Since the summer of 1990 there is only one German currency.

1 Deutsche Mark = 100 Pfennig (Pf)
Coins in circulation: 1, 2, 5, 50 Pf; 1, 2, 5 DM
Notes: 5, 10, 20, 50, 100, 500, 1,000 DM.

Automatic money dispensing machines are less common in Germany than in some other places and in general accept only the Eurocheque card. Germans don't often pay by cheque and even less often by credit card. But bank transfers are quite common. Careful: bank commissions are considerable. It is advisable to have traveller's cheques.

Usual bank hours are: 8:30 a.m. to 1:00 p.m. (13:00) and from 2:30 p.m. to 4:00 p.m. (14:30-16:00); Thursday till 5:30 (17:30). Banks are closed on Saturdays and Sundays.

POST AND TELEPHONE

Post offices are open from Monday to Friday from 8:00 a.m. to 6:00 p.m. (18:00), Saturdays from 8:00 a.m. to 12 noon.

Basic telephone rate is 0.30 DM (1992). In hotels or bars the basic rate might be 0.60 DM. Coin telephones predominate. Card phones are still uncommon.

The whole of Germany is now covered by one international dialling code (01049). There are also city codes e.g. 69, 40, 89 (Frankfurt, Hamburg, Munich). Berlin, both East and West, is now 30.

LODGING

From camping facilities to castle hotels, a wide range of accommodation awaits you. Local tourist offices have lists of what is available. You can also get in touch directly with large hotel chains like:

DEHCGA/Kronprinzenstraße 46/D-5300 Bonn 2
Castle Hotels/Gast im Schloß e. V./D-3526 Trendelburg

For vacation villages, camping sites, rentals, farm vacations etc. contact the German National Tourist Office, Nightingale House, 65 Curzon Street, London, W1Y 7PE. Tel: (071) 4956129.

Youth Hostels: If you have an international card from the Youth Hostel Federation, you will be able to stay at any youth hostel. For information, contact: Deutsches Jugendherbergswerk, Bismarkstraße 8, D-4930 Detmold.

A particularly warm welcome awaits you in your bed and breakfast (maybe dinner too) in local homes in the East.

The Jugendtourist organization offers various accommodation options at attractive prices: Jugendtourist, Alexanderplatz 5, Pf 57, Berlin 1026 or DETOURA, Wilhelm-Pieck-Straße 49, Berlin 1054.

EXCHANGES

For information on student or teacher exchanges, contact the German Academic Exchange Service, 17 Bloomsbury Square, London WC1A 2LP. Tel: (071) 404 4065 or: Pädagogischer Austauschdienst, Nassestraße 8, D-5300 Bonn 1.

Young people seeking employment in Germany should contact the Verein für Internationale Jugendarbeit, Adenauerallee 37, D-5300 Bonn 1.

The address of the German Embassy is 23 Belgrave Square, London SW1X 8PZ Tel: (071) 235 5033.

SPORTS AND RECREATION

Youth hostels arrange sports programmes in all areas of Germany. *See Lodging.*

PRACTICAL INFORMATION

SHOPPING

In general, shops are open from 9:00 a.m. to 6:30 p.m. (18:30) and closed on Sundays, holidays and Saturday after 2:00 p.m. (14:00) except for the first Saturday of the month when shops stay open until 6:00 p.m. (18:00). Shops in some cities are open on Thursday evenings.

TIPPING

It is customary to round off the amount due and to tell the waiter to keep the (usually small) change.

THE ENVIRONMENT

The Germans are great ecologists and individually observe simple environmental protection measures. There are separate receptacles for glass, old paper, batteries, aluminium, plastic. Most bottles are deposit bottles. Germans even recycle plastic mineral water bottles. Of course petrol is unleaded - *bleifrei* - in the country that invented the catalytic converter.

BUSINESS

If you are interested in doing business in Germany, get in touch with the German Consulate (see *Exchanges*) or the Anglo-German Chamber of Commerce, 16 Buckingham Gate, London, SW1E 6LB. Tel: (071) 233 5656.

THE EAST

Ever since the crumbling of the Berlin Wall in November, 1989 the country's energies have been focused on the East. The GDR's official tourist agencies which offered tours like "Land of Luther" for foreigners with hard currencies, still exist but a gradual transformation is taking place as private tourist facilities are developed and expanded. In the meantime travel to the East is for the adventurous. There is plenty to delight the traveller in this little known land, including some magnificent scenery and a warm welcome from the people.

BIBLIOGRAPHY

If you would like to know more about Germany and the Germans, here is a small selection of recent pertinent works:

Ardagh, John *Germany and the Germans* new revised edition, London, Penguin Books 1992.

Balfour, Michael *The tides of power* London, Routledge 1992

Breuilly, John (ed) *The state of Germany* Harlow, Longman 1992

Carr, William *A history of Germany 1815-1900* 4th edition London, Edward Arnold 1991

Craig, Gordon A *The Germans* London, Penguin Books 1982, reprinted with an afterword 1991

Fritsch-Bournazel, Renate *Europe and German reunification* Oxford, Berg Publishers 1992

Fulbrook, Mary *A concise history of Germany* updated edition, Cambridge University Press 1993

Insight Guides: *The new Germany* London, APA Publications 1992.

ABBREVIATIONS

Major cities (local administrative centres) are abbreviated on vehicle registration plates.

Aachen	AC	München	M
Berlin	B	Mannheim	MA
Bonn	BN	Münster	MS
Düsseldorf	D	Mainz	MZ
Dortmund	DO	Nürnberg	N
Essen	E	Oldenburg	OL
Frankfurt/Main	F	Regensburg	R
Göttingen	GÖ	Stuttgart	S
Hannover	H	Saarbrücken	SB
Bremen	HB	Wuppertal	W
Heidelberg	HD	Wiesbaden	WI
Hamburg	HH	*Cities in the former GDR:*	
Köln	K	Leipzig	L
Karlsruhe	KA	Dresden	DD
Kiel	KI	Rostock	HRO

PRACTICAL INFORMATION

VOCABULARY

Words occurring in EXPRESS TRACK are listed in alphabetical order in this German-English Vocabulary. Words with multiple meanings have been defined only in the senses used in the book. In parentheses after the English definition you will find the unit and lesson number where the word first appeared.
Principal parts of common irregular verbs are on pages 220-221.

*In parentheses
you will find the article and plural form of nouns,
the past participle of verbs, and „sich" if the verb is reflexive.*

A

Aal (der, -e): eel (2.2)
Aalsuppe (die, -n): eel soup, stew (2.2)
ab: from, beginning (2.1)
abbiegen (abgebogen): to turn off (4.3)
abdecken (abgedeckt): to clear the table (3.3)
Abend (der, -e): evening (1.2)
Abendessen (das, -): evening meal, dinner (1.2)
aber: but (1.2)
Abflug (der, ¨e): flight departure (1.1)
abgeben (abgegeben): to submit (2.1)
Abgeordnete (der, -n): deputy (3.3)
abheben (abgehoben): to lift (receiver)(1.4)
abholen (abgeholt): to pick up (2.5)
Abitur (das, -e): exam qualifying for university admission (4)
abnehmen (abgenommen): to take off (1.4)
abschließen (abgeschlossen): to lock up (4.3)
Abschluß (der, -üsse): finals (4)
Abstellraum (der, ¨e): storeroom (3)
Abteil (das, -e): compartment (1)
Abteilung (die, -en): department (2.4)
Abteilungsleiter (der, -): departmental manager, head of department

ach so: Oh, I see (1.3)
acht: eight (1.3)
achtzehn: eighteen (1.3)
achtzig: eighty (1.3)
Adler (der, -): eagle (4)
Adoptiveltern (die, -): adoptive parents (3)
Adoptivkind (das, -er): adopted child (3)
Afrika (-): Africa (1)
Ägypten (-): Egypt (1)
aktiv: dynamic, active
Algerien (-): Algeria (1)
Allerheiligen (das): All Saints' Day (4)
alle: all (1.4)
also: thus, therefore (2.2)
als: as/than (2.2)(3.4)
alt: old (2.4)
Alter (das, -): age (3.2)
Ameise (die, -n): ant (4)
Amerika (-): America (1)
Ampel (die, -n): traffic light (4.3)
Amsel (die, -n): blackbird (4)
amüsieren (sich, amüsiert): to have a good time (2.3)
Ananas (die, -): pineapple (2)
Anbau (der): cultivation, growing (4.2)
anbauen (angebaut): to cultivate, grow (4.2)
anbieten (angeboten): to offer (3.3)
Anfang (der, ¨e): beginning (4.3)
anfangen (angefangen): to begin (1.4)

Anfrage (die, -n): demand (4.4)
angeln (geangelt): to fish (3)
angenehm: pleasant (1.1)
Angestellte (der, -n): employee (2)
Angola (-): Angola (1)
Angst (die, ¨e): fear (4.3)
ängstlich: fearful, anxious (4.3)
anhaben (angehabt): to have on, wear (3.2)
anhalten (angehalten): to stop (1.3)
Ankauf (der, ¨e): purchase (1.3)
Ankunft (die, ¨e): arrival (1.1)
Anlage (die, -n): facility, equipment, installation (4.5)
annehmen (angenommen): to assume (4.5)
Anrufbeantworter (der, -): answering machine (4.1)
anrufen (angerufen): to call up (1.4)
anschnallen (sich, angeschnallt): to buckle up (4.3)
ansehen (angesehen): to look at (3.3)
anspringen (angesprungen): to start (4.3)
anspruchsvoll: demanding (3.4)
anstatt...zu: instead of (4.1)
anstoßen (angestoßen): to toast, clink glasses (1.5)
anstrengend: tiring (2.1)
Antarktis (die): Antarctica (1)
Antenne (die, -n): antenna (4.3)
Antwort (die, -en): answer (2.1)
antworten (geantwortet): to answer (2.1)

Anzug (der, ¨e): suit (2.4)
Apfel (der, ¨): apple (2)
Apfelsine (die, -n): orange (2)
Apotheke (die, -n): pharmacy (2.5)
Apotheker (der, -): pharmacist (2)
Aprikose (die, -n): apricot (2)
April (der): April (2.1)
Ar (der, -): 100 square metres (4)
Arbeit (die, -en): work (1.5)
arbeiten (gearbeitet): to work (1.5)
Arbeitsplatz (der, ¨e): workplace (1.5)
Arbeitszeit (die -en): working hours (4.5)
Architektur (die, -en): architecture (3.4)
Argentinien (-): Argentina (1)
Arm (der, -e): arm (2)
Art (die -en): style, kind (2.2)
Artikel (der, -): article (2.1)
Arzt (der, ¨e): doctor (2.5)
Asien (-): Asia (1)
Ast (der, ¨e): branch (4)
attraktiv: attractive (2.4)
auch: also (1.5)
aufdecken (aufgedeckt): to set the table (3.3)
auffallen (aufgefallen): to be noticeable (3.2)
aufführen (aufgeführt): to perform (3.5)
Aufgabengebiet (das, -e): funtions, range of duties (4.5)
Aufgabe (die, -en): task (1.5)
aufgeben (aufgegeben): to make/file (a report) (3.1)
aufhängen (aufgehängt): to hang up (1.4)
aufhören (aufgehört): to stop (1.4)
auflegen (aufgelegt): to hang up (receiver)(1.4)
aufmachen (aufgemacht): to open (3.3)
Aufschlag (der, ¨e): service (tennis)(3)
aufschreiben (aufgeschrieben): to note, write down (4.2)
aufsetzen (aufgesetzt): to draw up, write (4.5)
aufstehen (aufgestanden): to stand up, get up (3.3)

Aufstiegschance (die, -n): promotion prospects (4.5)
aufwachsen (aufgewachsen): to grow up (3)
auf: on at (1.4)
Auge (das -n): eye (2)
August (der): August (2.1)
Ausbildung (die -en): training (4.5)
Ausflug (der, ¨e): excursion (3.4)
ausgeben (ausgegeben): to spend, spend; (jemandem) to treat (someone) (3.5)
ausgehen (ausgegangen): to go out (3.5)
ausgezeichnet: excellent (3.5)
auskennen (sich, ausgekannt): to know one's way around (4.3)
Auskunft (die, ¨e): information (1.4)
ausnutzen (ausgenutzt): to exploit (3.5)
ausrichten (ausgerichtet): to pass on (a message) (1.4)
ausschalten (ausgeschaltet): to turn off (3.3)
aussehen (ausgesehen): to resemble (3.3)
außerdem: besides (3.3)
Aussicht (die, -en): panoramic view (3.4)
Ausstellung (die, -en): exhibition (1.1)
Austern (die): oysters (2)
Australien (-): Australia (1)
ausverkaufen (ausverkauft): to sell out (3.5)
Ausweis (der,: e): identity card (1.2)
aus: out of, from (1.1)
Auto (das, -s): car (1.5)
Autobahn (die, -en): highway (1)
Autobahngebühr (die -en): motorway toll (4.3)
Automat (der, -en): vending machine (4.3)
Autoreise (die -n): car journey (1)

Bäcker (der, -): baker (2)
Bad (das, ¨er): bath (1.2)
Bademantel (der, ¨): dressing gown (3)
Badewanne (die, -n): bathtub (3)
Badezimmer (das, -): bathroom (3.3)
Bahnhof (der, ¨e): railway station (1)
Bahnhofsbasar (der, -e): station supermarket (2)
Ball (der, ¨e): ball, balloon (3)
Banane (die, -n): banana (2)
Bankangestellte (der, -en): bank employee (1.3)
Bär (der, -en): bear (2.2)
basteln (gebastelt): to do craft work (3)
Bauchschmerzen (die): stomachache (2.5)
Baum (der, ¨e): tree (3.4)
beachten (beachtet): to respect (4.3)
Beamte (der, -n): official (2)
beeilen (sich, beeilt): to hurry (3.3)
beenden (beendet): to finish (1.4)
befehlen (befohlen): to order (command)(3.1)
befreien (befreit): to liberate (2.4)
begegnen (begegnet): to meet (3.2)
begeistert: enthusiastic (3.5)
beginnen (begonnen): to begin (1.4)(3.1)
bei: at, with (1.5)
beide: both (2.2)
Beifall (der): applause (3.5)
Beilage (die, -n): side dish, garnish (2.2)
Bein (das, -e): leg (2)
bekannt: well-known (3.4)
bekommen (bekommen): to get, receive (1.3)
Belgien (-): Belgium (1)
Belgier (der, -): the Belgian *(m)* (1)
Belgierin (die, -nen): the Belgian *(f)* (1)
Benzin (das): petrol (4.3)
bequem: comfortable (3.4)
bereitstellen (bereitgestellt): to get ready, make available (3.3)
Berg (der, -e): mountain (3.4)

Bergsteigen (das): mountain climbing (3)

Bericht (der, -e): report (2.1)

berichten (berichtet): to report (3.3)

Berufsschule (die, -n): vocational or technical school (4)

beruhigen (sich, beruhigt): to calm down (3.2)

beschreiben (beschrieben): to describe (3.2)

besichtigen (besichtigt): to visit take a look at (2.3)

Besichtigung (die, -en): visit (2.3)

besorgen (besorgt): to get, procure (3.5)

besprechen (besprochen): to discuss (4.1)

Besprechung (die, -en): discussion (4.1)

bessern (sich, gebessert): to improve (2.5)

bestellen (bestellt): to order (goods)(2.2)

Bestellung (die, -en): order (4.4)

besuchen (besucht): to visit (1.4)

Besucher (der, -): visitor (2.1)

Besuch (der, -e): visit (2.1)

Besucherzahl (die, -en): number of visitors (2.1)

Betreff (der): reference (4.4)

Betrieb (der -e): enterprise (4.5)

Bett (das, -en): bed (1.2)

bevor: before (4.1)

bewerben (sich, beworben): to apply for (4.5)

Bewerbung (die, -en): application (4.5)

Bewerbungsschreiben (das, -): letter of application (4.5)

Bewerbungsunterlagen (die): resumé, supporting documents (4.5)

bezahlen (bezahlt): to pay (1.3)

Bezahlung (die, -en): payment (4.4)

Biene (die, -n): bee (4)

Bier (das, -e): beer (1.5)

Biergarten (der, ¨): beer garden (2)

Bierstube (die, -n): tavern (2)

bieten (geboten): to offer (3.1)

binden (gebunden): to tie (3.1)

Binnenmarkt (der): domestic market (4.5)

Bioladen (der, ¨): health food shop (4.2)

biologisch: biological, organic (4.2)

Birke (die, -n): birch (4)

bißchen (ein): a little (3.3)

bitten (gebeten): to ask for (3.1)

bitte: please (1.2)

Blatt (das, ¨er): leaf (4)

blau: blue (2.4)

bleiben (geblieben): to stay (3.3)

Blick (der, -e): glance (2.3)

Blinker (der, -): indicator (4.3)

blond: blond (3.2)

bloß: merely (3.4)

Blume (die, -n): flower (3.3)

Blumenkohl (der, -e): cauliflower (2)

Bluse (die, -n): blouse (2.4)

Boden (der, ¨): floor (3)

Bohne (die -n): bean (2)

Bosnien: Bosnia (1)

braten (gebraten): to roast (4.2)

brauchen (gebraucht): to need (1.3)

brechen (gebrochen): to break (3.1)

Brei (der, -e): puree, mash (2.2)

bremsen (gebremst): to brake (4.3)

brennen (gebrannt): to burn (3.1)

Bridge (das): bridge (3)

Brief (der, -e): letter (2.1)

Briefkasten (der, ¨): post box (4.4)

bringen (gebracht): to bring (3.1)

Bruder (der, ¨): brother (3)

Brust (die, ¨e): breast (2)

Buch (das, ¨er): book (1.1)

Buchhalter (der, -): accountant (2)

Buchhändler (der, -): bookseller (2)

Buchmesse (die, -n): book fair (1.2)

Buchung (die, -en): booking, reservation (1)

Bühnenbild (das, -er): decor, sets (3.5)

Bühne (die, -n): stage (3.5)

Bulgarien (-): Bulgaria (1)

bummeln (gebummelt): to stroll (2.5)

Burg (die, -en): fortress (3.4)

Burkina Faso (-): Burkina Faso (1)

Bus (der, -se): bus (1.5)

Busreise (die, -n): bus trip (1)

Buß und Bettag (der): Day of Prayer and Repentance

Bussard (der, -e): buzzard (4)

Büstenhalter (der, -): brassiere (2.4)

Butter (die): butter (2)

Café (das, -s): café (1.3)

Chef (der, -s): chief, boss (2)

Chile (-): Chile (1)

China (-): China (1)

Clown (der, -s): clown (3.2)

Computer (der, -): computer (2.4)

Cousin (der, -s): cousin (3)

Cousine (die, -n): cousin *(f)* (3)

Croatien: Croatia (1)

dahin: to there, over there (2.3)

Dame (die, -n): lady (2.4)

Damespiel (das, -e): draughts (3)

damit: so that (4.3)

Däne (der, -n): the Dane *(m)* (1)

Dänemark (-): Denmark (1)

Dänin (die, -nen): the Dane *(f)* (1)

danke: thank you (1.2)

dann: then (1.5)

daß: that (3.2)

Datenschutz (der): data protection (4.5)

Datum (das, -ten): date (2.1)

dazwischenkommen (dazwischengekommen): to intervene (4.1)

da: there (1.1)

Decke (die, -n): ceiling, blanket (3.3)

decken (gedeckt): to set the table (3.3)

Demonstration (die, -en): protest demonstration (4.3)

denken (gedacht): to think (2.4) (3.1)

denn: because (2.1)

derzeit: at present (4.4)

Deutsche (der, -n): the German *(m)* (1)

Deutsche (die, -n): the German *(f)* (1)
Deutschland (-): Germany (1)
deutsch: German (1.2)
Dezember (der): December (2.1)
Deziliter (der): decilitre (4)
Dienstag (der): Tuesday (2.1)
Diesel (der): diesel (4.3)
Diplom (das, -e): diploma (4)
Diplomarbeit (die, -en): dissertation (4.5)
direkt: direct (1.4)
Dissertation (die, -en): thesis, dissertation (4)
Doktorprüfung (die, -en): doctoral exam (4.4)
Donnerstag (der): Thursday (2.1)
Doppelzentner (der): 100 kilogrammes (4)
Doppelzimmer (das, -): double room (1.2)
dort: there (1.2)
dorthin: to there (2.4)
drei: three (1.3)
dreißig: thirty (1.3)
dreiundzwanzig: twenty-three (1.3)
dreizehn: thirteen (1.3)
dringend: urgent (4.1)
Durchsage (die, -n): public announcement, paging (3.1)
dürfen: to be permitted, allowed (2.1)
Durst (der): thirst (2.2)
Dusche (die, -n): shower (1.2)

E

Ecke (die, -n): corner (2.3)
Ehefrau (die, -en): spouse *(f)* (3)
Ehemann (der, ¨er): spouse *(m)* (3)
ehrlich: honest (2.3)
Ei (das, -er): egg (2.2)
Eichhörnchen (das, -): squirrel (4)
eigentlich: really (3.5)
einfach: simple (4.1)
einfrieren (eingefroren): to freeze (4.2)
Eingang (der, ¨e): entrance (3)
einhundert: one hundred (1.3)
einigen (sich, geeinigt): to agree (3.3)
Einkauf (der, ¨e): purchase (1.3)

einkaufen (eingekauft): to shop (1.3)
Einkaufszettel (der, -): shopping list (4.2)
einladen (eingeladen): to invite (3.1)
einlegen (eingelegt): to make preserves, pickle (4.2)
einmal: once (2.2)
einpacken (eingepackt): to wrap up (2.4)
einparken (eingeparkt): to park (4.3)
eins: one (1.3)
einsteigen (eingestiegen): to get in (4.3)
einstellen (eingestellt): to regulate (4.3), to hire (4.5)
Einstellungsgespräch (das, -e): job interview (4.5)
eintreten (eingetreten): to go in (3.1)
Eintrittskarte (die, -n): admission ticket (3.5)
einundzwanzig: twenty-one (1.3)
Einzelheit (die, -en): detail (4.5)
Einzelzimmer (das, -): single room (1.2)
Eisenbahn (die,: en): railway (1)
Elefant (der, -en): elephant (4)
Elektriker (der, -): electrician (2)
elf: eleven (1.3)
Elfenbeinküste (die): Ivory Coast (1)
Eltern (die): parents (3.2)
Empfang (der, ¨e): reception, front desk (1.2)
Empfangsdame (die, -n): receptionist, desk clerk (1.2)
empfehlen (empfohlen): to recommend (2.2)
Ende (das, -n): end (3.5)
Endiviensalat (der, -e): endive salad (2)
endlich: finally (1.5)
Engländer (der, -): Englishman (1)
englisch: English (1.2)
Ente (die, -n): duck (2)
entfernt: distant (3.4)
entlassen (entlassen): to discharge, let go (4.5)
entnehmen (entnommen): to gather from (4.4)

Entschuldigung (die, -en): pardon (1.1)
entspannen (sich, entspannt): to relax (3.4)
Erbse (die, -n): pea (2)
Erdbeere (die, -n): strawberry (2)
Erdgeschoß (das, -sse): ground floor (3)
Erfahrung (die, -en): experience (4.5)
erholen (sich, erholt): to recover, rest (3.4)
Erholungsgebiet (das, -e): recreation area (3.4)
erkälten (sich, erkältet): to get a cold (2.5)
Erkältung (die, -en): cold (2.5)
erstklassig: first class (3.5)
erstmal: first of all (3.2)
Erwachsene (der/die, -n): adult (3)
erwarten (erwartet): to await, expect (4.5)
Esel (der, -): ass (4)
essen (gegessen): to eat (2.2)(3.1)
Essig (der, -e): vinegar (2.2)
Essiggurke (die, -): gherkin (2.2)
Eßzimmer (das, -): dining room (3)
Etage (die, -n): floor, storey (2.4)
etwas: something (1.4)
Europa (das): Europe (1)
europäisch: European (4.4)
Europarat (der): Council of Europe (3.3)
Exemplar (das, -e): copy (1.5)
exotisch: exotic (4.4)
Exportstopp (der, -s): trade boycott (4.4)
extra: expressly (2.4)

F
---

fabelhaft: fabulous (3.5)
Fachgymnasium (das, -sien): specialized secondary school (4)
fahren (gefahren): to travel, drive (1.5)(3.1)
Fahrkarte (die, -n): ticket (1)
Fahrrad (das, ¨er): bicycle (3.3)
Fahrschein (der, -e): train ticket (1)

Fahrt (die, -en): trip (1)
Falke (der, -n): falcon (4)
Fall (der, "e): case (2.1)
fallen (gefallen): to fall (3.1)
falsch: false (1.2)
faul: lazy (3.4)
Februar (der): February (2.1)
fechten (gefochten): to fence (3)
feiern (gefeiert): to celebrate (4.4)
Feld (das, -er): field (3.4)
Fenchel (der, -): fennel (2)
Fenster (das, -): window (3)
Ferien (die): vacation (4.4)
Fernsehen (das): television (3.3)
fernsehen (ferngesehen): to watch TV (3.3)
Fernseher (der, -): television set (3.3)
fertigmachen (fertiggemacht): to finish (4.1)
fertig: finished (2.1)
Film (der, -e): film (3.5)
Finanzaffaire (die, -n): financial scandal (1.5)
finden (gefunden): to find (1.2)(3.1)
Finger (der, -): finger (2)
Finnland (-): Finland (1)
Fisch (der, -e): fish (2.2)
Flasche (die, -n): bottle (1.5)
Fleisch (das): meat (2.2)
Fleischer (der, -): butcher (4.2)
Flieder (der): lilac (4)
fliegen (geflogen): to fly (3.1)
fließen (geflossen): to flow (3.1)
Flöte (die, -n): flute (3)
Flughafen (der, "): airport (1.1)
Flugreise (die, -n): plane trip (1)
Flugzeug (das, -e): aeroplane (1.1)
Flur (der, -e): hall, lobby (3)
Fluß (der, "sse): river (3.4)
Föhn (der): hairdryer (3)
folgen (gefolgt): to follow (3.2)
Forelle (die, -n): trout (2)
Foto (das, -s): photo (2.1)
fragen (gefragt): to ask (2.1)
Frankreich (-): France (1)
Franzose (der, -n): Frenchman (1.2)
Französin (die, -nen): Frenchwoman (1)
französisch: French (1.2)
Frau (die, -en): woman, Mrs. (1.1)

Freilandhuhn (das, "er): free-range chicken (4.2)
Freitag (der): Friday (2.1)
freuen (sich, gefreut): to be glad (4.4)
Freundin (die, -nen): girlfriend (3.2)
frieren (gefroren): to be cold (3.1)
frisch: fresh (4.2)
Frischei (das, -er): fresh egg (4.2)
Frischkornmüsli (das): fresh grain muesli (4.2)
Frischkost (die): fresh produce (4.2)
Fruchtsaft (der, "e): fruit juice (2)
Frühstück (das): breakfast (1.2)
frühstücken (gefrühstückt): to eat breakfast (1.2)
früh: early (3.3)
führen (geführt): to lead (2.3)
Führerschein (der, -e): driving licence (1.2)
fünf: five (1.3)
fünfzehn: fifteen (1.3)
fünfzig: fifty (1.3)
für: for (1.2)
Fußballspiel (das, -e): football game (3)
Fußball (der): football (3.4)
Fuß (der, "sse): foot (2.3)
füttern (gefüttert): to nourish, feed (4.4)

Gang (der, "e): corridor (3)
Gans (die "e): goose (2)
ganz: whole, wholly: 2.1)
Garten (der, "): garden (3.4)
Gast (der, "e): guest (1.5)
Gatte (der, -n): spouse *(m)* (3)
Gattin (die -nen): spouse *(f)* (3)
Gebäude (das, -): building (3)
geben (gegeben): to give (1.4)(3.1)
Gebühren (die): fees (1.3)
gefährlich: dangerous (3.4)
gefallen (gefallen): to like (3.3)
gegen: against; approx. (3.2)
Gegend (die, -en): region (3.4)
Gehalt (das, "er): salary (4.5)
gehen (gegangen): to go (3.1)
Gehilfe (der, -n): assistant (2)

gehören (gehört): to belong to (3.3)
Geige (die, -n): violin (3)
gelb: yellow (2.4)
Geld (das): money (1.3)
Gelee (das, -s): jelly (2.2)
Gelegenheit (die, -en): occasion, opportunity (3.5)
gemeinsam: together (4.4)
Gemüse (das): vegetables (2)
genau: exact (1.4)
genießen (genossen): to enjoy (3.1)
Gepäck (das): baggage (1)
gerade: just (3.3)
geradeaus: straight ahead (4.3)
gerne: gladly (2.2)
Geschäftsleitung (die, -en): management (4.5)
geschehen (geschehen): to happen (3.1)
Geschenk (das -e): gift, present (2.4)
geschieden (sein): (to be) divorced (3)
Geschwindigkeitsbegrenzung (die, -en): speed limit (4.3)
Gesicht (das, -er): face (2)
gesperrt: blocked, closed (4.3)
gestern: yesterday (1.4)
Gesundheit (die): health (4.2)
gesund: healthy (2.5)
Getränk (das, -e): drink (2.2)
gewähren (gewährt): to grant (4.4)
gewinnen (gewonnen): to win, gain (3.1)
gießen (gegossen): to pour water (4.4)
Glas (das, "er): glass (1.5)
glauben (geglaubt): to believe (1.5)
gleich: right away (2.3)
Gleis (das, -e): track (1)
Glück (das, -e): happiness (3.5)
Golf (das): golf (3)
Gott (der): God (2.1)
Gramm (das): gramme (4)
greifen (gegriffen): to seize, grasp, grip (3.1)
Griechenland (-): Greece (1)
Grieche (der, -n): the Greek *(m)* (1)
Griechin (die, -nen): the Greek *(f)* (1)
Grippe (die, -n): flu (2.5)

Großbritannien (-): Great Britain (1)
Großhandel (der, -): wholesale trade (4.4)
groß: big (2.4)
Größe (die, -n): size (3.2)
Großmutter (die, "): grandmother (3)
Großvater (der, "): grandfather (3)
Grundschule (die, -n): primary school (4)
grün: green (2.4)
Gruppenreise (die, -n): group trip, tour (1)
grüßen (gegrüßt): to greet (2.5)
Guitarre (die, -n): guitar (3)
Gurke (die, -n): cucumber (2.2)
gut: good (1.5)
Gymnasium (das, -sien): academic secondary school (4)
Gymnastik (die): gymnastics (3)

Haare (die)(pl): hair (2)
Haarfarbe (die, -n): hair colour (3.2)
haben (gehabt): to have (1.2)
Hafen (der, "): harbour (2.3)
Hahn (der, "e): cock, rooster (4)
halb: half (1.4)
Halbbruder (der, "): half brother (3)
Halbschwester (die, -n): half sister (3)
Halle (die, -n): hall (1.4)
Halsschmerzen (die): sore throat (2.5)
halten (gehalten): to hold (3.1)
Halteverbot (das, -e): no parking, parking prohibited (1.3)
Hammel (der, -): mutton (2)
Hand (die, "e): hand (2)
Händler (der, -): dealer (4.2)
Handschuh (der, -e): glove (2.4)
Handtuch (das, "er): hand towel (3)
hängen (gehängt): to hang (3.1)(3.4)
Hase (der, -n): hare (2)
Hauptschule (die, -n): secondary school (4)
Haustür (die, -en): house door (4.3)

Haut (die, "e): skin (2)
heben (gehoben): to lift (3.1)
heißen (geheißen): to be named (1.1)(3.1)
Heizung (die, -en): heating (3)
Hektar (der): hectare (4)
helfen (geholfen): to help (1.5)(3.1)
Hemd (das, -en): shirt (2.4)
herausgeben (herausgegeben): to publish (1.5)
Herd (der, -e): stove (5.3)
hereinkommen (hereingekommen): to come in (3.3)
Herr (der, -en): Mr., gentleman (1.1)
herrlich: magnificent, splendid (4.4)
herstellen (hergestellt): to produce (4.5)
hervorragend: excellent (2.2)
Herz (das, -en): heart (2)
heute: today (1.4)
hier: here (1.1)
Himbeere (die, -n): raspberry (2.2)
Himbeergelee (das, -s): raspberry jelly (2.2)
Himmel (der): sky (4.1)
Himmelfahrt (die): Ascension (4)
hinreißend: ravishing (3.5)
hinten: behind (1.3)
Hintern (der, -): posterior (2)
Hirsch (der, -e): stag (4)
Hochschule (die, -n): university, college of higher education (4)
Hocker (der, -): stool (3)
hoffen (gehofft): to hope (2.2)
hoffentlich: let's hope (2.3)
holen (geholt): to fetch, get (1.1)
Holländer (der, -): the Dutchman (1)
Holländerin (die, -nen): the Dutch woman (1)
Holz (das, "er): wood (4.4)
Hose (die, -n): trousers (2.4)
Hotel (das, -s): hotel (1.2)
Huhn (das, "er): chicken (4.3)
Hühnchen (das, -): pullet (2)
Hummel (die, -n): bumblebee (4)
Hummer (der, -): lobster (2)
Hund (der, -e): dog (4)
hundert: hundred (1.3)
Hunger (der): hunger (2.2)
Husten (der): cough (2.5)
Hut (der, "e): hat (2.4)

Idee (die, -n): idea (2.3)
Imbißstube (die, -n): snack bar (2)
immer: always (1.5)
in: in (1.1)
inbegriffen: included (4.4)
Indien (-): India (1)
Indonesien (-): Indonesia (1)
Informatik (die): computer science (4.5)
Information (die, -en): information (1.4)
Ingenieur (der, -e): engineer (2)
innerhalb: within (4.4)
Instrument (das, -e): instrument (3)
Inszenierung (die, -en): staging, mise en scène (3.5)
interessieren (sich, interessiert): to be interested (2.3)
interviewen (interviewt): to interview (2.5)
Ire (der, -n): Irishman (1)
Irin (die, -nen): Irishwoman (1)
Irland (-): Ireland (1)
Irrtum (der, "er): error (1.4)
Israel (-): Israel (1)
Italien (-): Italy (1)
Italiener (der, -): Italian *(m)* (1)
Italienerin (die, -nen): Italian *(f)* (1)
italienisch: Italian (1.2)

ja: yes (1.5)
Jacke (die, -n): jacket (2.4)
Jagd (die, -en): hunt (3)
jagen (gejagt): to hunt (3)
Jahr (das, -e): year (2.4)
Januar (der): January (2.1)
Japan (-): Japan (1)
japanisch: Japanese (1.2)
jederzeit: any time (4.4)
jemand: someone (3.1)
jetzt: now (1.1)
Johannisbeere (die, -n): currant (2)
Jordanien (-): Jordan (1)
Journalist (der, -en): journalist *(m)* (1.1)
Journalistin (die, -nen): journalist *(f)* (1.1)
Judo (das): judo (3)
Jugend (die): youth (3)

Jugendliche (der, -n): adolescent (3)
Jugoslawien (-): Yugoslavia (1)
Jugoslawin (die, -nen): Yugoslav *(f)* (4.2)
Juli (der): July (2.1)
Junge (der, -n): boy (2.4)
jung: young (2.4)
Juni (der): June (2.1)

K

Käfer (der): beetle (4.3)(4)
Kaffee (der, -s): coffee (1.3)
Kalb (das, -¨er): calf (2)
Kamm (der, ¨e): comb (3)
Kanada (-): Canada (1)
Kaninchen (das, -): rabbit (4)(3.2)
Kantine (die, -n): canteen (2)
kaputt: broken (3.3)
Karat (das, -e): carat (4)
Karfreitag (der): Good Friday (4)
Karriere (die, -n): career (4.5)
Karte (die, -n): card (2.2)
Kartenspiel (das, -e): card game (3)
Kartoffel (die, -n): potato (2.2)
Käse (der): cheese (2)
Kasse (die, -n): pay desk, till (2.4)
Kastanienbaum (der, ¨e): chestnut tree (4)
Katalog (der, -e): catalogue (4.4)
Katze (die, -n): cat (4)
Kaufhaus (das, ¨er): department store (3.1)
Kaufmann (der, -leute): merchant, salesman (2)
kaum: scarcely (4.3)
Kaution (die, -en): bail, security (3)
Keks (der, -e): biscuit
kennen (gekannt): to know, be familiar with (1.1)(1.3)
kennenlernen (kennengelernt): to meet (4.4)
Kenntnis (die, -se): knowledge (4.5)
Kfz-Schlosser (der, -): motor mechanic (2)
Kiefer (die, -n): pine (4)
Kilogramm (das): kilogramme (4)
Kilometer (der, -): kilometre (4)
Kind (das, -er): child (2.4)

Kindergarten (der, ¨): kindergarten (4)
Kinderzimmer (das, -): children's room (3)
Kindheit (die): childhood (3)
Kino (das, -s): cinema (3.5)
Kirche (die, -n): church (4.3)
Kirsche (die, -n): cherry (2)
klatschen (geklatscht): to applaud (3.5)
Klavier (das, -e): piano (3)
Kleid (das, -er): dress (2.4)
klein: small (2.4)
Kleine: (der/die, -n): the little boy, girl (3.2)
Kleingeld (das): change (1.3)
Klimaschutz (der): protection of the climate (4.2)
klingeln (geklingelt): to ring (3.3)
klingen (geklungen): to sound, resound (3.1)
knabbern (geknabbert): to nibble (3.3)
knapp: brief, limited, tight (2.1)
Kneipe (die, -n): bar (2)
Knoblauch (der): garlic (2)
Koffer (der, -): suitcase (1)
kommen (gekommen): to come (1.1)(3.1)
Konditor (der, -en): pastry cook (4.2)
können (gekonnt): to be able, can (1.2)
Konto (das, -en): bank account (1.3)
Konzert (das, -e): concert (3.5)
Kopf (der, ¨e): head (2)
Korn (der): grain; grain spirit (2)
Körper (der, -): body (2)
Kost (die): food, board (4.2)
kosten (gekostet): to cost (2.4)
Kostüm (das, -e): women's suit (2.4)
Krabbe (die, -n): crab, shrimp (2)
krank: sick (2.5)
Krankenhaus (das, ¨er): hospital (2.5)
Krankenschwester (die, -n): nurse (2)
Krankenwagen (der, -): ambulance (2.5)
Krankheit (die, -en): illness (2.5)
Kraut (das, ¨er): herb (4)
Kräutertee (der): herbal tea (2)

Krebs (der, -e): crayfish (2)
Kreditkarte (die, -n): credit card (1.3)
Kreuzung (die, -en): intersection (4.3)
Kreuzworträtsel (das, -): crossword puzzle (3)
kriegen (gekriegt): to get (3.5)(4.2)
Kriminalliteratur (die): crime novels/stories (1.5)
Krokodil (das, -e): crocodile (4)
Krokus (der, -se): crocus (4)
Kubikmeter (der, -): cubic metre (4)
Kubikzentimeter (der, -): cubic centimetre (4)
Kuchen (der, -): cake (2)
Küche (die, -n): kitchen (2.5)
Kuh (die, ¨e): cow (4)
Kühlschrank (der, ¨e): refrigerator (3)
Kunde (der, -n): client (4.5)
kündigen (gekündigt): to resign (4.5)
Kunst (die, ¨e): art (3.4)
Künstler (der, -): artist (3.4)
Künstlerin (die, -nen): artist *(f)* (3.4)
Kur (die, -en): cure, treatment (at a health resort) (4.1)
Kurort (die, -e): spa, health resort (4.1)
Kurs (der, -e): rate (1.3)
kurz: short (3.2)

L

lachen (gelacht): to laugh (3.4)
Lachs (der, -e): salmon (2)
Lagerbestand (der, ¨e): stock, inventory (4.4)
Lampe (die, -n): lamp (3)
Landschaft (die, -en): landscape (3.4)
lange: long (1.3)
langsam: slow(ly) (2.5)
langweilen (sich, gelangweilt): to be bored (2.3)
lang: long (3.4)
lassen (gelassen): to let (3.1)
Lastkraftwagen (der, -): lorry (4.3)
laufen (gelaufen): to run (3.1)

Lebenslauf (der, ¨e): curriculum vitae, resumé (4.5)
Lebensmittelabteilung (die, -en): food department (3.2)
Lebensmittelzusatz (der, ¨e): food additive (4.2)
lecker: delicious (4.2)
ledig: single (3)
leeren (geleert): to empty (4.4)
Legehenne (die, -n): laying hen (4.2)
Lehre (die, -n): apprenticeship (4)
Lehrer (der, -): teacher (2)
leicht: easy, light (4.2)
leider: unfortunately (2.2)
leihen (geliehen): to lend (3.1)
leistungsgerecht: corresponding to job performance (4.5)
Leiter (der, -): director (2)
Lektor (der, -en): publisher's reader (1.5)
lesen (gelesen): to read (1.5)(3.1)
Leute (die): people (3.4)
Libanon (der): Lebanon (1)
Libyen (-): Libya (1)
lieb: dear, kind (4.3)
lieber: preferably, rather (2.2)
Lieferung (die, -en): delivery (4.4)
Lieferzeit (die, -en): delivery time (4.4)
liegen (gelegen): to be situated, lie (2.3)
Lift (der, -e): elevator (1.2)
links: to the left (1.2)
Linse (die, -n): lentil, lens (2)
Liter (der, -): litre (4)
lügen (gelogen): to lie (prevaricate)(3.1)
Luxemburg (-): Luxembourg (1)

machen (gemacht): to make (1.3)
Mädchen (das, -): girl (2.4)
Magister (der, -): master's degree (4)
Mai (der): May (2.1)
Maikäfer (der, -): may-bug (4)
Marienkäfer (der, -): ladybird, (4)
malen (gemalt): to paint (3)
Maler (der, -): painter (2)
man: one (1.2)

manchmal: sometimes (1.5)
Mandarine (die, -n): tangerine (2)
Mann (der, ¨er): man (2.4)
Mantel (der, ¨): coat (2.4)
Manuskript (das, -e): manuscript (1.5)
Marketing-Manager (der, -): marketing manager (4.5)
Markstück (das, -e): one-mark coin (1.3)
Marktplatz (der, ¨e): market place (4.3)
Marokko (-): Morocco (1)
März (der): March (2.1)
Maschine (die, -n): aeroplane (1.1)
Massentierhaltung (die, -en): factory farming (4.2)
Maß (das, -e): measure (4.4)
Mauersegler (der, -): swift (4)
Maus (die, ¨e): mouse (4.4)
Medikament (das, -e): medication (2.5)
Meer (das, -e): sea (2.3)
Mehrwertsteuer (die, -n): VAT (Value Added Tax)(4.4)
Meile (die, -n): mile (4)
meinen (gemeint): to mean, think, say (4.2)
Meise (die, n): titmouse (4)
meisterhaft: masterly (3.5)
melden (sich, gemeldet): to report, announce, contact (4.1)
Melone (die, -n): melon (2)
Mensa (die, -sen): cafeteria (university)(2)
Mensch (der, -en): human being (2.3)
Messe (die, -n): fair (1.1)
Meter (der, -): metre (1.3)
Metzger (der, -): butcher (4.2)
Mexiko (-): Mexico (1)
Miete (die, -n): rent (3)
Mieter (der, -): tenant (3)
Mietvertrag (der, ¨e): lease (3)
Milch (die): milk (2)
Milligramm (das): milligramme (4)
Millimeter (der, -): millimetre (4)
Million (die, -en): million (1.3)
mindestens: at least (3.5)
Mineralwasser (das, -): mineral water (1.5)
mit: with (1.2)

Mitarbeiter (der, -): collaborator (1.5)
Mittag (der, -e): noon (1.4)
Mittagessen (das, -): lunch (1.2)
mitteilen (mitgeteilt): to announce, communicate (4.2)(4.5)
Mitteilung (die, -en): message, communication (4.1)
Mittwoch (der): Wednesday (2.1)
mögen (gemocht): to like, want (1.3)(2.2)
möglich: possible (1.2)
Möhre (die, -n): carrot (2)
Monat (der, -e): month (1)
Montag (der): Monday (2.1)
Morgen (der, -): morning (1.4)
Morgenmantel (der, ¨): dressing gown (2.4)
morgens: mornings (1.4)
morgen früh: tomorrow morning (1.4)
Möwe (die, -n): gull (4)
Mücke (die, -n): gnat (4)
Mund (der, ¨er): mouth (2)
Münze (die, -n): coin, medal (1.3)
Muschel (die, -n): mussel (2)
Museumshafen (der, ¨): museum harbour (2.3)
Musik (die): music (3)
Muskel (der, -n): muscle (2)
müssen (gemußt): to have to, must (1.3)
Mutter (die, ¨): mother (2.5)
Mutti (die, -s): Mum, Mummy (2.5)
Mütze (die, -n): cap (2.4)

Nachbar (der, -n): neighbour (4.1)
nachdem: after (4.1)
nachdenken (nachgedacht): to reflect, think about (3.4)
nachher: later (3.3)
nachlaufen (nachgelaufen): to run after (3.2)
Nachmittag (der, -e): afternoon (1.4)
Nachname (der, -n): surname (1.1)
Nachricht (die, -en): news (3.3)
nächste (der): next (3.1)
Nachtisch (der, -): dessert (2.2)
Nacht (die, ¨e): night (1.2)

nach: after (2.1)
nackt: naked (3.4)
Nadel (die, -n): needle (4)
Nahrung (die, -en): nourishment, food (4.2)
Name (der, -n): name (1.1)
Nase (die, -n): nose (2)
Natur (die): nature (3.4)
natürlich: of course, naturally (1.2)
Nebenkosten (die): expenses (3)
Neffe (der, -n): nephew (3)
nehmen (genommen): to take (3.1)
nein: no (1.2)
Nelke (die, -n): carnation (4)
nennen (genannt): to name (3.1)
nett: nice (2.5)
Netz (das, -e): net (3)
neu: new (2.4)
Neujahr (das): New Year (4)
neun: nine (1.3)
neunzehn: nineteen (1.3)
neunzig: ninety (1.3)
Neuseeland (-): New Zealand (1)
nicht...mehr: no more (2.4)
Nichte (die, -n): niece (3)
Nichtraucherabteil (das, -e): nonsmoking compartment (1)
nichts: nothing (2.3)
nie: never (1.5)
Niederlande (die): The Netherlands (1)
Nigeria (-): Nigeria (1)
noch: still, yet (2.1)
nochmal: once again (4.4)
noch nicht ganz: not yet entirely (2.1)
norddeutsch: North German (2.5)
normalerweise: normally (1.5)
Norwegen (-): Norway (1)
nötig: necessary (3.3)
November (der): November (2.1)
Nudeln (die): noodles (2)
nur: only (2.2)

ob: if, whether (3.3)
Ober (der, -): waiter (2.2)
Obergeschoß (das, -osse): upper floor (3)
Oberschenkel (der, -): thigh (2)

Obst (das): fruit (2)
öffnen (geöffnet): to open (3.1)
oft: often (1.5)
ohne: without (1.2)
ohne...zu: without ...-ing (4.1)
Ohr (das, -en): ear (2)
ökologisch: ecological (4.2)
Oktober (der): October (2.1)
Oma (die, -s): granny (3)
Onkel (der, -): uncle (3)
Opa (der, -s): grandpa (3)
Oper (die, -n): opera (3.5)
Opernplatz (der, ¨e): opera ticket (3.5)
Ordnung (die, -en): order (1.4)
ostdeutsch: East German (2.5)
Ostermontag (der): Easter Monday (4)
Ostern (das): Easter (4)
Österreich (-): Austria (1)
Österreicher (der, -): the Austrian (m) (1)
Österreicherin (die, -nen): the Austrian (f) (1)
Ozonloch (das): hole in the ozone layer (4.2)

P

paddeln (gepaddelt): to paddle (3)
Paprikaschote (die -n): red pepper (2)
parken (geparkt): to park (4.3)
Parkplatz (der, ¨e): parking place (4.3)
Passantin (die, -nen): passer-by (f) (1.3)
passen (gepaßt): to suit (4.1)
passieren (passiert): to happen (3.2)
Paß (der, ¨sse): passport (1.2)
Personal (das, -e): personnel (4.5)
Personalabteilung (die, -en): personnel department (4.5)
Personalausweis (der, -e): identity card (1.2)
Personalchef (der, -s): personnel manager (2)
Personenkraftwagen (der, -): passenger car, automobile (4.3)
persönlich: personal(ly) (1.5)

Petersilie (die): parsley (2)
Pfennig (der, -e): pfennig (1.3)
Pferd (das, -e): horse (4)
Pferderennen (das, -): horse race (3)
Pfingsten (das): Whitsun (4.4)
Pfingstmontag (der): Whit Monday (4)
Pfirsich (der, -e): peach (2)
Pflaume (die, -n): plum (2)
Pfund (das, -e): pound (1.3) (4)
Picknick (das, -e): picnic (3.4)
picknicken (gepicknickt): to picnic (3.4)
Pilz (der, -e): mushroom (4)
Platz (der, ¨e): place (2.3)
plötzlich: sudden(ly) (3.1)
Polen (-): Poland (1)
Polizeibeamte (der, -n): police officer (3.1)
Polizeirevier (das, -e): police station (3.1)
Polizist (der, -en): policeman (2)
Porree (der): leek (2)
Portugal (-): Portugal (1)
Portugiese (der, -n): the Portuguese (m) (1)
Portugiesin (die, -nen): the Portuguese (f) (1)
Post (die): post office, mail (2.1)
Postfach (das, ¨er): post office box (4.4)
Postkarte (die, -n): postcard (4.4)
Praktikant (der, -en): trainee
Praktikum (das, -ka): practical training/work (4)
Preis (der, -e): price (4.4)
Preisliste (die, -n): price list (4.4)
Pressebericht (der, -e): press report (2.1)
prima: super, great (2.5)
Prinzessin (die, -nen): princess (2.4)
probieren (probiert): to try, taste (2.2)
produzieren (produziert): to produce (4.5)
Programmierer (der, -): programmer (2)
Projekt (das, -e): project (4.1)
Prozentsatz (der, ¨e): percentage (4.4)

Prüfung (die, -en): exam (4.4)
Publikationsmöglichkeit (die, -en): possibility of publication, chance of getting something published (1.4)
Publikum (das): public, audience (3.5)
publizieren (publiziert): to publish (2.4)
Pullover (der, -): sweater (2.4)
Puppe (die, -n): doll (2.4)
putzen (geputzt): to clean (3.3)

Quadratkilometer (der, -): square kilometre (4)
Quadratmeter (der, -): square metre (4)
Quadratmillimeter (der, -): square millimetre (4)
Quark (der, -e): curd cheese (2)

Rabatt (der, -e): discount, price reduction (4.4)
raten (geraten): to advise (3.1)
Rathaus (das, ¨er): City Hall (4.3)
Ratte (die, -n): rat (4)
Raucherabteil (das, -): smoking compartment (1)
Raum (der, ¨e): room, space (3)
Realschule (die, -n): secondary school (4)
Rechnung (die, -en): bill, check (restaurant) (2.2)
Rechnungsdatum (das, -ten): billing date (4.4)
recht haben: to be right (4.5)
rechts: to the right (1.2)
rechtzeitig: on time (4.1)
Recycling (das): recycling (4.2)
Redakteurin (die, -nen): editor *(f)* (2.5)
Regal (das, -e): shelf (3)
regelmäßig: regularly (4.4)
regeln (geregelt): to adjust, regulate (4.5)
Regen (der, -): rain (2.3)
der saure Regen: acid rain (4.2)

Reh (das, -e): roe (deer) (4)
Reiher (der, -): heron (4)
Reisebüro (das, -s): travel bureau (1)
Reis (der): rice (2)
Reise (die, -n): trip, voyage (1)
Reisende (der/die, -n): traveller (1)
Reiten (das): riding (3)
rennen (gerannt): to run (3.1)
reservieren (reserviert): to reserve (1.2)
Restaurant (das, -s): restaurant (2.2)
Rezept (das, -e): prescription (2.5)
Rezeption (die, -en): reception, front desk (1.2)
richtig: correct, right (1.2)
riechen (gerochen): to smell (3.1)
Riesenerfolg (der, -e): huge success, triumph (3.5)
Rind (das, -er): beef (2)
Rock (der, ¨e): skirt (2.4)
Rose (die, -n): rose (4)
rot: red (2.2)
Rotkohl (der, -e): red cabbage (2)
Rotwein (der, -e): red wine (2)
Rücken (der, -): back (2)
Rucksack (der, -): rucksack, backpack (3.4)
Rückspiegel (der, -): rear view mirror (4.3)
rückwärts: backward (4.3)
rudern (gerudert): to row (3)
rufen (gerufen): to call (1.1) (3.1)
Rumänien (-): Romania (1)
Rußland: Russia (1)

sagen (gesagt): to say (2.1) (3.3)
Sahne (die, -n): cream (2)
Salat (der, -e): salad (2.2)
Salz (das, -e): salt (2.2)
Salzkartoffel (die, -n): boiled potatoes (2.2)
Samstag (der): Saturday (2.1)
Saudi-Arabien (-): Saudi Arabia (1)
saufen (gesoffen): to drink, guzzle (3.1)
Sauwetter (das): foul weather (2.3)
Saxophon (das, -e): saxophone (3)
Schachbrett (das, -er): chessboard (3)

schade!: pity! (2.3)
Schaf (das, -e): sheep (4)
schaffen (geschafft): to succeed in (4.3)
Schafskäse (der): sheep's milk cheese (4.2)
Schalter (der, -): window (1.3)
Schatz (der, ¨e): treasure (2.5)
Schauer (der, -): shower (2.3)
Schauspieler (der, -): actor (3.5)
Scheck (der, -s): cheque (1.3)
scheiden (sich scheiden lassen): to get divorced (3)
Schein (der, -e): banknote (1.3)
scheinen (geschienen): to shine; seem (2.3)(3.1)(4.3)
schenken (geschenkt): to offer, give (4.4)
Schiff (das, -e): ship (2.3)
Schild (das, -er): sign (4.3)
Schinken (der, -): ham (2)
Schlachter (der, -): butcher (2)(4.2)
schlafen (geschlafen): to sleep (3.1)(3.3)
Schlafzimmer (das, -): bedroom (3)
Schlagzeug (das, -e): percussion instrument (3)
schlecht: bad (1.5)
schließen (geschlossen): to close (3.1)
schlimm: serious (2.5)(4.3)
Schlips (der, -e): tie, cravat (2.4)
Schloß (das, ¨sser): castle (3.4)
Schluß (der, -üsse): end (3.5)
Schlüssel (der, -): key (1.2)
schmackhaft: tasty (4.2)
schmecken (geschmeckt): to taste (2.2)
Schmerz (der, -en): pain (2.5)
Schmetterling (der, -e): butterfly (4)
Schnaps (der, ¨e): brandy, spirits (2)
schneiden (geschnitten): to cut (3.1)
schnell: rapid, fast (2.5)
Schnitzel (das, -): cutlet (4.2)
Schnupfen (der, -): cold in the head, sniffles (2.5)
Schokolade (die, -n): chocolate (3.2)

VOCABULARY

Scholle (die, -n): sole (2.2)
schonen (sich, geschont): to spare oneself (4.4)
schon: already (3.1)
schön: beautiful (1.1)
Schrank (der, "e): cupboard (3)
schreiben (geschrieben): to write (1.2)(3.1)
Schreibtisch (der, -e): writing table, desk (3)
schreien (geschrien): to cry out (3.1)
Schriftsteller (der, -): writer (m) (1.1)
Schriftstellerin (die, -nen): writer (f) (1.1)
Schuh (der, -e): shoe (2.4)
Schulter (die, -): shoulder (2)
Schwager (der, -): brother-in-law (3)
Schwägerin (die, -nen): sister-in-law (3)
Schwalbe (die, n): swallow (4)
schwarz: black (2.4)
Schweden (-): Sweden (1)
schweigen (geschwiegen): to be silent (3.1)
Schwein (das, -e): pig (2); pork (4)
Schweiz (die): Switzerland (1)
schwer: heavy, difficult (4.3)
Schwester (die, -n): sister (3)
Schwesterchen (das, -): little sister (4.3)
Schwiegereltern (die): in-laws (3)
Schwiegermutter (die, "): mother-in-law (3)
Schwiegersohn (der, "e): son-in-law (3)
Schwiegertochter (die, "): daughter-in-law (3)
Schwiegervater (der, "): father-in-law (3)
Schwimmen (das): swimming (3)
schwimmen (geschwommen): to swim (3.1)(3)
sechs: six (1.3)
sechzehn: sixteen (1.3)
sechzig: sixty (1.3)
Seebad (das, "er): seaside resort town (4.1)

See (der, -n): take (2.3)
seekrank: seasick (2.3)
Seemeile (die -n): nautical mile (4)
Sehenswürdigkeit (die, -en): tourist attraction (3.4)
sehen (gesehen): to see (2.3)
sehr: very (2.2)
Seife (die, -n): soap (3)
sein (gewesen): to be (1.1)
Sekretärin (die, -nen): secretary (2)
Sekt (der, -e): sparkling wine (1.5)
selten: rare, rarely, seldom (1.5)
Senegal (der): Senegal (1)
September (der): September (2.1)
Serbien: Serbia (1)
Sessel (der, -): armchair (3)
setzen (sich, gesetzt): to sit down (3.3)
sicher: certain, sure (1.2)
sicherheitshalber: for safety's sake (4.3)
sicherlich: certainly (4.4)
sieben: seven (1.3)
siebzig: seventy (1.3)
singen (gesungen): to sing (3.1)(3.5)
Sitz (der, -e): seat (4.3)
sitzen (gesessen): to sit (3.1)
Skilaufen (skigelaufen): to ski (3)
Skulptur (die, -en): sculpture (3.4)
die Slowakei: Slovakia (1)
Slowenien: Slovenia (1)
so... wie: as ... as (2.5)
Socke (die, -n): sock (2.4)
Sofa (das, -s): sofa (3)
sofort: right away (2.2)
sogar: even (2.2)
Sohn (der, "e): son (1.4)
Solist (der, -en): soloist (3.5)
sollen (gesollt): to be supposed to, expected to, should, ought (2.1)
Sondermüll (der): toxic waste (4.2)
Sonne (die): sun (2.3)
Sonnenblume (die, -n): sunflower (4)
sonnen (sich, gesonnt): to sun oneself (3.4)
sonntag (der): Sunday (2.1)
sonst: otherwise (3.2)
Sorge (die, -n): care (3.2)
Soße (die, -n): sauce (2.2)

Sowjetunion (die): Soviet Union (1)
Sozialleistung (die, -en): fringe benefits (4.5)
Spanien (-): Spain (1)
Spanier (der, -): Spaniard (m) (1)
Spanierin (die, -nen): Spaniard (f) (1)
spannend: exciting, suspenseful (1.5)
Spaß (der, "e): fun (2.5)
spät: late (1.4)
später: later (2.3)
spätestens: at the latest (4.1)
Spatz (der, -en): sparrow (4)
Spaziergang (der, "e): walk, stroll (2.3)
Speck (der): bacon (2.2)
Speise (die, -n): food, dish (2.2)
Speisekarte (die, -n): menu (2.2)
Speiselokal (das, -e): eating place (2)
Spiegelei (das, -er): fried egg (2.2)
Spiel (das, -e): game (2.4)
spielen (gespielt): to play (2.4)
Spitzenhemd (das, -en): lace chemise (2.4)
Sport (der): sport (3)
Sporthalle (die, -n): gymnasium (3)
sportlich: sporty, athletic (3.4)
Sprachkenntnisse (die): knowledge of languages (4.5)
sprechen (gesprochen): to speak (3.1)
springen (gesprungen): to jump (3.1)
Spüle (die, -n): sink (3)
Staatsexamen (das, -n): public examination (4)
Stachelbeere (die, -n): gooseberry (2)
Stadtpark (der, -s): city park (2.3)
Stadtplan (der, "e): city map (4.3)
Stadt (die, "e): city (2.3)
Stamm (der,: "e): trunk (4)
Stand (der, "e): stand (1.4)
Star (der, -s): starling (4)
Stau (der, -s): traffic jam (4.3)
stehen (gestanden): to stand; be stated (1.3)(3.1)
steigen (gestiegen): to climb (2.5)(3.1)
sterben (gestorben): to die (3.1)
Steuer (das, -): tax (4.3)

Stimme (die, -n): voice (1.4)
stinken (gestunken): to stink (3.1)
Strafzettel (der, -): parking ticket (4.3)
Straße (die, -n): street (1)
streiten (gestritten): to dispute (3.1)
Strom (der, ˝e): electric current (3)
Strumpf (der, ˝e): stocking (2.4)
Strumpfhose (die, -n): tights (2.4)
Stück (das, -e): piece (1.3)
studieren (studiert): to study (4)
Stuhl (die, ˝e): chair (3)
Stunde (die, -n): hour (1.4)
suchen (gesucht): to look for (2.4)
Suchmeldung (die, -en): missing person report (3.1)
Südafrika (-): South Africa (1)
Süddeutschland (-): South Germany (2.2)
süddeutsch: South German (2.5)
Suppe (die, -n): soup (2.2)
Syrien (-): Syria (1)

Tag (der, -e): day (1.1)
Tagesschau (die): TV news programme (3.3)
tanken (getankt): to fill up with petrol (4.3)
Tanne (die, -n): fir (4)
Tante (die, -n): aunt (3)
Tanz (der, ˝e): dance (3)
tanzen (getanzt): to dance (3)
Tatsache (die, -n): fact (1.5)
tausend: thousand (1.3)
Taxi (das, -s): taxi (1.1)
Taxistand (der, ˝e): taxi stand (1.3)
Teddybär (der, -en): teddy bear (2.4)
Tee (der, -s): tea (2)
Teenager (der, -): adolescent, teenager (3)
Teich (der, -e): pond (3.4)
Telefon (das, -e): telephone (1.2)
telefonieren (telefoniert): to telephone (1.2)
Telefonnummer (die, -n): telephone number (1.4)
Telefonzelle (die, -n): telephone booth (1.2)
Temperatur (die, -en): temperature (2.5)

Tennisplatz (der, ˝e): tennis court (3)
Teppich (der, -e): carpet (3)
Termin (der, -e): appointment, deadline (2.1)
Terminkalender (der, -): appointment book, diary (4.4)
teuer: dear (2.2)
Theater (das,-): theatre (3.5)
Theaterstück (das, -e): drama, theatre, play (3.5)
Thunfisch (der, -e): tuna (2)
Tier (das, -e): animal (4)
Tip (der, -s): tip (2.1)
Tisch (der, -e): table (2.1)
toben (getobt): to go wild (3.5)
Tochter (die, ˝): daughter (2.4)
Toilette (die, -n): toilet (3)
toll: super, great (2.3)
Tonne (die, -n): ton (4)
töpfern (getöpfert): to throw pots (3)
total: total (4.1)
tragen (getragen): to carry (3.1)(3.2)
treffen (getroffen): to meet (1.2)(3.1)
Treibhauseffekt (der, -e): greenhouse effect (4.2)
Treppe (die, -n): staircase (3)
Treppenhaus (das, ˝er): stairwell (3)
treten (getreten): to walk (3.1)
trinken (getrunken): to drink (1.3)(3.1)
Trompete (die, -n): trumpet (3)
trotz: despite (4.4)
trotzdem: nevertheless (4.2)
die Tschechische Republik — The Czech Republic (1)
tschüß: 'bye, cheerio (4.1)
Tulpe (die, -n): tulip (4)
Tunesien (-): Tunis (1)
tun (getan): to do, put ((1.4)(3.1)
Turkei (die): Turkey (1)
Turm (der, ˝e): tower (3.4)
Tür (die, -en): door (3.3)
typisch: typical (2.2)

U-Bahnstation (die, -en): subway station (4.3)
über: over, above (1.4)
überall: everywhere (3.1)
überholen (überholt): to pass (4.3)
überlastet: overburdened (4.4)
überlegen (überlegt): to think over (2.3)
übernachten (übernachtet): to spend the night (4.4)
übernehmen (übernommen): to take over (2.1)
übertreiben (übertrieben): to exaggerate (4.5)
überzeugen (überzeugt): to convince (4.5)
übrigens: by the way (2.1)
Uhr (die, -en): watch, clock, o'clock (1.4)
um...zu: in order to (4.1)
umdrehen (sich, umgedreht): to turn around (2.3)
umgehend: immediately (4.1)
Umleitung (die, -en): detour (4.3)
umtauschen (umgetauscht): to change (1.3)
umweltbewußt: environmentally aware (4.3)
umweltfreundlich: environmentally friendly (4.2)
Umweltschutz (der): protection of the environment (4.2)
unangenehm: disagreeable (1.1)
und: and (1.3)
und so weiter: and so forth (3.5)
Unfall (der, ˝e): accident (4.3)
Ungarn (-): Hungary (1)
ungefähr: about (1.5)
uninteressant: uninteresting (1.1)
Universität (die, -en): university (4)
unmöglich: impossible (1.2)
unsicher: uncertain (1.2)
Unterhemd (das, -en): vest (2.4)
Unterhose (die, -n): underpants, (2.4)
Unternehmensberater (der, -): consultant (2.1)
unternehmungslustig: enterprising (3.4)
Unterstützung (die, -en): support (4.5)
Urgroßmutter (die, ˝: great grandmother (3)

VOCABULARY

Urgroßvater (der, ˮ): great grandfather (3)
Urlaubszeit (die, -en): holiday time (4.5)

Vanillesoße (die, -n): vanilla sauce (2.2)
Vater (der, ˮ): father (2.5)
Vati (der, -s): Dad, Daddy (2.5)
verabreden (sich, verabredet): to make an appointment (4.3)
Veranstaltung (die, -en): show, performance (3.5)
verantwortlich: responsible (1.5)
verbunden: bound (4.1)
Vereinigten Staaten (die): U.S.A. (1)
verfahren (sich, verfahren): to take a wrong turn, lose one's way driving (4.3)
Verfügung (die, -en): disposition (4.4)
vergessen (vergessen): to forget (2.1)(3.1)
vergeßlich: forgetful (4.4)
verhalten (sich, verhalten): to behave (4.5)
Verhandlung (die, -en): negotiation (3.3)
verheiratet: married (3)
Verkaufsleiter (der, -): sales director (2)
Verkaufsmanager (der, -): sales manager (4.5)
Verkauf (der, ˮe): sale (1.3)
verkaufen (verkauft): to sell (1.3)
Verlag (der, -e): publishing house (1.4)
verlegen (verlegt): to publish (1.5)
Verleger (der, -): publisher (1.1)
Verlegerin (die, -nen): publisher (f) (1.1)
verlieren (verloren): to lose (3.1)
Vermieter (der, -): landlord (3)
veröffentlichen (veröffentlicht): to publish (1.5)
verreisen (verreist): to set off on a journey (4.1)

verschlechtern (sich, verschlechtert): to get worse (2.5)
verschwinden (verschwunden): to disappear (3.1)(3.2)
versichern (versichert): to assure (3.2)
Verspätung (die, -en): delay (1.5)
versprechen (versprochen): to promise (3.4)
verstehen (verstanden): to understand (1.2)
vertagen (vertagt): to adjourn (3.3)
Vertrieb (der, -e): distribution (4.5)
Verzeihung (die, -en): pardon (1.1)
viel: much, many (1.4)
vielleicht: perhaps (1.5)
vielseitig: many sided (5.4)
vier: four (1.3)
Viertel (das, -): quarter (1.4)
Viertelstunde (die, -n): quarter of an hour (1.4)
vierzehn: fourteen (1.3)
vierzig: forty (1.3)
Vietnam (der): Vietnam (1)
Vollkornbrot (das, -e): wholegrain bread (4.2)
von: of, from (1.4)
vor allem: above all (3.5)
voraussetzen (vorausgesetzt): to require (4.5)
Vorfahrtsstraße (die, -n): major road (4.3)
vorführen (vorgeführt): to present, show (3.5)
vorhaben (vorgehabt): to have the intention (3.5)
vorher: before (4.3)
vorhin: previously (3.1)
Vormittag (der, -e): forenoon, morning (1.4)
vormittags: in the morning (1.4)
Vorname (der, -n): first name (1.1)
vorne: in front (1.3)
vorschlagen (vorgeschlagen): to propose, suggest (2.3)
Vorschule (die, -n): preschool (4)
Vorspeise (die, -n): appetizer (2.2)
Vorstellung (die, -en): performance (3.5)

Wagen (der, -): car (4.3)
Wagenschlüssel (der, -): car key (4.3)
wählen (gewählt): to choose, dial a number (1.4)
während: during (4.4)
wahrscheinlich: probably (3.2)
Wal (der, -e): whale (4)
Wald (der, ˮer): woods, forest (3.4)
wandern (gewandert): to go hiking (3)
Wanderweg (der, -e): hiking trail (3.4)
wann?: when? (1.2)
Ware (die, -n): merchandise, ware (4.5)
Wartehalle (die, -n): waiting room (1)
warten (gewartet): to wait (1.1)
warum?: why? (1.3)
was?: what? (1.1)
Waschbecken (das, -): washbasin (3)
waschen (gewaschen): to wash (3.1)(3.3)
Wäsche (die, -): lingerie (2.4)
Waschlappen (der, -): facecloth, face flannel (3)
Waschmaschine (die, -n): washing machine (3)
Wasser (das): water (1.5)
Wasserski (das): water skiing (3)
wechseln (gewechselt): to change (1.3)
Wechselstube (die, -n): bureau de change (1.3)
Weg (der, -e): way, path (4.3)
wegen: on account of (4.4)
Weihnachten (das): Christmas (4)
weil: because (2)
Wein (der, -e): wine (1.5)
Weinkeller (der, -): wine cellar (2)
Weinstube (die, -n): wine bar (2)
Weintraube (die, -n): grape (2)
weiß: white (2.4)
Weißkohl (der, -e): cabbage (2)
Weißwein (der, -e): white wine (2)
weitergehen (weitergegangen): to walk on (1.3)
weit weg: far away (2.3)
welcher (-es, -e): which, what (2.4)
Welt (die, -en): world (2.1)

weltweit: worldwide (2.1)

wenig: little (2.2)

wenn: when, if (4.1)(4.4)

wer: who (1.4)

werden (geworden, worden): to become, get (2.3)

werfen (geworfen): to throw (3.1)

Werkstoff (der, -e): raw material (4.5)

Wespe (die, -n): wasp (4)

westdeutsch: West German (2.5)

Weste (die, -n): waistcoat (2.4)

Wetter (das): weather (2.3)

wichtig: important (1.2)

widerstehen (widerstanden): to resist (3.2)

wie?: how? (1.1)

wieder: again (2.3)

wiederkommen (wiedergekommen): to come back

Wiese (die, -n): meadow (3.4)

wieviel?: how much? (1.3)

Wild (das): wild game (2)

Wildschwein (das, -e): wild boar (4)

willkommen: welcome (1.1)

Windsurfing (das): wind surfing (3)

wirklich: really (1.5)

Wirtschaft (die, -en): tavern, economy, commerce (2)

wissen (gewußt): to know (3.3)

Witwe (die, -n): widow (3)

Witwer (der, -): widower (3)

wo?: where? (1.2)

Woche (die, -n): week (2.1)

Wochenmarkt (der, ¨e): weekly market (4.2)

woher?: from where? (1.1)

wohin?: where to? (2.3)

Wohl (das): welfare; wellbeing (1.5)

Wohnung (die, -en): flat (3)

Wohnzimmer (das): living room (3.3)

wollen (gewollt): to want (2.1)

worum: about what (3.2)

wunderbar: wonderful (3.4)

wünschen (gewünscht): to wish (2.2)

Wurm (der, ¨er): worm (4)

Wurst (die, ¨er): sausage (2)

Würstchen (das, -): little sausage (2)

Yuppie (der -s): Young Urban Professional (2.1)

Zahl (die, -en): number, amount (1.4)

Zahn (der, ¨e): tooth (3.3)

Zahnbürste (die, -n): toothbrush (3)

Zahnpasta (die, -ten): toothpaste (3)

Zahnschmerz (der, -en): toothache (2.5)

Zaïre (-): Zaire (1)

Zebra (das, -s): zebra (4)

zehn: ten (1.3)

zeichnen (gezeichnet): to draw (3)

Zeichnung (die, -en): drawing (3)

zeigen (gezeigt): to show (1.5)

Zeit (die, -en): time (1.4)

Zeitung (die, -en): newspaper (3.3)

Zentiliter (der, -): centilitre (4)

Zentimeter (der, -): centimetre (4)

Zentrum (das, -en): centre (2.3)

Zettel (der, -): slip of paper (4.2)

Zeugnis (das, -se): certificate (4.5)

Ziege (die, -n): she goat (2)

ziehen (gezogen): to pull (3.1)

Zigarette (die, -n): cigarette (4.3)

Zimmer (das, -): room (1.2)

Zimmerschlüssel (der, -): room key (1.2)

Zoll (der, ¨e): customs (1)

zu: to, at (2.1) (3.2)

zuerst: at first (2.3)

zu Fuß: on foot (2.3)

Zug (der, ¨e): train (2.5)

Zugreise (die, -n): train journey (1)

zukunftssicher: with a secure future (permanent position) (4.5)

zumachen (zugemacht): to close (3.3)

zurückkommen (zurückgekommen): to come back (2.5)

zurückrufen (zurückgerufen): to call back (4.1)

zusammen: together (2.5)

Zusammenarbeit (die, -en): collaboration (1.5)

zusammenarbeiten (zusammengearbeitet): to collaborate, work together (1.5)

zusammenschrumpfen (zusammengeschrumpft): to shrink (4.2)

zuschauen (zugeschaut): to look at (3.5)

Zuschauer (der, -): spectator (3.5)

zwanzig: twenty (1.3)

zwei: two (1.3)

zweimal: twice (2.2)

zweiundzwanzig: twenty-two (1.3)

zwölf: twelve (1.3)

VOCABULARY

THE MOST COMMON IRREGULAR VERBS

INFINITIVE	IMPERFECT	PAST PARTICIPLE	ENGLISH
anfangen	*fing an*	*angefangen*	to begin, start
befehlen	*befahl*	*befohlen*	to order, give a command
beginnen	*begann*	*begonnen*	to begin
bieten	*bot*	*geboten*	to offer
binden	*band*	*gebunden*	to tie, bind
bitten	*bat*	*gebeten*	to ask for
bleiben	*blieb*	*geblieben*	to stay, remain
brechen	*brach*	*gebrochen*	to break
brennen	*brannte*	*gebrannt*	to burn
bringen	*brachte*	*gebracht*	to bring
denken	*dachte*	*gedacht*	to think
einladen	*lud ein*	*eingeladen*	to invite
empfehlen	*empfahl*	*empfohlen*	to recommend
essen	*aß*	*gegessen*	to eat
fahren	*fuhr*	*gefahren*	to travel, go
fallen	*fiel*	*gefallen*	to fall
fliegen	*flog*	*geflogen*	to fly
fließen	*floß*	*geflossen*	to flow
frieren	*fror*	*gefroren*	to freeze; be cold
geben	*gab*	*gegeben*	to give
gehen	*ging*	*gegangen*	to go, walk
genießen	*genoß*	*genossen*	to enjoy
geschehen	*geschah*	*geschehen*	to happen
gewinnen	*gewann*	*gewonnen*	to win
greifen	*griff*	*gegriffen*	to seize, grip
halten	*hielt*	*gehalten*	to hold
hängen	*hing*	*gehangen*	to hang
heben	*hob*	*gehoben*	to lift
heißen	*hieß*	*geheißen*	to be named
helfen	*half*	*geholfen*	to help
kennen	*kannte*	*gekannt*	to know, be familiar with
klingen	*klang*	*geklungen*	to sound, resound
kommen	*kam*	*gekommen*	to come
lassen	*ließ*	*gelassen*	to let, allow
laufen	*lief*	*gelaufen*	to run
leihen	*lieh*	*geliehen*	to lend
lesen	*las*	*gelesen*	to read
liegen	*lag*	*gelegen*	to lie (be recumbent); be situated
lügen	*log*	*gelogen*	to lie, prevaricate

INFINITIVE	IMPERFECT	PAST PARTICIPLE	ENGLISH
nehmen	*nahm*	*genommen*	to take
nennen	*nannte*	*genannt*	to name
raten	*riet*	*geraten*	to advise
rennen	*rannte*	*gerannt*	to run
riechen	*roch*	*gerochen*	to smell
rufen	*rief*	*gerufen*	to call
(sich) saufen	*soff*	*gesoffen*	to drink (animal), guzzle, "booze"
scheinen	*schien*	*geschienen*	to shine; seem
schließen	*schloß*	*geschlossen*	to close
schlafen	*schlief*	*geschlafen*	to sleep
schneiden	*schnitt*	*geschnitten*	to cut
schreiben	*schrieb*	*geschrieben*	to write
schreien	*schrie*	*geschrien*	to cry out, scream
schweigen	*schwieg*	*geschwiegen*	to be silent
schwimmen	*schwam*	*geschwommen*	to swim
sehen	*sah*	*gesehen*	to see
sein	*war*	*gewesen*	to be
singen	*sang*	*gesungen*	to sing
sitzen	*saß*	*gesessen*	to sit
sprechen	*sprach*	*gesprochen*	to speak
springen	*sprang*	*gesprungen*	to jump
stehen	*stand*	*gestanden*	to stand
steigen	*stieg*	*gestiegen*	to climb
sterben	*starb*	*gestorben*	to die
stinken	*stank*	*gestunken*	to stink
sich streiten	*stritt*	*gestritten*	to quarrel, dispute
tragen	*trug*	*getragen*	to carry
treffen	*traf*	*getroffen*	to meet
treten	*trat*	*getreten*	to walk, tread
trinken	*trank*	*getrunken*	to drink
tun	*tat*	*getan*	to do; put
vergessen	*vergaß*	*vergessen*	to forget
verlieren	*verlor*	*verloren*	to lose
verschwinden	*verschwand*	*verschwunden*	to disappear
waschen	*wusch*	*gewaschen*	to wash
werden	*wurde*	*geworden*	to become
werfen	*warf*	*geworfen*	to throw
ziehen	*zog*	*gezogen*	to pull, draw, tug

Verbs in **bold type** use „sein" to form the perfect tenses (auxiliary verb + past participle).

PHOTO CREDITS